THE STORY OF THE CHRISTMAS NO. 1

MISTLETOE & VINYL

MARC BURROWS

M^cNIDDER | &
GRACE

Published by McNidder & Grace
Jedburgh
Scotland
United Kingdom
www.mcnidderandgrace.com

First Published 2025
© Marc Burrows

A catalogue record for this work is available from the British Library.

ISBN   9780857162854
eISBN 9780857162861

Cover design: Tabitha Palmer, Wales
Cover illustrations by Philip Hughes and Russ Williams
Designer: JS Typesetting Ltd, Porthcawl, Wales
Printed and bound in the United Kingdom by Short Run Press, Exeter

For Melanie

Foreword
NO POP, NO STYLE, ALL STRICTLY RUDOLPH

The fact that Christmas is a fake holiday created by an American corporation to sell more carbonated sugar should come as no surprise at all. However, its subsequent success leading to an exponential cultural response, which every year inspires yet more outlandish contenders, has been bizarre to witness. The cheesy Christmas jumper thing, the hordes of drunk Santas running around cities thing, the fucking mawkish John Lewis advert thing. Utter madness.

My own take is that, fake as it may be, Christmas is completely brilliant but should be totally banned from ANY mention until 9:00 a.m. sharp on the first of December. Then you would have this whole amazing, mad launch day when the shops suddenly have all their Christmas stock in, the adverts all start, the songs would be released, and the Santas would start drinking. We would also be spared the sight of advent calendars in early September.

I was born at a strangely problematic time for a young music fan. 1962. Too non-existent for Rock n Roll and Skiffle. Too young for The Beatles, The Stones, Merseybeat, Motown, Psychedelia, Ska and Bluebeat. Too immature for glam. Too confused for Bowie. Too suburban for first wave punk. Too scruffy for the New Romantics. Each new musical movement seemed to have a rock solid reason for me to be precluded from membership. I needily drifted from band to band as a desperate arriviste. A callow outsider, lacking the hipster credentials or nerdy knowledge that inclusion in any of these new waves (sic) demanded.

However, every year around early November, there was the bizarre spectacle of the nations arbiters of melody, rhythm and taste, throwing their hat into the ring with a seasonally flavoured song, in order to have a tilt at being the *Christmas No. 1!* The result of this seasonal bun fight was revealed to the nation on Christmas Top of the Pops, shortly before the Queen's Christmas message. This timing always seemed a little perverse to me. Her Majesty fruitlessly trying to gee up the Commonwealth or bravely lament her own annus horribilis, while thousands of people in Kettering, St Ives and Kirkcaldy were still shouting at each other about how bad/good the George Michael song was. But in Barking, Essex, I too could shout about it as well! Every single December even us outsiders had some skin in the game.

Marc Burrows has decided to plunge headfirst into the icy waters of this wackiest of races to the Christmas No. 1 spot. In this frenzied digital era of hundreds of different charts, is it even a thing any more? Why and when did we start caring about it? What is its future? Yes, poor Marc has decided to wrestle all of these questions to the frigid shores, and then beat them into submission with a robust striped cinnamon candy cane of in depth analysis and weapons grade festive whimsy. This book is an essential guide for those of us who hate or indeed love this annual struggle for artistic commercial dominance. It will answer some questions, settle some arguments, but I sense, will start many more.

And before you ask, the greatest Christmas song of all time is 'Bugger My Buttocks For Christmas' by Howling Wilf. It's on YouTube. Happy Christmas.

Phillip Jupitus
Fife
2025

CONTENTS

Prologue
MERRY CHRISTMAS
(I WON'T DO WHAT YOU TELL ME)

A true story of taking the power back

December 2008, and the Christmas chart is hovering on the horizon. Christmas No. 1. The crown jewel of pop. The only time we know of, in the long calendar of the year, when anything can happen in the UK Top 40. When all bets are off, while, oddly, a lot of bets are also literally *on*. Charity records with stars in big headphones singing into mics. Novelty records and comedians. Pop giants. The ghosts of Christmas past. It's all part of the fun, closely tracked by press and public alike. It's the one point of the year when people with no interest in the pop chart are paying attention to the Top 10. It's also the only time when a giant pink foam monster called Mr Blobby – a character created to prank celebrities on a Saturday night TV show – could beat the biggest pop band in the UK to No. 1. *Anything* can happen.

For the last three years, the UK Christmas No. 1 has been the "winner's single" from the reigning *X Factor* champion, and it's not even been close. Simon Cowell's behemoth is the country's most popular music show, beamed into homes every Saturday and Sunday teatime and then discussed obsessively in playgrounds and offices and school gates and factory floors, and in the tea rooms at the Houses of Parliament and the newsroom of the *Guardian* for the rest of the week. Technically, the prize for the winning act is a record contract and the immediate release of their first single, but since the show climaxes the week before Christmas, everyone knows what that *really* means: Christmas No. 1. In the bag. This year, 13.1 million people tune in to watch South London shop girl Alexandra Burke duet with Beyoncé and subsequently *trounce* boyband JLS in the final. Her winner's single, which goes on sale digitally the moment the show ends, is a cover of Leonard Cohen's 1984 masterpiece 'Hallelujah', given a gooey pop spit 'n' shine. It now has a key change. And a gospel choir. It sounds a long way from Cohen, or indeed Jeff Buckley, whose 1994 cover of the song is a beloved classic in its own right, but it *does* sound like a hit. Burke is brilliant as well – a charismatic diva onstage with a belting voice, and the very definition of likeable relatability offstage. As the CDs hit the shops, Ladbrokes and William Hill are giving odds of 1/8 it'll go to the top of the charts, which is barely worth queuing in the bookie's for.

In the past, *Who will be Christmas No. 1?* has been a big story, which the media always appreciates in a traditionally slow news week. Not this year. Not for a few years, really. There have, however, been some whispers of discontent among the populace at large. Comedian Peter Kay, cross-dressed in character as pastiche pop idol Geraldine McQueen, has put out a single of his own, 'Once Upon a Christmas Song', co-written with Take That's Gary Barlow[1] and the proceeds going to a children's charity. In the press release, "Geraldine" is among the first to really put her acrylic-tipped finger on something that's starting to bother the nation: "Simon Cowell is the Grinch that stole the Christmas single … I'm stealing it back for the people of Britain – and the NSPCC."

It's tentative, but music fans are starting to organise in an attempt to rescue the Christmas No. 1. In 2005 the rules had changed and legal downloads of MP3s could be counted toward the singles chart, and that carries some interesting possibilities: a Facebook group has formed in an attempt to strike a blow for "real music", whatever that means, and get Buckley's version of 'Hallelujah' to

---

[1] Who, having been beaten down into the Christmas No. 2 slot twice, in 1993 and 2006 (once by a barely credible monster created for TV with little musical clout and once by Mr Blobby) was out for revenge.

No. 1 instead of Cowell's. Another group see Buckley himself as a pretender, and are pushing for Cohen's original version. No one is running these campaigns with any efficiency, though. There's no proper focus.

Sitting at home in Essex, and recognising the possibilities in all of this, are music fans Jon Morter and Tracy Hayden. They're not music industry professionals by any means – Jon works in logistics for a high-end audio and electronics brand and Tracy is a photographer. They're parents of young children, they have normal jobs, a love of Christmas and decent music in general and an interest in comedy and social media. The couple decide to throw a curveball into the race and start a Facebook group of their own to get Rick Astley's classic 80s hit 'Never Gonna Give You Up' to No. 1 instead, because it would be funny to Rickroll the charts.[2] A lot of people agree, and the campaign gets some traction. In fact, Rick Astley is in the Top 5 on various download charts as the end of the week approaches.

Alas, it wasn't to be; not for Jeff Buckley, Leonard Cohen or Geraldine and certainly not for Jon, Tracy and Rick. Simon Cowell knows what he's about – previous winners' singles had been schmaltzy and forgettable, but 'Hallelujah'? That's a stone-cold classic, whoever's singing it. Add that to the *X Factor* hype train and it's a foregone conclusion. It sells 120,000 copies on its first day, growing to 571,000 by the end of the week. When the chart is announced, it's an easy Christmas No. 1. Jeff Buckley is at No. 2, Geraldine at No. 5, Leonard Cohen at 36. Rick Astley, to the astonishment of the Facebook campaign organisers, is at 73. Jon Morter suspects foul play on Sony's part.[3] Still, the couple have learned a lot of lessons about Facebook campaigns, chart positions, PR and the music industry in general. When December 2009 rolls around, they will be ready.

---

[2] An early social media trend, emerging that year, saw millions of people encouraging each other to click an internet link to see something fantastic, only to find it was 'Never Gonna Give You Up'. It seemed funny at the time.

[3] "It was controversial in the end because it got nobbled, and I'll take that to my grave – it was nobbled, right?"

One year later …

It is 14 November. There is just over a month to go until the Christmas No. 1 is announced, and Jon and Tracy have just repurposed an unused fan group on Facebook. At the time, this was fairly easy to do – you just had to find a group where the admins had either lost interest, been booted off the platform or been temporarily suspended, leaving it rudderless, and then hit the "become admin" button. "Bang!" says Jon. "It's your group now." This particular group, which has around 8,000 members already, is for British fans of the US rock band Rage Against the Machine, and they rename it "RAGE AGAINST THE MACHINE FOR CHRISTMAS NO.1".

The plan is to get the band's 1992 alt rock classic 'Killing in the Name' to the top of the chart ahead of whatever the *X Factor* is putting out that year. It's a perfect choice – a rebel anthem that, like many of the band's songs, is rooted in the rejection of capitalist conformism and authoritarian control. The song was originally inspired by a freed American slave who wrote about the power of rejecting his master. At its heart it's about the freedom of saying no. Of resisting. It's also a wildly popular rock classic. There isn't a club in the world that hasn't spun 'Killing in the Name' at every rock and metal night held in the last 20 years, and the dance floor will always go off. 'Killing in the Name' ticks all the boxes – the message is perfect, and there is no greater antithesis of manufactured, plasticised pop than a rock-rap band of avowedly political, left-wing agitators. It represents, as Rage say on another of their songs, a desire to "take the power back". It works. It really does. It's such a bold, simple statement. The song ends with frontman Zack de la Rocha screaming "Fuck you, I won't do what you tell me!" over an irresistible, *heavy as all hell* groove; a moment that imprints itself onto the soul. Okay, it's not Christmassy, but as a rejection of the spoon-fed entitlement of the mainstream music industry, it's unarguably brilliant. It's authentic and rebellious and undeniably cool, and represents everything a reality singing competition on ITV absolutely isn't. If anything could make a statement, if any song could say: "We will not take this any more. We draw a line. Here. Today", it is this one. Plus, as Tracy says, "I remember just sitting there laughing to myself about how funny it would be to have Rage Against the Machine on

Top of the Pops, right before the Queen's Speech. I just wanted that to happen."

By 2 December the group has hit 10,000 members. A Twitter account is created on 3 December and immediately starts to go viral. On 4 December the *NME* website gives the story its first real media boost: *Rage Against The Machine to take on* The X Factor *for Christmas No. 1*. The group now has 45,000 members and online bookies Betfred have set the odds of 'Killing in the Name' being Christmas No. 1 at 10/1. It is, as Jon and Tracy say online, "worth a punt!". By the time the next episode of the *X Factor* airs – on Saturday, 5 December – the group is 150,000 strong. Two days later, with the three *X Factor* finalists now selected and with a week to go before the final, Jon and Tracy's group has 300,000 members and is growing fast. So popular is the group, in fact, that Jon keeps having to beg people to keep their powder dry – only sales made between Sunday, 13 December to midnight on Saturday, 19 December will count for the Christmas No. 1.

Celebrities, including the Sex Pistols' John Lydon and comedian Bill Bailey, share the link. The story is growing, and the press, starved these past four years, *love* a Christmas No. 1 story. The BBC's 6 Music radio station, especially the Shaun Keavney breakfast show, get behind the campaign, interviewing Tracy and creating a special jingle. That Saturday, online bookmaker, Betfred declares 'Killing in the Name' to be the favourite in the Christmas No. 1 race. William Hill are offering 7/4, Bet365 offer 8/11. Tracy has the idea of doing some real good and sets up a page on the charity donation site JustGiving, raising money for the homeless charity Shelter, and links it to the *Rage For Christmas* Facebook group. Jon and Tracy then go out grocery shopping. When they get home, a few hours later, they've already raised several thousand pounds.

The media now have the scent and Jon and Tracy are finding themselves in demand. Jon has already been on BBC London. "It's a rallying cry," he says, "it's been taken on by thousands as a defiance to Simon Cowell's 'music machine' … we've got nothing personally against him, we just do not want yet another Christmas chart-topper from *that* show."

As the group hits 550,000 members, it's becoming clear that the Christmas No. 1 truly means something to people. That it's part of

British culture, and there's a real resentment of the *X Factor* foregone conclusions of recent years. Throw in too that Simon Cowell himself comes off as smug, having made a TV career out of condescending to a succession of pop wannabes. Pricking that balloon of arrogance, supporting the underdog – it's a very British instinct. Cowell doesn't help himself. Appearing at a press conference on 10 December, he addresses the campaign for the first time, much to the surprise of its organisers. "If there's a campaign, and I think the campaign's aimed directly at me, then it's stupid," he says. "I think it's quite a cynical campaign." Cowell goes on to point out that "everyone has this slightly distorted view of Christmas number ones being incredible, but they're often ghastly. We haven't exactly taken away anything special." The dismissive comments have the effect of galvanising those who already resent Cowell's entitlement while providing a huge publicity bump to the campaign. Tracy and Jon, who fully expected the *X Factor* to ignore them, are astonished and delighted. "He lost it, he threw his toys out of the pram, which was the worst thing he could have done," says Tracy.

The next day, the Facebook page hits 600,000 people and book-ies slash odds on 'Killing in the Name' winning. "The *X Factor* has had a monopoly over the Christmas No. 1, but there is a real buzz about Rage Against The Machine," William Hill's Rupert Adams tells *NME*. "We might just have the biggest upset in chart history!" Simon Cowell's comments are repeated that morning on Channel 5's current affairs chat show *The Wright Stuff*, and though panellist Oz Clarke makes a reasonable point that "rage and killing isn't quite what you want for Christmas", the consensus from both the guests in the studio and callers at home is that it's time to bloody Cowell's nose. The fundraising for Shelter, which is nearing £10,000 by now, is also a source of much good will.

It's at this point that Jon and Tracy start to hear whispers com-ing from inside Sony Records and its Simon Cowell-run subsidiary, Syco, that the company is spooked. *X Factor* is a golden goose that props up much of the label's annual activities. They can't afford for this crucial single to fail. Someone has set up a website called "RageFactor", styling itself as an official focal point for the cam-paign. It has originated from Sony. The call to action is "BUY THE SONG NOW" – and this is the last message Jon and Tracy want out there. Sales don't count until midnight on Saturday, so it's an encouragement for people to waste their vote. A clever misdirect by the enemy? Jon is able to trace the owner and pressure them into taking their site down until the following week, but it's enough to indicate that Sony are both scared and not above some dirty tricks.

The *X Factor* final goes out live on Sunday, 13 December and is watched by 16.2 million people. Those are absurd numbers, a true national television moment. Affable Geordie teen Joe McElderry is declared the winner and his debut single, a cover of a song written for Miley Cyrus called 'The Climb', goes on immediate sale. Joe's single will be available on CD on Wednesday, but the download is out now and *the race is on*. He has some catching up to do – Jon and Tracy fired their own starter pistol as the clock ticked passed 00.01 the previous night, encouraging fans to buy the single from multiple digital outlets: iTunes, HMV, Amazon, Tesco, 7digital and more. The song has already leapt up the download charts on each platform.

Monday. Six days before the chart is announced. Poor Joe McElderry, running on two hours sleep, is dispatched to do the breakfast TV circuit. He doesn't mention the words "Rage Against the Machine" once – not on *GM:TV*, not on *This Morning*. The ITV shows know better than to bring it up and feed the publicity machine. The immediate surge has pushed 'The Climb' into the lead on the various download charts. There's a general consensus that, despite the rabble at the gate, *X Factor* will still work its magic. Ladbrokes give it 1/8, the same odds it gave Alexandra Burke the previous year. "Joe is the toast of fans up and down the country," says spokesman Nick Weinberg. "Christmas chart success is virtually assured". Meanwhile, the "RAGE AGAINST THE MACHINE FOR CHRISTMAS NUMBER 1" group has vanished from Facebook. Jon suspects that Sony has encouraged mass reporting of the page, accusing it of spam. He ends up on the phone with Facebook's PR team, who are claiming the problem is "a bug". A suspiciously well-timed bug. "Well, look, if the group's not returned, I'm going on national TV and telling them why," says Jon. He's already been in the news, talking to *The Global Herald* about how Facebook's actions are limiting the donations to Shelter coming from the page – currently at £20,000. Several back-up groups are created, just in case, but funnily enough, as the sun sets on Monday, the group reappears.

Tuesday. Five days to go. 'Killing in the Name' is ahead, with 83,276 downloads compared to 77,401 for 'The Climb', but everyone knows that Sony has one very big card left to play. Tomorrow is when Joe McElderry's single will be released on CD. HMV alone are stocking 500,000 copies – the store's biggest order for a CD single in a decade. There is no physical version of 'Killing in the Name' widely available. Simon Cowell tells the *Daily Star* that "Joe WILL be No. 1". He seems very sure. He's also, clearly, livid at the challenge. Absolutely furious. "Why not let the kid have his moment?" he says. "It's all very Scrooge. It's miserable to put down young talent. We should celebrate him." Meanwhile, somewhere in Los Angeles, Zack de la Rocha is told by a server in a bakery that his song is currently blowing up in the UK. His response? "What?!" The rest of his band are waking up to the attention too. "Rage's 'Killing in the Name' & *The X Factor's* goofy Christmas single are neck and neck for num one spot on UK chart,"[4] writes guitarist Tom Morello on Twitter. "England! Now is your time!". The members of Rage Against the Machine have entered the game.

Wednesday. Four days to go. In Joe McElderry's native South Shields, crowds queue in the early hours, in freezing conditions, outside HMV. The *X Factor* winner is signing copies of 'The Climb' here today. HMV boss Gennaro Castaldo is feeling bullish. "We are expecting that most customers will actually buy this single in a store rather than online", he tells the *Daily Mail*, pointing out *that* the market for the *X Factor* is "much broader" than the appeal of a song as extreme as 'Killing in the Name'. 'The Climb' has done 110,000 downloads in three days. It's worth noting that Alexandra Burke's 'Hallelujah', the previous year, did 126,000 in the first 24 hours alone. That's a hell of a drop. 'Killing in the Name' is still 60,000 records ahead. Bookies are reporting a surge in bets for Rage Against the Machine, with odds slipping to 5/4. Poor Joe is now at 4/7. RATM guitarist Tom Morello appears on the BBC 6

---

[4] This was the days when Twitter restricted posts to 140 characters.

Music Breakfast show, down the line from LA, announcing that he will donate his portion of any profits to Youth Music, a British music charity, so that "a new generation of rockers can take on the establishment."

Simon Cowell is doing himself no favours in the pages of *NME*. He's featured on the cover under the headline "The Grinch Speaks", interviewed by the magazine's editor, Krissi Murison. He repeats his claim that *X Factor* has somehow "saved" the Christmas No. 1. "There's a tradition of quite horrible songs," he says. "I think I've done everyone a favour". Joe McElderry, meanwhile, tells the *Daily Mirror* that he still hasn't heard 'Killing in the Name'. "It's out of my hands," he says of the race. "Obviously I'd love, love LOVE a No. 1 … I'm just going to work hard and try my best. Good luck to them as well." He's a nice boy ….

Thursday. Three days to go. 'Killing in the Name' is still ahead of 'The Climb', but the gap is closing. "You won't do the swearing part, will you?" It's eight o'clock in the morning, UK time, and the four members of Rage Against the Machine – Zack de la Rocha, Tom Morello, Timmy C and Brad Wilk – have assembled in a studio in Los Angeles. It's midnight for them, and this is the first time they've played together in over a year. This will be the only live appearance of the surprise campaign. It's being beamed across the planet to UK breakfast radio; not on Radio 1, the BBC's mainstream pop station, not on 6 Music, the corporation's home of alternative music, but on BBC Radio 5, the Beeb's talk-based news, current affairs and sport station. Because it is legitimate *news*. "Simon is an interesting character," says Zack de la Rocha. "He seems to have profited greatly off humiliating people on live television and has a unique position of capturing the attention of people and the airwaves. We see this as a necessary breaking of that control." Tom Morello chips in: "People are tired of being spoon-fed one schmaltzy ballad after another. They want to take back their own charts. We're honoured they've chosen our song to be the rebel anthem to topple the *X Factor* monopoly. It's a little dose of anarchy." The quartet rip into 'Killing in the Name'. A scrappy but brilliant version. When it gets to the expletive-ridden outro, you can sense the relief in the studio as Zack cuts out the swearing in the build-up. That is, until the song kicks into its vicious final movement. "FUCK YOU I WANT DO WHAT YOU TELL ME!" Zack screams, offering both middle fingers to the webcam. "FUCK YOU, I WON'T DO WHAT YOU TELL ME!" He gets *fuck you* in four times before host Shelagh Fogarty can be heard yelling, "Get it off! Get it off!" There is quite the commotion. "Buy Joe's single!" says Shelagh, as Nicky Campbell apologises profusely.[5] The BBC later issues an apology. "We had spoken to the band repeatedly beforehand and they had agreed not to swear. When they did we faded the band out and said sorry immediately."[6]

It feels like a turning point. There is another surge in bets on 'Killing in the Name' winning. Bookmakers William Hill decide to temporarily suspend betting on this year's Christmas No. 1, since 98% of bets are for Rage. Paddy Power also closes their book, declaring Rage the likely winner. Ladbrokes, however, are once again backing Joe McElderry, offering 2/7 on 'The Climb' winning and an unlikely 9/4 on 'Killing in the Name'. "We saw a steady stream of money for Rage at the beginning of the week," spokesman Nick Weinberg tells the *Daily Mirror*, "but last night Joe rediscovered the X Factor in the eyes of punters." HMV's Gennaro Castaldo agrees: "It's going to be a much closer race than predicted, but we remain confident Joe will do it." However, there are problems in the *X Factor* camp: there have been delays getting the physical singles out to stores, with only ASDA and HMV currently stocking it. Hopes for 'The Climb' are pinned entirely on physical copies being shifted in massive quantities, so this is a real worry. Still, wherever they can be found, those copies are shifting in huge numbers.

Friday. Two days to go. 'Killing in the Name' is ahead by just 8,923 downloads, and Jon and Tracy are going into overdrive, posting links to the various sales platforms and highlighting how many times a person can buy the track. Amazon is selling it for 29p. Sir Paul McCartney is the latest celebrity to come out in favour of 'Killing in the Name'. "It would be kind of funny if a band like Rage Against the Machine got it," he told *Sky News*, "because it would prove a

---

[5] She will later have to apologise herself for this comment, following complaints of bias.

[6] Could they really be *that* surprised? The clues are right there in the song.

point." Joe is on *BBC Breakfast*, still bright-eyed, still smiling, working his arse off. His mentor on the show, newly appointed nation's sweetheart Cheryl Cole, is not happy with how things are panning out. "He put his heart and soul into every single week of the *X Factor* and I cannot bear to see him lose out to a mean campaign that has nothing to do with his efforts," she tells the *Daily Record*. "If that song, or should I say campaign, by an American group is our Christmas number one, I'll be gutted for him and our charts." The national mood is buoyant. Snow and frost across the country are bringing a Christmassy glow, and sometimes it feels like the Christmas No. 1 battle is the only thing anyone can talk about. "Pop music," notes Caitlin Moran in *The Times* that day. "Simultaneously the most important and ridiculous thing in the world."

Saturday. One day until Christmas No. 1 is announced. According to online retailer 7digital, 'The Climb' has pulled ahead by 11,000 copies as *X Factor* fans hit the Saturday high streets. Sony will be hoping for more, but the cold weather and snow across much of the country is keeping people at home. Meanwhile, poor Joe McElderry has finally heard 'Killing in the Name'. "They can't be serious!" he tells the *Sun*. "I had no idea what it sounded like. It's dreadful and I hate it. How could anyone enjoy this? Can you imagine grandmas hearing this over Christmas lunch?! ... I wouldn't buy it. It's a nought from me. Simon Cowell wouldn't like it. They wouldn't get through boot camp on the *X Factor*. They're just shouting!"

With just hours to go before the chart week officially finishes, Rage Against the Machine have an ace up their sleeve, "Attention Freedom Fighters!" Tom Morello says in a statement. "RAGE VS. X Factor WILL BE DECIDED BY SATURDAY'S SALES. Spread the word! Knock on doors! Host downloading parties! Knock over ladies buying X Factor! The clock is ticking. And if 'Killing in the Name' is number one WE ARE COMING. And it will be the victory party to end all victory parties." The long and short of it is that the band promise to play a huge, free show in London should 'Killing in the Name' clinch Christmas No. 1. On Twitter, with just 10 minutes to go, Morello still has the bit between his teeth. "Finish line is in sight! Will David smite Goliath? Will Luke Skywalker destroy the Death Star? Will Frodo defeat Sauron? UK - it's now or never. Will the next 10min determine the fate of a nation's musical soul? WHICH FUCKING SIDE ARE YOU ON!! To the barricades!! One last download!"

It might not be enough. According to some estimates, 100,000 copies of 'The Climb' have been sold today. According to others, however, 'Killing in the Name' has also been downloaded 100,000 times today. As the sun goes down on a freezing, buzzing Britain, all we can do is wait. Behind the scenes a relaxed Simon Cowell phones Jon and Tracy at home and congratulates them on a campaign well fought. "Oh well, look, I've done all right out of this because my staff are working four times as hard now," he says, "and now I know they can work that hard, they're always going to work that hard." He suggests they meet up for a drink at some point.[7]

Sunday, 20 December. The Christmas No. 1 will be announced by Scott Mills on Radio 1 at 7 p.m. With a few hours to go, the CEO of 7digital, the online music store, takes to Twitter and calls the race in favour of Rage Against the Machine. "Judging by our sales and our market share … I reckon RATM has done it but need to wait until 6.30 p.m.-ish to find out." The comments are reported immediately by the *Guardian* and *NME* websites. A nation holds its breath. As the clock ticks toward 7 p.m. Joe McElderry is heading to Radio 1's Great Portland Street studios, so he can be interviewed in the event of a win. Jon is in a cab travelling across London to do interviews of his own. The cab doesn't have a working radio. Tracy is at home, cooking the kids' dinner and listening in. Where Simon Cowell is right now is unknown, but it's probably somewhere nice. Jon and Tracy have already had "you didn't hear it from us, right?" tip-offs from journalists at the *Guardian* and t*Mirror* so they know what's coming. You can probably assume that Joe and Simon do too.

Over on Radio 1, the Top 40 countdown has reached the No. 3 record – Lady Gaga's pop banger 'Bad Romance'. But who will be played next? "Let's find out," says Scott Mills, tense music in the background, all drama and seriousness, "who is this week's number two on the official chart –" dramatic pause – "2009 –" dramatic pause – "for Christmas." Dramatic pause. A space age voice says

---

[7] They never do.

"TWO". The tense music stops. There is silence. Dead air. Nothing. An excruciating one … two … three seconds. "It's Joe." *Rage Against the Machine are No. 1*. Scott sounds disappointed. The inspirational opening piano of 'The Climb' starts. It sounds oddly disappointed, too. Somehow sadder now. The studio is inundated with texts and emails. "I bought the Rage song, but now I feel sorry for Joe. Sorry Joe!" says Tara from Cornwall. "No! Joe should have won!" says Becky in Worcester. "You can't even sing along to Rage![8] You can sing along to Joe! Joe is the real winner, and everyone knows it!" "GET IN THERE! AWESOME! THE PEOPLE HAVE SPOKEN!" says Big Norm in Cumbria. Scott Mills, bewildered, has never seen a reaction like this. "Thanks for listening tonight," he says. "We did invite Joe into the studio but he … didn't make it." You can't blame him, really. Meanwhile Jon and Tracy's phones are lighting up. Later, Zack de la Rocha is down the line on Radio 1. "We're great, we're very very ecstatic and excited about the song reaching the No. 1 spot," he says. "And I just want to say we want to thank everyone for participating in this incredible, organic grass roots campaign … It's about the spontaneous action taken by young people in the UK to topple this very sterile pop monopoly. When young people decide to take action they can make what's seemingly impossible, possible." Tom Morello tweets to call it "THE ANARCHY CHRISTMAS MIRACLE OF 2009!!!!!"

'Killing in the Name' has sold 502,672 copies in a week. The biggest one-week download sales in British chart history, and the best one-week sales ever for a rock band on any format. It's a record unlikely to ever be broken. 'The Climb', meanwhile, was no slouch, notching up 450,830 sales between digital and CD copies. In total, it's a 45% increase on singles sales week on week, so maybe the real winner is … music? Some 800,000 people have joined Jon and Tracy's Facebook group; 150,000 have joined the "incase it goes down" back-up group. Most impressively, £64,726 has been raised for Shelter. Simon Cowell is typically magnanimous in defeat. "I am genuinely impressed by the campaign they have run. It has been a good campaign with no dirty tricks and without any funding. They have been passionate and worked hard," he tells the *Daily Mirror*.

---

[8] You *absolutely* can.

"I offered them jobs at my record company … I wanted them to come and work for us. I was deadly serious, but they haven't taken me up on the offer." This particular comment is reported in dozens of newspaper stories and reports. Jon and Tracy, incidentally, never hear a peep directly. Which, at the very least, saves them the bother of turning it down. The betting industry, meanwhile, is smarting. There were a *lot* of bets put on a Rage win before the odds started to slip. At one point a 'Killing in the Name' Christmas No. 1 was going at 150/1. Well over £1,000,000 is paid out. "It's the biggest Christmas shock of all time," Coral spokesman Gary Burton tells the *Daily Mirror,* "and although it has cost the industry over £1 million, it at least now keeps the interest going, after the *X Factor* dominance almost killed off the festive chart betting forever."

It's been an exhausting, exhilarating week. Ultimately, the real winner is, well, the Christmas chart. For the first time in years, it has felt exciting again. That, after all, is what this has been all about. Protecting something sacred. Tracy says it best. "Music is our memories. Christmas is something you usually remember quite clearly, growing up, and the soundtrack to that time and period is really important. So it's nostalgia and history and where you've come from and your family. You don't want it ruined … Christmas number one is now part of our DNA." I'm not sure if she's talking about herself and Jon, or literally everybody. Either way, I think I see what she means. Caitlin Moran was right. Pop music – the most important and ridiculous thing in the world. Not just for Christmas. But, also, especially at Christmas.

A week goes by. Christmas comes and goes. Joe McElderry's 'The Climb' goes to No. 1. All is calm. All is bright.

Chapter 1
THE GHOST OF CHRISTMAS PAST

Being a brief history of Christmas music before the charts, told in three parts

A Christmas No. 1 is, to put in the simplest terms, the record at the top of the official UK singles charts in the week during which 25 December falls. And that's it. Officially, that's all there is to it. So why do we *care* so much? No other country on Earth gives a figgy pudding for the Christmas chart – at least no more so than at any other time of the year. A No. 1 at Christmas was once extremely financially desirable, pretty much everywhere – back when a single on vinyl, CD or cassette was a perfect stocking filler and people bought them by the truckload. It meant being the top seller in the biggest sales week of the year. In the age of streaming, however, when physical singles barely exist, the massive sales incentive has largely been removed. Albums are another matter, of course, especially since vinyl became sexy again. But the Christmas singles chart? It should mean no more than any other time of the year. So why *do* we still care? Because across the decades (I'd argue across the *centuries,* in fact) Britain has made music the heart of Christmas, and Christmas the heart of the year. A UK Christmas No. 1 *isn't* just a No. 1 at Christmas. It means more than that. Or, at least, it did. Once upon a time.

To understand why this is, we need to go back. *Way* back. In order to arrive at the point where we have a true Christmas No. 1, in a meaningful British *more than simply topping a cha*rt sense, three elements needed to be in place, and it's going to take a few centuries to get there. First, we need Christmas music, and we need to understand how music and Christmas are inexorably linked. Secondly, we need that music to be commercialised, packaged and sold. We need *pop* music. And ideally a chart to measure its success. And thirdly, we need to add one to the other in a way that magnifies both. A Christmas No. 1 isn't *just* a Christmas song. Sometimes it's not *even* a Christmas song. It's also not just a No. 1. It's something else. Something more. Something special. And it began thousands of years ago.

Part one: Do you hear what I hear?

As long as there has been Christmas, there has been Christmas music. When the people of Bethlehem were asked to "hark!", it was because the herald angels were *singing*. The birth of Christ even featured, according to the modern carol, a little drummer boy.[1] Throughout the ages, more than any other festival in the calendar, Christmas has been celebrated in song. In fact, our urge to sing and dance at the turning of the year goes back even further than the birth of Christ. Most societies throughout history have celebrated midwinter feasts, marking a point in the calendar in which, as Steven Moffat once wrote in another fine British festive tradition – the *Doctor Who* Christmas special – we are "halfway out of the dark". Those celebrations invariably include music – it's built into the human experience. The Romans, for example, marked the new year with a period of debauchery known as the Kalends of January, which followed the more religious Saturnalia festival. Its riotous fun was habit-forming: Christian leaders were still tutting about it as late as the sixth century. One account, attributed to an early church elder, complains about the local population's annual tendency to be

---

[1] Much to the annoyance of Mary and Joseph, who had finally gotten the baby down in the manger after he'd been grizzling all night, and did not appreciate some kid turning up to play a *drum*.

"raved in drunkenness and impious dancing" as they celebrated in the bleak midwinter.[2]

It was AD 336 when the Catholic church declared 25 December, a few days after the traditional pagan and Roman winter solstice, to be Christ's birthday – deliberately mapping a Christian holy day onto the rhythms of the existing calendar, and inadvertently welding it to party season as a result. The Vatican has been trying to convince us of the solemn spirituality of Christmas ever since, with limited success. An instinctive rowdiness has remained present in our midwinter celebrations, an urge to party we simply can't shake off. It's embedded too deep, with the singing of Christmas songs "generally done" as a Reverend Henry Bourne of Newcastle wrote in 1775, "in the midst of Rioting and Chambering,[3] and Wantonness". Singing and dancing our way through a Christmas party is an instinct recognisable to the people of pre-Christian Rome, seventeenth-century Tyneside and the customers of a twenty-first century pub having a mass singalong to Mariah Carey on a Christmas Eve. The good Reverend Bourne had the same complaint that Cliff Richard did 200 years later – that there wasn't anywhere near enough *Christ* in *Christmas*. The twist, which has been true pretty much from Day One, is that at a fundamental level, there never really had been.

Early, irreligious Christmas celebrations were about chaos, and music was always a part. For centuries Britain retained the tradition of a Lord of Misrule, an Abbot of Unreason or a King of the Bean (so called because they were selected by finding a dried bean in a special cake). A member of the court or household, usually quite a lowly one, was put in charge of mischievous Christmas proceedings, sometimes even with temporary authority over their lord or

---

[2] Christmas historian Clement A. Miles speculates that this quote came from Caesarius of Arles, a leading bishop in the fifth and sixth century who dedicated his life to stamping out enduring pagan traditions and instilling a more pious and well-behaved Catholic Christianity in the population. He was also involved in wars against the German Visigoths, putting him in opposition to both rampaging goths *and* "drunken ravers". He'd have absolutely hated the 1990s.

[3] *Chambering* being where the *Wantoness* ultimately occurs.

king, overseeing various pranks and debauchery.[4] Inevitably this would involve organising the music. Mediaeval courts and guilds employed a band of musicians known as waytes to play at banquets and parties across the Christmas period and often the Bean King or Lord of Misrule was a musician himself – he would certainly be accompanied by them. These traditions, tied to Christmas as a mid-winter festival and a hangover from the Roman Kalends of January, had nothing to do with the baby Jesus and everything to do with a release of tension and a pricking of tedium as people endured the long, dark winters of Northern Europe. It's especially true in Britain, where our relationship to Christmas has always been expressed as a joyous and messy celebration rather than with pious spirituality. It's perhaps telling that, though there are Latin hymns celebrating the birth of Christ dating from the eighth or ninth century,[5] the earliest *English* Christmas carol we know of, written somewhere around the 1400s, is a drinking song:

> *Lords, by Christmas and the host,*
> *Of this mansion hear my toast –*
> *Drink it well –*
> *Each must drain his cup of wine,*
> *And I the first will toss off mine:*
> *Thus I advise.*
> *Here then I bid you all Wassail,*
> *Cursed by he who will not say,*
> *Drinkhail!*
> *May joy come from God above,*
> *to all those who Christmas love.*

---

[4] One popular game, known as Hot Cockles, involved a player burying their face in a companion's lap and being spanked from behind – they would then have to guess which of the other guests had administered the spank. If they guessed correctly, the spanker then assumed the position and became the spankee. Hot cockles, indeed.

[5] The earliest recognisable one is the twelfth-century 'Veni, Veni Emmanuel', later translated into English as 'O Come, O Come Emmanuel' – and still sung today, to a beautiful melody that itself dates back to fifteenth-century France and is possibly even older. There is a lovely version by Sufjan Stevens' on his 2006 collection *Songs For Christmas*.

It's telling that the reference to God here is almost added as an after-thought. This was a wassailing song – a practice that stuck around for centuries, in which parties of revellers would go door to door during the Twelve Days of Christmas,[6] singing songs and offering a draught of booze from a special bowl in return for small gifts of money or food. It's a tradition that endures today in carol singing from door to door.

Almost all of the early English Christmas carols mention food and drink as often as they mention baby Jesus. (Check out, for example, the 'Boar's Head Carol', a sixteenth-century celebration of, well, eating a boar's head, the "bravest dish in the land".) Our songs have always celebrated the *celebration* itself. In the late 1600s we *wished you a merry Christmas*; in the late 1900s we *wished it could be Christmas every day*; and at the start of the 2000s we begged you not to *let the bells end*. The cheeky wink from the Darkness in that last example is far more appropriate than you'd think – British Christmas songs have been predominantly about bawdy fun for centuries. "To mask and to mum[7] kind neighbours will come," says the fifteenth-century carol 'All Hail to the Days', "With wassails of nut-brown ale/ To drink and carouse to all in the house/ As merry as bucks in the dale."

This bawdiness is one of the reasons that the Puritans tried so hard to stamp out the holiday and all of its trappings following the English Civil War. In 1647, before Charles I had even been re-lieved of his head, the celebration of Christmas was banned entirely by the new Puritan government, who associated it with pointless Papist fripperies and unseemly indulgence among the aristocracy

---

[6] A lot of early Christmas traditions are centred in the weeks *after* 25 December, culminating on Twelfth Night (5 January), rather than on Christmas Eve or Christmas Day itself. In the modern era we've rather dragged the holiday forward, spreading it across December – and it's pretty much done by 2 January. Hence the Christmas No. 1 is the song at the top of the charts when the day itself comes around. No one really cares much who's at the top the following week.

[7] Mummery was, essentially, a sort of theatrical, masked cross-dressing, done door to door, and yet another Christmas tradition that revolved around switching social roles.

and common folk alike – ironically lumping the Church's celebrations in with the sort of ribald midwinter revelling the Catholics had been trying to uncouple from Christmas for a thousand years. Christmas traditions, especially those involving singing and dancing, were driven underground, though they could never be stamped out. In Kent people rioted rather than give up Christmas. Others refused to open their businesses on Christmas Day as demanded by Parliament, and many simply held their parties anyway. The ban became largely unenforceable. A new folk song, 'The World Turned Upside Down', in which the singer laments that "Old Christmas is kickt out of Town", became popular to the point it was still being sung a hundred years later during the American Revolution.

The holiday was restored, along with the monarchy, in 1660, though some of its rougher edges had, alas, been forever buffed down. Lords of Misrule, Bean Kings, Boy Bishops[8] and all of their accompanying chaos largely fell out of fashion. What remained was the music – odes to food, drink, games, family and celebration mingling with the nods to the Nativity. By the end of the century a number of the songs we still sing today were being bellowed with gusto in pubs, halls and households across the land: 'We Wish You a Merry Christmas', 'Deck the Halls', 'God Rest Ye Merry Gentlemen' and more. The sound, at least, of Christmas in 1700 will be familiar to any British child of the twenty-first century. As the writer Nicholas Breton had put it, over a century before Oliver Cromwell tried to spoil everything, "the holidayes and musicke must bee in tune, or else never: the youth must dance and sing."

Part two: God Rest Ye Merry Gentlemen

If the birth of Christ gave us Christmas itself, pagan partying gave it its celebratory tone and mediaeval revelry gave it its voice, the Victorians were the people who packaged it all up, including the music – and sold it back to us. The customs and celebration of Christmas had emerged from the Puritan era a bit dusty but essentially intact – the singing, the drinking, the feasting, and yes, even

---

[8] Like a Lord of Misrule, but a boy who gets to, temporarily, be a Bishop. Some churches even had little Bishop's hats and crooks made especially.

the religion, all continued much as they had done before. What changed in the nineteenth century wasn't so much *what* the British did at Christmas, but *how* it was done.

It was Victorians, fervent capitalists that they were, who made Christmas an *industry*. They didn't create carol singing, but they did popularise the sale of carol books and sheet music. They didn't invent gift giving, but they did invent department store Christmas displays. They didn't create festive feasting, but they did create the Christmas food industry. In doing so, they pulled off a remarkable trick – they managed to make Christmas simultaneously more commercial *and* more sentimental.

No one embodied this contradiction better than Charles Dickens. His 1843 story *A Christmas Carol*, which has become one of the central texts of Christmas in the Western world,[9] is both a celebration of commercial Christmas and a warning. Ebenezer Scrooge's redemption comes from embracing the season's sentimentality *and* spending power in equal measure – he learns to love Christmas through seeing acts of cruelty and want, kindness and charity, family and friendship, but he manifests that love by buying a massive turkey and giving Bob Cratchit a pay rise. Dickens understood instinctively that British Christmas was both a spiritual and commercial undertaking, a time for both prayer and party, song and shopping. Though there's very little mention of music in *A Christmas Carol*, the spirit of the book can be found in most of the festive iconography and much of the tradition that came in its wake, music included – the notion that Christmas is a time for charity when we think of those less fortunate than ourselves, and that warmth and familial closeness is the idealised norm, meaning that their absence is felt keenly and starkly. Those are key themes of many of the Christmas hits of the late twentieth century.

---

[9] There are, essentially, only three Christmas stories. The Nativity, the gift giver (Santa Claus, Babushka, Père Noël, the Yule Lads, the Christkind etc) and *A Christmas Carol*. Every Christmas story we have is a version of one of those three, and it's the last that has defined the idea of what modern Christmas "should" be, a combination of revelry and charity, peace and partying. That's all Dickens: he united the two poles.

The Victorians didn't so much tame Christmas as create two parallel versions. This was the beginning of a culture that would give us the nostalgic, cosy and limp spirituality of 'Mistletoe and Wine', the mercy mission of 'Do They Know It's Christmas?' *and* the boozy riot of 'Merry Xmas Everybody', then place them next to one other on a compilation and make us pay for all three of them a few times over. The respectable version of Victorian Christmas is familiar to any modern observer: family gatherings, carol concerts, children's toys and department store spectacles. But alongside this sanitised Christmas, another version endured – one that looked remarkably like the mediaeval celebrations that had come before. In pubs, music halls and working-class neighbourhoods, the rowdier traditions lived on.

For centuries local officials had hired bands of musicians – the original waytes, known by the nineteenth century as *waits* – to perform at civic occasions, particularly during Christmas. These were disbanded by the Municipal Reform Act of 1835 which fundamentally rewrote the rule book of local government. Local revellers, however, were not easily put off from spreading musical Christmas cheer and for the rest of the century waits were formed and reformed unofficially every year, playing boisterously and loudly through the season, mostly at night. No longer on the local payroll, they essentially busked their way through December, often taking contributions to simply go away. Victorian satire is full of depictions of street musicians having projectiles and buckets of water hurled at them from windows. A cartoon showing a harassed-looking woman throwing shoes at a man playing a horn appears in an 1890 edition of *Punch* magazine, captioned waggishly "all things come to he who waits". The fine British tradition of moaning about the music of Christmas being inescapable and annoying had begun. The road to Whamageddon! starts here.

The tradition of singing carols in pubs had been a huge part of Christmas music for generations, and one that still endures in parts of Derbyshire and South Yorkshire. The Royal Hotel in Dungworth, near Sheffield, for example, hosted carolling sessions for 200 years, from late November to early January, with lots of specific local variations.[10] A 1978 report in *Melody Maker* confirms that these were not reverential, polite occasions. Songs were bellowed with "no airs and graces, roared out with vigour ... Loud and lusty with no time for the sweet, lilting cadences of the carols sung at most Christmas services. The singers in the bar, shoulder to shoulder, pints in hand, mostly singing from memory." It had been that way for centuries.[11]

Lustily sung though they might be, the village carols were still, essentially, hymns rooted in Christian tradition. In music halls across Britain, however, a distinctly irreligious Christmas music tradition had emerged and would thrive well into the twenty-first century. As variety entertainment flourished across the country, Christmas inevitably became part of the show. The halls invariably gave the Christmas season up to pantomimes – absurd comedies borrowed from the traditions of Italian clowning and anglicised into musical spectaculars, made raucous and commercial, and thoroughly embedded in working class culture. While the more well-heeled Drury Lane in London attempted to keep a veneer of theatrical respectability across its annual extravaganzas, most music hall pantos were in the rowdy and decidedly impolite traditions of British midwinter. A sheet of pantomime songs published in 1890 lists such thoroughly disrespectable titles as 'La-Diddly-Umpty-Umpty-Ay', 'A Regular Rosy Red', 'Do Buy Me That, Mamma Dear' and 'Pinky Ponky Poo'. 'Silent Night' this was not. The performers who worked these halls – singers, comedians and musicians – understood instinctively what later pop stars would rediscover: that British Christmas was primarily about celebration, and that celebration needed a soundtrack.

---

[10] The landlord of the Royal Hotel once claimed there were 28 local versions of 'While Shepherds Watched their Flocks '.

[11] It's a tradition that, regretfully, is starting to die. The Royal Hotel itself closed its doors in 2024, saying that business had slowed to a crawl following the COVID-19 pandemic. As landlord Dave Lambert told the *Star*, "We made some really lovely friends and had some great times. But those people don't come in now, or they're dead." There are still a few dozen pubs in the North of England that keep the tradition of village carols alive.

It was in the nineteenth century that Christmas music first became big business. The sheet music industry started to boom around the 1840s as printing became cheaper and more accessible, accompanied by the tightening of copyright laws and the increased affordability of pianos for pubs and middle-class homes. Publishers like Novello produced carol collections for homes and choirs, while works like Stainer's *Christmas Carols New and Old* and William B. Sandys' *Christmas Carols Ancient and Modern* helped standardise the Christmas musical repertoire. The growing middle-class market for sheet music meant traditional carols and new Christmas songs could be mass-produced and sold across the country. As prices dropped and literacy became more widespread, printed chapbooks and single-sheet "broadside ballads" brought collections of lyrics to the working classes. This was the beginnings of a recognisable music industry, in which songs themselves became sellable commodities. From its very beginning, the industry knew that Christmas was a useful and lucrative marketing opportunity.

For all their innovations, expansion of the middle classes and reputation for stuffy politeness, the Victorians, like the Puritans before them, couldn't quite tame the music of Christmas. The season remained a time when normal rules could be broken, when classes mixed more freely, and when celebration took precedence over propriety. Victorian newspapers regularly complained about rowdy Christmas celebrations in much the same way mediaeval church leaders always had, and Mary Whitehouse and Cliff Richard later would – and with about as much success. What the Victorians really created was the infrastructure for modern Christmas. They developed the commercial mechanisms that would later sell Christmas records, and – perhaps most importantly – demonstrated how sentiment and commerce could work together. They showed that Christmas celebration could be packaged and sold without losing its essential character.

They also, inadvertently, created the perfect conditions for what would come next. As the nineteenth century drew to a close, new technologies were emerging which would transform how Britain celebrated Christmas. The arrival of recorded music, radio and eventually television would create new ways of sharing. The musical traditions that had survived from mediaeval times through the

Victorian era were about to find new forms of expression, building a bridge between the wassailing songs of mediaeval Britain and the Christmas hits of the twentieth century. Now all that was needed was a way of tracking the success of that music, and a means by which it could be heard across the nation.

Part three: I'm dreaming of a ...

It was in the Roaring Twenties that Britain's music press began to emerge. The first edition of *The Melody Maker*, the music paper which would run in various forms until 2001, was published in January 1926, dedicated to jazz and dancehall music and initially aimed at musicians and music industry. Its second edition, hitting stands the following month, featured the paper's first chart. Or, at least, a chart of sorts – a list of "hits of the season" based rather arbitrarily on the sheet music subscription club run by the paper's proprietor, Lawrence Wright.[12] *Melody Maker's* first Christmas No. 1 would follow at the end of the year – 'While the Sahara Sleeps' by Horatio Nichols,[13] not that the seasonal top spot was given any particular prominence.

Though the paper's editorial content barely mentions festive music at all, and there are no seasonal songs among the "hits of the season", the December edition still tells us much about the importance of music to a 1920s Christmas. There's an editorial celebrating the December hardships of the working bandsman ("musicians' wives and children are left at the fireside to play time-honoured games and weave fairy tales without the benign presence of the family Santa Claus"), underlining the central role played by showbands and orchestras during the season. There's a call-out for members of Lawrence Wright's subscription club, promising a special "Christmas parcel of modern winning dance orchestrations" and a classified ad for the music publisher's Dix, with a fairly terrifying

---

[12] The first No. 1 was 'The Tin Can Fusiliers', a composition by Mr. Horatio Nichols – which also, by absolutely no coincidence at all, happened to be the pen name of one Lawrence Wright. The same issue declared Nichols to be "the world's greatest popular composer".

[13] Who saw that coming, eh?

looking "Father DixMas". Music, more than ever, was at the heart of the season, providing both the pulse of the party and, via records, instruments and sheet music, the ideal gift.

At the same time, the media model that would be essential in creating national music moments was starting to build momentum. The BBC's founding in 1922 created Britain's first mass broadcast medium, transforming Christmas from a collection of local traditions into a shared cultural moment. Where once every pub and music hall had its own Christmas entertainments, the entire nation could now experience the same songs, the same shows and, from 1932, even hear the same King giving the same Christmas message, all at the same time. The Corporation developed a particular genius for blending the two parallel Christmases created by the Victorians – mixing carols from King's College Chapel with variety shows and popular entertainment, creating a template for broadcasting that endured into the twenty-first century, where *Carols From Kings* and *Top of the Pops* would share the Christmas Day schedule.[14]

This coincided with the arrival of recorded music in homes was changing how Britain experienced its Christmas soundtrack. The gramophones that had begun appearing in middle-class parlours in the 1910s were becoming widely available and more affordable, and the catalogue of available titles was growing all the time, pressed onto 10", 78 rpm shellac. The music industry, which had cut its teeth selling sheet music, recognised the commercial potential immediately. The first Christmas issue of *Melody Maker* carries an ad for the His Master's Voice (HMV) record label boasting "a selection of irresistible rhythmic melodies recorded by exclusive 'His Master's Voice' artists" and promising that they are "just the records you want for Christmas entertaining". Another advert declares simply "Christmas poser solved … GRAMOPHONE RECORDS!"

---

[14] 2023 was the first Christmas Day since 1965 to not feature a *Top of the Pops* Christmas special. By itself, that speaks volumes about pop's place at the heart of Christmas celebration – *Top of the Pops*, once Britain's premier pop showcase, hadn't been broadcast regularly since 2006 but had held on to its Christmas Day slot for, almost, another 20 years. The 2023 broadcast was relegated to a lowly teatime slot on BBC 2 on 28 December. *Carols from Kings* is still on.

It was, however, classical, rather than "light" (pop) music that dominated the early record industry's Christmas rush. It took the Second World War to change that. With British troops stationed around the world, the BBC's role in maintaining morale became crucial. Christmas broadcasts took on new significance, with the BBC's Forces Programme and Home Service stations creating shared moments between soldiers and their families back home. It was in this context that "Forces' Sweetheart" Vera Lynn became the first real star of Christmas music, her heartfelt performances of songs like 'White Christmas', a huge seller in 1942, providing comfort and connection to separated families.

It's during the war years that we have our first true sales charts, based on something more substantial than a subscription club run by the man who owned *Melody Maker*. The Wholesale Music Distributors' Association (and, later, the Music Publishers Association), kept track of orders of sheet music and produced a weekly rundown of bestsellers, published in *Melody Maker* and other papers and, later, on Radio Luxembourg. Though sales of 78 rpm records themselves are harder to track, this would be our first real, sales-based look at what pieces of music were enjoying popularity in any given week. The first song that can legitimately lay claim to the title "Christmas No. 1", the bestselling song in the week of Christmas, was 1940's 'There'll Come Another Day',[15] made popular that year by Vera Lynn, though several artists released recordings around the same time. Much like Lynn's other big war-time numbers, 'We'll Meet Again' and '(There'll Be Bluebirds Over) The White Cliffs of Dover,' it's a melancholic and yearning piece with the general theme of *it'll all be okay in the end, just hang on in there.* You can see why it would appeal to a population on a war footing, left at home while husbands and fathers shipped abroad to fight. Along with rousing patriotism (George Fornby's 'Bless 'Em All' was also a huge hit at the time) these blends of melancholy

---

[15] The surviving chart data begins on 30 December of the previous year, so we don't actually know what the bestseller of Christmas 1939 was. However, since the final No. 1 that year was 'I'm Sending a Letter to Santa Claus', a hit at the time for both Arthur Askey and Gracie Fields, it's a fairly safe assumption that it probably held the spot the previous week as well.

optimism were, understandably, a general theme of the wartime Christmas charts.

The only true holiday song to get a look in during this period is the aforementioned 'White Christmas'. It entered the 1942 sheet music charts in early September, hit No. 1 mid November and stayed there until the end of the year. Bing Crosby's version was also the UK's bestselling 78 record across December, with versions by Vera Lynn, Hutch and Victor Silvester also selling well. In fact, 'White Christmas' went on selling consistently, on paper and on disc, and later online, from that point onwards for, well ... pretty much forever. 'White Christmas' might just be the most important Christmas song ever written, establishing themes of wistful nostalgia, a yearning for the Christmases "I used to know", and a celebration of the old-timey imagery that would become an absolutely key theme in seasonal music, films and stories of all sorts as the twentieth century progressed. It's certainly the bestselling Christmas song – the *Guiness Book of World Records* estimates over a hundred *million* copies are out there in the world in one form or another, with versions recorded by Bing Crosby accounting for over half.[16] In fact, 'White Christmas' isn't just the bestselling *Christmas* song of all time, it's the bestselling *song* of all time – and since the way music is distributed has changed so radically, that's a position it is unlikely to ever lose.

This gently epoch-shaking ballad had been penned by songwriting titan Irving Berlin in 1940. Berlin, already the most influential American songwriter of his era,[17] had spent long periods of

[16] Crosby recorded 'White Christmas' several times, beginning with a duet on the soundtrack for the movie *Holiday Inn* (it won him an Oscar). The notable recordings are the solo take that was released on a 78 rpm disc in 1942, and a second recording tracked in 1947 after the original master wore out. It's the latter that's probably most familiar. Crosby would go on to record dozens of live versions over the years. His final recording of the song was just a month before his death, for the TV special *Bing Crosby's Merrie Olde Christmas,* recorded in the UK in September 1977.

[17] Berlin, in his fifties by this point and a legend in the industry, had established himself as a successful songwriter in the first decade of the twentieth century, but it was his 1911 hit 'Alexander's Ragtime Band' that supercharged everything. To say that it invented modern pop is a stretch, but it certainly laid its foundations.

the late '30s living out of LA hotels, writing for Hollywood, and found himself, like the wartime families of 1940s Britain, separated from his loved ones at Christmas and pining for a simpler time. A Russian-born Jew (his given name was Israel Beilin), Berlin had emigrated to the United States around the turn of the century and remembered well the New York Christmases of his childhood and teens: the snowy streets, the bitter cold and the accompanying fireside cosiness and familial warmth in the glow of the Christmas tree, which the Jewish Berlin had to view through the windows of his neighbours[18] – all a far cry from the lonely blue skies and palm trees of California.[19] Feeling rather sorry for himself, he had channelled all of that into the intimate, yearning and, somehow, though it's not really present in the lyrics themselves, desperately sad 'White Christmas'. It took him another few years to nail the song down, but when he did, during an all-nighter back in New York in the first week of January 1940, he knew he'd struck gold. According to Helmy Kresa, Berlin's principal arranger and orchestrator, the

Berlin's then uncommon blend of syncopated African-American ragtime beats with white vaudeville charm – and an overemphasised, key-changing chorus (a novel trick that defied centuries of songwriting tradition) – created something universally accessible. You could sing to it, dance to it; it was white, it was Black, it was hummable, and, more than anything, it was American. The song changed Berlin's life, but it also changed music, helping to finally give the United States a sound of its own, distinct from its European ancestry. Not many songwriters can claim to have changed culture. Berlin did it at least twice, and lived past the age of 100, getting to see the scope of the world he'd created – though since he was famously quite crotchety and bad-tempered, he probably wasn't hugely impressed by what he had wrought.

[18] Once he had a family of his own he made a point of going BIG on Christmas for the sake of his children, though the season would always be tinged with sadness for him – his second child, a son called Irving Junior, had died on Christmas Day in 1928 at just three weeks old. Once Berlin's children left home, he and his wife never celebrated Christmas again.

[19] The original lyrics for 'White Christmas' opened with a verse setting out the stall – describing the shining sun, the green grass and the swaying palm trees. This section, rarely performed, was resurrected for Darlene Love's brilliant version on 1963's classic *A Christmas Gift For You from Phil Spector*.

following morning he declared that 'White Christmas' was "not only the best song I ever wrote ... it's the best song *anybody* ever wrote."

It was recorded by Bing Crosby in 1941 for the film *Holiday Inn*, winning a 'Best Original Song' Oscar in the process. Crosby sang it with purring warmth into microphones capable of delivering a vocal intimacy not possible until relatively recently,[20] and it connected instantly, and not just in the US. December 1942 saw seven different versions of 'White Christmas' released on 78 in the UK, all of them massive sellers. So completely pervasive, so perfectly *Christmassy* was it, that a *New Music Express* review of Mantovani's version, just a decade later, was offhandedly describing it as a "standard". The words "instant classic" have rarely been so appropriate.

The Missing Charts, a book by Steve Waters published in 2013, used historical data collected by the late music industry archivist Colin Brown to compile theoretical charts, covering sales of 78 rpm records between 1940 and the birth of the "official" chart in 1952. Brown had spent the late 1940s glad-handing music publishers and record companies to obtain data from their sales reps and buyers, and had hung on to those figures for half a century. After his death, Waters used that data to create a reasonably comprehensive snapshot of physical record sales in the pre-chart era. According to Brown's figures, 'White Christmas' was Christmas No. 1 in 1942, 1945, 1946, 1947, 1948, 1949, 1950 and 1951.[21]

---

[20] The intimacy with which the early crooners were able to sing was revolutionary when electrical recording was introduced in the mid 1920s. Before that, acoustic recording meant singers had to project powerfully into a recording horn – anything subtle would be lost. The new electric microphones changed everything, allowing vocalists to sing as if they were whispering sweet nothings directly into the listener's ear. This more intimate style raised eyebrows in conservative quarters, being considered rather too sensual for polite society. Crosby, who began his career just as this technology was emerging, mastered the technique early. It's probably the only time in his whole career anyone could consider Bing Crosby the least bit sexy.

[21] If you're wondering about 1943 and 1944 – it stalled at No. 2 behind the Mills Brothers' 'Paper Doll' and Harriet Cohen's 'The Cornish Rhapsody', respectively.

'White Christmas' was one of only a handful of Christmas songs to be a hit during the war years, and it changed Christmas culture as it passed through. It introduced to the canon something which the hard-partying Brits had previously wanted little to do with: nostalgic American schmaltz. Though that schmaltz would be hard to come by for a while: the BBC's Dance Music Policy Committee (nicknamed the 'Anti-Slush committee') was formed specifically to keep maudlin music off the airwaves, lest it damage morale.[22] Once the war was over, however, such songs would become a feature of the season. As the decade progressed, American artists increasingly defined the sound of commercial Christmas. By 1950 we had 'Rudolph the Red-Nosed Reindeer', a song so classic-sounding you assume it must date back at least a century. In fact, as of the time of writing, it's still in copyright. The tale of the scarlet-snozzed Rudolph was originally written as a promotional story for the Montgomery Ward department store in 1939 and had been turned into a song by the Singing Cowboy Gene Autry a decade later. It's a good example of how thoroughly commercialised Christmas music had become: Autry's recording was followed by Bing Crosby's, and would be covered by British artists like Donald Peers. Then there was 'Let It Snow! Let It Snow! Let It Snow!' (written during a Los Angeles heat wave in 1945) and, far better, 1944's 'Baby, It's Cold Outside' (originally a party piece written by Broadway composer Frank Loesser to perform with his wife at society gatherings); 'The Christmas Song (Chestnuts Roasting on an Open Fire)', a huge hit for Nat King Cole in 1945; 'Sleigh Ride' (1948), 'Silver Bells' (1950), 'Frosty the Snowman'(1950) and 'It's Beginning to Look a Lot Like Christmas' (1951). Older Christmas songs, nineteenth-century carols like 'Deck the Halls' and 'God Rest Ye Merry Gentlemen' and secular ditties like 'Jingle Bells', were also dusted off, as were more recent slices of Americana; 1930s songs

---

[22] According to BBC records, one committee member was heard to say, "we have recently adopted a policy of excluding sickly sentimentality which, particularly when sung by certain vocalists, can become nauseating and not at all in keeping with what we feel to be the need of the public in this country." As the *Daily Telegraph* said at the time, "If our Armed Forces really like this sort of thing, it should be the duty of the BBC to hide the fact from the world."

that had been largely forgotten but would quickly become classics as the rising tide of 'White Christmas' raised all boats – among them 'Winter Wonderland' and 'Santa Claus is Comin' to Town', the latter now holding the title for the most commonly performed Christmas song. America's Tin Pan Alley songwriters were finally catching onto something they'd previously missed: Christmas could be a goldmine. The best of this new crop, 'Have Yourself a Merry Little Christmas' (performed by Judy Garland in the film *Meet Me In St. Louis*) and 'I'll Be Home For Christmas' (recorded by Crosby himself in 1943) were, like 'White Christmas', achingly sad paeans to home and hearth, imagining some "proper" version of Christmas, "just like the ones we used to know", centred around peace, kindness, family and, inevitably, snow, that was, at this moment, just out of reach.[23] In a way these songs both did something that the Catholics and the Puritans had failed to achieve – taking all the messy, riotous partying out of the season.

The songbook of modern Christmas pop was growing, but it was almost all coming from the United States. British songwriters were adding very little to the canon. The American music industry had developed a sophisticated system of professional songwriting, centred around New York's Tin Pan Alley, where teams of writers crafted hits with almost industrial efficiency. These writers – Irving Berlin himself, Johnny Mercer, Frank Loesser and their contemporaries – were masters at balancing commerce and emotion, creating songs that could be both successful products and cultural touchstones. They had elevated songwriting into a craft, even a science, with their own formulas and techniques for reaching audiences. Berlin was the perfect example – a Jewish immigrant who understood exactly how to capture the Christian holiday's broader cultural appeal, just as he had done with 'Easter Parade' and countless other standards. He'd learned his trade writing for Broadway and vaudeville where success relied on finding universal experiences in specific moments. The same skills that helped him tap into America's

---

[23] Bing's 'I'll Be Home for Christmas' was one of those records banned by the BBC's 'Anti-Slush Committee' for being too soppy for wartime airwaves – it was felt such yearning for hearth and home was likely to leave the brave boys on the frontlines rather despondent.

patriotic spirit with a song like 'God Bless America' allowed him to crystallise the emotional peak of Christmas into a simple wish for snow, coded into which was so much more: home, peace, family, tradition, comfort. The sophistication of the American music industry, combined with Britain's post-war embrace of American culture through Armed Forces Radio and the influx of US servicemen, created the perfect conditions for these songs to flourish. British artists would cover them enthusiastically but seemed hesitant to create their own. It would take another generation, and the arrival of rock and roll, before home-grown writers finally caught up.

By 1951 all the elements that would culminate in the phenomenon of the Christmas No. 1 were in place. We had the technology to distribute Christmas music to the masses. We had the BBC creating shared cultural moments. We had a music industry that understood both the commercial and sentimental power of the season. The following year would see the launch of the first true singles chart, tracking actual sales of music discs, and with it the birth of the Christmas No. 1 pop record; though it would take another 20 years for that to really mean something. When it did, it would draw on everything that had come before – the rowdy traditions of mediaeval wassailing, the commercial instincts of the Victorians, the music hall's slice of *mother wouldn't approve* sauce, the Americana paeans for cosy days of yore and the BBC's ability to create moments of national togetherness. The Ghost of Christmas Past had given us a hell of a Christmas present.

Chapter 2
CHRISTMAS (YEAH, YEAH, YEAH)

Being a tale of Festive Music in the modern pop era

The first *official* UK Christmas No. 1, as in the disc that was selling the most copies in the week prior to Christmas Day, in the first year in which there was a (mostly) reliable chart to record it, was the croonsome Al Martino's December 1952 hit 'Here in my Heart'. There are various earlier songs that can claim the Christmas No. 1 in the decades prior – but no-one was marking the achievement – in 1952, came something new. A music magazine decided to put together a list of the top-selling records and compiled it by collecting reasonably reliable data. It wasn't completely accurate and could be gamed fairly easily – it would be replaced as the "official" chart by another magazine within a few years[1] – and, really, no chart was considered properly authoritative until the independent British Market Research Bureau (BMRB) started to compile one from rigorously collected sales data in 1969. But still, 1952 marks the watershed. A true singles chart based on sales of actual discs. And it turned up just in time for Christmas.

The magazine that broke this ground was *New Musical Express*, later of course known as *NME*. It was a relaunch of the ailing

---

[1] The Official Charts Company, the body that oversees the UK singles chart in the present day, switches to the more comprehensive and less easily gamed Top 50 featured in the trade paper *Record Retailer*.

Musical Express,[2] an industry rival to *The Melody Maker* that had recently fallen on hard times and been bought out by music impresario Maurice Kinn, who moved its offices to London's Denmark Street, the centre of the British music industry, and hired a whole new staff, headed by music press veterans Percy Dickins and editor Ray Sonin. Sales were slow to begin with, until Kinn, Dickins and Sonin[3] hit upon an idea that was both fairly simple and completely revolutionary – print a list of the top-selling records in the country. They'd pinched the concept from *Billboard*, the US industry magazine that had regularly ran a Hit Parade tracking the songs most popular on American jukeboxes and radio stations as well as through sales data. *NME, however,* was only interested in pure sales – establishing a key difference between the British and American singles chart that endures to this day. The plan was simple: phone around 20 or so record shops and get a list of their biggest-selling singles that week, then get the company accountant to compile the results. "Announcing the first record Hit Parade!" ran the headline in the issue of 14 November. "For the first time in the history of the British popular music business, an authentic weekly survey of the bestselling 'pop' records has been devised and instituted." It was a genius move. Immediately, the music industry was paying closer attention to *NME* than any of its rivals, and access and advertising both shot up, as did circulation as readers returned every week to see, in real time, what was hot and what was not. Sales increased 50% by the end of the year. By the mid '50s it was selling 100,000 copies a week. Radio Luxembourg even based a weekly show on the chart.

The Hit Parade had a genuine cultural impact. The paper's editors could now see the emergence of sales trends and spot the holes

---

[2] Or to give it its full title *Accordion Times and Musical Express*. There'd been a huge boom in accordion music in the 1930s, fuelled mostly by energetic and brightly dressed performances that splashed some colour into the drab streets of Depression-era Britain. The boom was short lived, and the genre's premium publication, *Accordion Times*, was soon combined into the newly launched *Musical Express*, where it quickly became a single column before vanishing completely from the masthead.

[3] All three claimed credit for this idea over the years.

in their coverage, and realised pretty quickly that the syncopated showband swing and the big band orchestras that *Melody Maker* had been favouring for decades were gradually being supplanted by newer, younger singers – pre-rock heartthrobs like Johnny Ray, Frankie Laine and Frank Sinatra, artists who weren't being especially well covered by the existing press. *NME* was able to pivot to them. It was the first music magazine to celebrate pop on the grounds that it was, well, *popular*, the first magazine to focus on what was *cool* as its priority. The charts made *NME* matter, and its proclamation of the UK's No. 1 record mattered most of all. Predictably, *Melody Maker* followed suit with a hit parade of its own fairly quickly, and was able to offer its weekly chart for republishing in national news-papers.[4] Suddenly the bestselling song in the country was *news*. The launch of the hit parade also coincided with the arrival of the 7" single in Britain – it was Christmas 1952, and the modern pop era had begun.

We should pause a second here to pay some tribute to Al Martino, the Italian-American crooner who, per *NME's* hit parade, claimed not only he first UK Christmas No. 1 but the first UK No. 1 full stop. 'Here In My Heart' is not necessarily an impor-tant record, nor an especially well remembered one – Martino had the misfortune to hit his early fame in an era immediately before rock and roll came along and changed the game, and he is prob-ably better remembered for his acting career than his hits; he was in *The Godfather*.[5] It's also not a song we'd typically associate with Christmas, though its release on 78 rpm shellac disc would certainly have been a popular gift that year. In truth, Martino is more pub quiz answer than classic pop idol. Which is a shame, because 'Here in my Heart' is rather good – a stirring, dramatic and romantic ballad that opens with a swell of cinematic strings and a lung-bursting, almost

---

[4] The *Maker* chart combined sales data with sheet music statistics from the Music Publishers Association. This gave it the veneer of accessibility needed to tempt the national press but rather muddied the waters – it's why the Official Charts Company uses *NME's* Hit Parade as the official charts of the 1950s.
[5] A role he played with some credibility – Martino's management contract had been bought out in the states by the Mafia. He fled to the UK in the '50s to escape the Mob.

operatic "Heeeeeeeeeeeeeeeeeere in my heeeeeeeeeeaaaaaaaaaart" from Martino, who then drops his voice to a croon to complete the line: "I'm alone and so lonely". Like many of the best Christmas No. 1s, from Mud's 'Lonely this Christmas' to Wham!'s 'Last Christmas' to East 17's 'Stay Another Day', it's built on heartbreak. The song had been a huge hit in the US, and would top the new UK Hit Parade for nine consecutive weeks. It's still, at the time of writing, one of only ten records to spend that long at No. 1. Though something of a footnote now, there are far worse songs that could have begun the tradition of Christmas No. 1.

What's interesting is what's *not* in the Christmas chart that year. Bing Crosby's recording of 'White Christmas' had been the unofficial Christmas No. 1 for eight of the previous ten years, including a seven-year run from 1945 to 1951. It's not, however, on the *NME*'s first chart at all, though a cover by Mantovani is. The absence of the Crosby version is something of a mystery. Tastes in the UK were indeed changing, with Labour's recent Festival of Britain inspiring a more forward-looking culture and a general move in pop music toward smore progressive and modern musical moods over slushy balladeers ... but that doesn't seem to apply to the Christmas chart, which has most of the same names as the previous year's big sellers: Vera Lynn, Nat King Cole, Frankie Laine and, yes, Bing Crosby, who appears twice, at No. 3 with 'The Isle of Innisfree' *and* at No. 8 with his version of 'Silent Night'. The presence of Mantovani's orchestral 'White Christmas' makes it even more peculiar. Was the Crosby version simply not widely stocked that year? Was the *NME* ringing around stores where it was inexplicably unpopular? Or, after a decade of dominance, had the public finally had enough?

In Crosby's absence, Martino's 'Here in my Heart' remains our *official* first Christmas No. 1, though it's a title it holds in name only. We recognise it as such now because it fits the technical definition, but we're still a long way from the emergence of the media-led phenomenon we came to recognise. No one especially cared. A No. 1? Sure. No. 1 at Christmas? No bigger a deal than any other. The building blocks were falling into place, however. We had a thriving market in singles and a more or less reliable chart to track it. Music was a huge part of the festivities, as is pretty clear from the *NME*'s 1952 Christmas issue, stuffed full of seasons greetings from the stars of the day (including a huge half-page, colour advert from Vera Lynn "wishing you all a Merry Christmas and a Happy New Year"), reports from Christmas gigs and any number of festive-themed small ads for records and sheet music. There was no real connection yet, though, between pop music and festive tradition – at least not one that went any deeper than soundtracking parties and concerts or being given as a gift. Music itself was part of Christmas, but pop had yet to find its role. A seismic shift in youth culture was necessary, one that would elevate pop into one of the most important art forms in the land and make its tethering at the heart of Christmas inevitable. Fortunately, there was one just around the corner.

According to the *NME* Hit Parade, the 1955 Christmas No. 1 was Dickie Valentine's faintly insipid novelty song 'Christmas Alphabet'.[6] It's not particularly well remembered, though it's interesting for a few reasons – it was the first Christmas No. 1 to actually be about Christmas, and it was the first to be available on a 45 rpm 7" disc, the spiritual home of the pop song. It also set a precedent that we would see again and again, right through the canon: Christmas No. 1s weren't always going to be good records. This, arguably, was the first genuinely bad song to take the title. The groundwork for Mr Blobby and LadBaby started here.

If you were reading *Record Mirror* rather than *NME*, however, things were slightly different. *Record Mirror* was a newer publication and pushing the formula that little bit further. *NME*, like *Melody Maker*, still assumed a large part of its readership were musicians or involved in the industry, or at least knowledgeable about the music world, and though the magazine had been leaning further and further into pure pop, it still carried some of the respectable weight

---

[6] 'Christmas Alphabet' was co-written by American lyricist Buddy Kaye, who had some form with this type of thing – his other notable hit was "A' You're Adorable', which went through the alphabet tagging a compliment to each letter. Every bit as punk rock as it sounds. For 'Christmas Alphabet', Kaye focused on just the eight that spelled out C-H-R-I-S-T-M-A-S. And by the last few letters he seems to be running out of ideas. A is for "the angels who make up the Christmas list", which angels don't traditionally do. Also, which list? The list of presents you send to Santa? The naughty or nice list? And the final S is for "old Santa who makes every kid his pet" – kind of creepy.

of the business. *Record Mirror*, launched in 1954, was a different proposition entirely. It was the first music paper to be aimed entirely at *fans*, and had a breezier, more lightweight tone, written from the correct assumption that fans were interested in their favourite artists' lives and opinions as much as their songs. It also, predictably, had a chart of its own, using a different set of vendors (the paper listed individual Top 10s for each contributing store). Though the *NME*, *Melody Maker* and *Record Mirror* charts were similar, they were not identical, and *Record Mirror* broke ranks that Christmas, declaring a different No. 1 – Bill Hayley & His Comets' international smash 'Rock Around the Clock'. The song had been a huge hit that year and had sat at the top of the *NME* chart for three weeks before being knocked out by Valentine's more seasonal shmaltz. *Record Mirror* had it at the top a whole week earlier than *NME* and kept it there until well into the new year.[7] Rock and roll had finally arrived in the UK. Across the next few years it would change the landscape, within a decade it would change the world.

From our perspective today, it's difficult to appreciate why a song like 'Rock Around the Clock' was such a jolt – familiarity has now left it dulled and aged. In 1955, though, this was like hearing punk rock, acid house and hip-hop all at once and for the very first time. Hayley was an unlikely rock idol, pushing 30 years old with a cornball persona and a kiss curl, but his jumping take on rockabilly was the perfect bridge between the dance bands of the past and the pure rock of the future. It's right there in 'Rock Around the Clock', which has a horn break that could have come from a Glenn Miller big band number and a guitar solo that would have sat comfortably on a record by Elvis. More than that, it was a pure good-time, begging us to, quite literally, party all day and all night. That opening line, "One, two, three o'clock, four o'clock *rock* is as exciting a start to a pop record as you'll find. Its sharp opposition to the candy floss-soft 'Christmas Alphabet' is a precursor to many seasonal chart battles of the future, which would pit Pink Floyd against ABBA (1979), Rage Against the Machine against Joe McElderry (2009) and the Darkness against Gary Jules (2003).

---

[7] The song would also return to the top spot in *NME* once the bloom had come off Christmas, and would become the UK's first million seller.

The fact that different record shops could produce such different results showed how fragmented British pop was becoming. While Dickie Valentine represented the old guard of variety entertainment and novelty songs, Bill Haley was the harbinger of something new – the racket and rumble of rock and the sound of teen rebellion: "Merry Christmas, I won't do what you tell me!" The competing charts tell an interesting story about British pop in transition; *Record Mirror*'s methodology produced different results to *NME* precisely because they asked different shops. British record-buying habits varied from location to location, generation to generation. What sold well in one shop might bomb in another. The idea of a definitive No. 1 record was still a fairly loose concept yo-yoing from town to town, chart to chart, person to person. The seasonal charts of the mid to late 1950s remained dominated by crooners, big bands, instrumentals and novelty songs, but a change was coming. While their parents might have been content with another Mario Lanza carol collection, Britain's teenagers, finally feeling their oats as the shadow cast by the Second World War lifted, were developing their own relationship with pop, and the music industry was starting to notice. The growing popularity of the cheaper 7" single, now starting to overtake the old 78s, was making music affordable and attainable at home, just as the growth of printing and literacy had a hundred years earlier. A Christmas hit could now be bought with pocket money. Teenagers could afford their own record players and choose their own Christmas soundtrack for the first time. Youth culture and the cult of the teenager had arrived. It would change everything.

By the early 1960s, British pop was finding its feet, and with it came new approaches to the music of Christmas. Once the Beatles arrived, there was no looking back. They supercharged the pop industry, setting it on the trajectory that it's still on today, focused on youth, excitement, energy and charm. The Fab Four's dominance of the charts meant they were inevitably going to claim some Christmas No. 1s, bagging a hat trick with 'I Want To Hold Your Hand' (1963),[8] 'I Feel Fine' (1964) and 'Day Tripper'/'We Can

[8] That year they also held the Christmas No. 2 with their previous single, 'She Loves You', *and* the top two spaces on *Record Mirror*'s album chart with *With the Beatles* and *Please Please Me*.

Work It Out', a double A-side (1965),[9] though none of them felt remotely seasonal. Not that the biggest band in the world ignored Christmas. From 1963 to 1969, they recorded special Christmas messages every year, pressing them onto flexi discs and sending them free to fan club members. These were loose, playful recordings – 1967's 'Christmas Time (Is Here Again)' is the closest they would get to a real Christmas song – and they caught the band's natural humour, mixing comedy sketches, jokey versions of carols and Beatles originals[10] with messages of thanks to their fans. They also established something crucial – that even the biggest band in the world could treat Christmas as an opportunity to have fun. Far from leading to a wave of beat group Christmas songs, however, these remained private communications between band and fans. Other groups would copy the fan club message idea, but nobody tried to transfer it to the pop market.

The Christmas hits of the mid '60s tell their own story. The Beatles themselves would claim the top spot again in 1967 with 'Hello Goodbye', but again not with a Christmas song. Even as British pop grew more sophisticated and ambitious, it seemed reluctant to tackle Christmas head-on. It just didn't feel like something that *cool* bands did. The Beatles might command the No. 1 spot without trying, but seasonal themed hits were genuinely rare, and when they came they were almost always old standards (various recordings of the sickly hymn 'Little Donkey' charted from the late '50s to the mid '60s for example) or novelties (Dora Bryan's music hall-flavoured 'All I Want for Christmas Is a Beatle', a Top 30 hit in 1963[11]). Brenda Lee's 'Rockin' Around the Christmas Tree', peaking at No. 11 in 1962, Chuck Berry's 'Run Rudolph Run' (No. 23, 1963) and Elvis's 'Blue Christmas' (No. 13, 1964) might be the only genuinely good Christmas-themed hits of the whole decade. And they were all recorded in the '50s. By Americans. In the psyche-

---

[9] They'd hold the record for the most Christmas No. 1s in a row until it was equalled by the Spice Girls in the 90s and then finally broken by, of all things, LadBaby's Sausage Roll based novelties in the 2020s.

[10] "Christmas day, all my troubles seem so far away . . ."

[11] Sample lyric: "I told my mum that nothing else would do/ There are four, so she can have one too."

delic era, when British pop was at its most adventurous, Christmas remained curiously resistant to the revolution. Instead there was a minor music hall renaissance led by the Scaffolds' 1968 Christmas No. 1, 'Lily the Pink', joined in the chart that week by the Bonzo Dog Doo-Dah Band's 'I'm the Urban Spaceman' and Danny La Rue's 'On Mother Kelly's Doorstep.'[12] Outside of contemporary pop songs that would be hits at any time of year, Christmas remained a time for novelty and a harking back to the "good old days".

The launch of Radio 1, the BBC's first pop-focused station, in September 1967 would begin to change this. Britain now had an official, national pop channel creating shared moments for young audiences and focused entirely on "young" music, with no space for Max Bygraves, Harry Secombe, Des O'Connor or Val Doonican. The BBC's television coverage was changing, too – *Top of the Pops*, the weekly chart TV show, had launched in 1964, and was immediately unmissable viewing for pop fans. The first *Top of the Pops* Christmas special was broadcast at lunchtime on Christmas Day, 1965. This was a crucial step, as it meant an airing of the Christmas chart on Christmas Day itself – and it would occupy the slot for the next 58 years. Pop was finally taking its place at the Christmas dinner table.

Just as important that year was a special festive episode of *Ready Steady Go!*, the much livelier music show broadcast by ATV (the BBC's commercial rival in London). Given a prime slot at 8 p.m. on Christmas Eve, this featured a grab bag of pop talent, including the Who, the Animals, the Kinks and Cilla Black farcing their way through a pantomime performance of *Cinderella*, with Keith Moon as Buttons, naturally, and culminating with Messrs Townshend, Daltry, Moon and Entwistle delivering a messy, skiffle version of 'Jingle Bells' before the whole cast took on 'White Christmas'. Elsewhere on the show, the Animals covered Elvis's 'Santa Claus is Back in Town', the Hollies tackled 'Winter Wonderland' and Herman's Hermits took on 'Rudolph the Red Nosed Reindeer'. The Kinks' Ray Davies was supposed to be writing a song especially for

---

[12] Of these, only La Rue's was a true music hall number – 'Lily the Pink' was a novelty flop from the US and 'Urban Spaceman' was an original song. All three had the flavour of the halls, though. Variety was still a force to be reckoned with.

the occasion, but having failed to complete it opted to perform the old novelty 'All I Want for Christmas (Is My Two Front Teeth)'. The whole thing was a Christmas riot, true to the anarchic, partying spirit of the season that went back centuries. British pop absolutely knew how to let its newly grown-out hair down for Christmas. It just hadn't yet worked out that you could write credible chart hits at the same time. By 1968 pop had cemented itself into Christmas Day. As well as *Top of the Pops*, BBC 1 broadcast *Christmas Night with the Stars*, a glitzy affair featuring the broadest of pop churches: Lulu, Petula Clarke, the Seekers, Louis Armstrong, Cliff Richard and Nana Mouskouri. The show, which began in the '50s, would run every Christmas night for years.

By the end of the 1960s all the elements needed for the Christmas No. 1 phenomenon were present. The youth market was firmly established, and the music industry had grown sophisticated enough to capitalise. Charts had gained authority – the various competing publications might occasionally disagree on positions, but the concept of a No. 1 record held real cultural weight. What was missing was someone to put it all together – to create Christmas records that could unite the rowdy spirit of mediaeval Britain with the commercial instincts of the Victorians and the cultural impact of the beat groups of the early '60s. Christmas music had to become, not just fun, but *cool*. As usual, it was left to a Beatle to show the way

Chapter 3
SO THIS IS CHRISTMAS

Or how John and Yoko brought Christmas back to pop

With one very notable exception, the last Christmas chart of the '60s (the week ending 20 December 1969) was a remarkably modern one, largely free of the usual silliness. It features zero Christmas-themed songs and a clutch of genuine pop masterpieces: Elvis Presley's gospel-led return to form had put him into the Top 5 with the unimpeachable classic 'Suspicious Minds', and the Beatles' sublime double A-side of 'Something' and 'Come Together' was still lurking in the Top 20, ten places above John Lennon's brilliantly angsty solo single 'Cold Turkey'. There was Marvin Gaye, Stevie Wonder, the Creedence Clearwater Revival and Nancy Sinatra. There was Jimmy Cliff's sun-kissed 'Wonderful World, Beautiful People' and the gritty blues of Fleetwood Mac's fantastic 'Oh Well'. And, sure, there was a fair smattering of textbook, old-school British showbiz (Des O'Connor, Cliff Richard, Cilla Black, Tom Jones) and cornball Americana (Kenny Rogers, Bobbie Gentry and Glen Campbell, Jim Reeves, the cringey right-on but enjoyably funky Blue Mink[1]) but there was also the Hollies' 'He Ain't Heavy, He's My Brother' and the melodic reggae groove of The Harry J All Stars'

---

[1] The band's 1969 hit 'Melting Pot', a right-on paean to racial diversity, is rather spoiled when it follows a plea to mix white and Black with a word now largely considered a slur against people of Chinese descent.

'Liquidator'. Mercifully, the Archies' inescapable 'Sugar, Sugar' had been dethroned after a truly testing eight weeks at the top.[2]

The record that had replaced it, claiming the final Christmas No. 1 of the decade (and staying in place to be the first No. 1 of the '70s), however, was textbook Christmas chart novelty – 'Two Little Boys' by Australian artist and all-round entertainer Rolf Harris.[3] It's an odd song, written in the US at the turn of the century and telling a tale set possibly in the Crimean War, possibly in the American Civil War and possibly in the Napoleonic Peninsular War (there's a lot of arguments about this). In the song, two small boys who played at soldiers with hobby horses as children, grow up and go to war. The first verse is treacly sweet ("Two little boys had two little toys/ Each had a wooden horse"). The second, however, takes a brutal turn: "Long years had passed, war came so fast/ Bravely they marched away/ Cannon roared loud, and in the mad crowd/ Wounded and dying lay." It's a hell of a rug pull. "Do you think I would leave you dying," goes the second chorus, "when there's room on my horse for two?" Sung in Harris' plaintive, lightly accented voice, it's surprisingly affecting. Harris, a very occasional recording artist who hadn't had a real hit in years and was more known as a TV personality, decided to record it after a performance on his BBC TV show prompted huge reactions. It was a good instinct – despite being ignored by the music press at first (none of the weeklies reviewed the single) the melancholy ditty connected powerfully with listeners and the single shifted in huge numbers, going straight in at 32 and climbing to No. 1 just in time for Christmas, where it sat for

---

[2] Actually 'Sugar, Sugar', by the completely fictional cartoon pop band the Archies, is a *fantastic* single – Velcro catchy with a brilliant, breezy groove and a surprisingly sexy tone. It was only its ubiquity that counted against it as the year drew to a close. It would stay in the Top 40 for 14 weeks.

[3] Harris, of course, would end his career in disgrace after being found guilty of twelve counts of indecent assault, four against underage girls. Like Jimmy Savile he had been a beloved children's entertainer, and the public fury was palpable. I'm bringing it up here because it feels odd to discuss Harris and *not* mention his crimes, even if they're irrelevant to the story. This sort of thing is going to come up a few times – Savile, Gary Glitter, Phil Spector, Michael Jackson. These men committed or were accused of dreadful crimes, and their victims deserve to be seen and represented.

the next six weeks. It would stay on the Top 40 until May of 1970, finally dropping out after 24 weeks on the chart.

This was a typical Christmas hit, the sort of thing that could appeal to grannies and children – people who didn't buy records at other times of the year. It's the kind of single that defies the ordinary rules of pop, that hit songs and artists should be cool, young, sexy and relatable. The Christmas chart provides a brief window, largely shut for the rest of the year, for this sort of throwback to rocket up the hit parade. The same thing had happened in the past with 'Christmas Alphabet' (1953), and it would happen again with 'Ernie (The Fastest Milkman in the West)' (1971), 'There's No One Quite Like Grandma' (1980) and 'Bob the Builder' (2000) – though 'Two Little Boys' proved to have far more staying power. Years later Margaret Thatcher, that famous patron of pop, listed 'Two Little Boys' as one of her favourite songs, alongside '(How Much Is That) Doggie in the Window'.

Another person impressed by Harris's record was John Lennon. To Lennon, 'Two Little Boys' wasn't simply a song *about* a war, it was a song that was explicitly *anti*-war. He would later send a telegram to Harris congratulating him on having such a huge hit with an anti-war song during the Vietnam War.[4] That year Lennon and his new wife, Yoko Ono, had decided to make peace their personal brand and had embarked on a Campaign for Peace with attention-grabbing stunts designed to promote their agenda: anti-war, pro-love, anti-establishment, pro-freedom. That sort of thing. The most famous was the bed-in, when the couple held court in their pyjamas for two weeks in the spring of 1969, first in Amsterdam (doubling as their honeymoon) and then in Montreal,

---

[4] Was 'Two Little Boys' a protest song? A musical nod to 'The Last Post' certainly speaks to a more tragic spin on the story. The narrative of the song itself, however, doesn't really feel "anti" anything – the line isn't "Do you think I would leave you dying DURING THIS STINKING WAR WE SHOULD NEVER HAVE BEEN SENT TO FIGHT?" Harris would record another version, in 2008, to mark the anniversary of Armistice Day, raising money for the Royal British Legion via the Poppy Appeal, an organisation that does a lot of fine work and is certainly "pro-soldier", but could hardly be described as "anti-war".

where they recorded 'Give Peace a Chance'. Lennon even returned the MBE he had been given, along with the other Beatles, four years earlier, writing to the Queen to say: "Your Majesty, I am returning my MBE as a protest against Britain's involvement in the Nigeria-Biafra[5] thing, against our support of America in Vietnam and against 'Cold Turkey' slipping down the charts."

On 15 December 1969, as 'Two Little Boys' was racing up the chart as fast as 'Cold Turkey' was slipping down it, several key cities around the world woke up to find the streets plastered in posters – a simple message printed in block capitals in black ink on a white background: "WAR IS OVER! IF YOU WANT IT". The posters were signed off at the bottom: "Happy Christmas from John & Yoko". Locations included a giant billboard in New York's Times Square, as well as other key points in Los Angeles, Rome, Toronto, Amsterdam, Athens, Paris, Helsinki, Berlin, Tokyo, Hong Kong and London, with the slogan translated into local languages. The same message was broadcast in radio adverts and was printed in newspapers, and that night John and Yoko's Plastic Ono Band, featuring Eric Clapton, George Harrison and Alan White among myriad others, performed an improvised set at a benefit for UNICEF at London's Lyceum Ballroom in front of a huge "WAR IS OVER!" banner. For good measure, a "WAR IS OVER!" postcard was sent to British Prime Minister Harold Wilson (who marked it "no reply" and had it put in what was known as "the nutty file"). The whole campaign was mass propaganda for peace; a message that war was something that could be stopped if enough people simply said no. It was powerful in its simplicity, and the inclusion of a Christmas greeting was no coincidence. As Yoko told WABC-FM's Howard Smith, just a few days later, "Christmas is a time of peace."

"We specifically did the poster event around the world," John elaborated at the time, "to try and get at least one plug in for 'peace on Earth' at Christmas. Because that's what it's about. That and 'Happy Birthday Christ', ya know.". *Peace on Earth and goodwill to all men* is, after all, is pretty much the oldest Christmas message

---

[5] The UK had backed its former colony of Nigeria in a war against the secessionist state of Biafra, during which, according to some estimates, 2 million Biafrans died of starvation and 100,000 were killed in military action.

there is … at least it is if you ignore the Roman ones about raving. "That implies no violence," said Lennon. "No starving children. No violent minds. No violent households. No frustration. No fear."

The couple were serious, too. A year later, following the release of Lennon's incredible *John Lennon/Plastic Ono Band* album, John and Yoko released a statement declaring that 1971 would be "Year 1 AP (After Peace)," adding, "We believe that the last decade was the end of the old machine crumbling to pieces. And we think we can get it together, with your help. We have great hopes for the new year." Peace, alas, was a little out of reach, even for one of the most famous couples on the planet: the Vietnam War rumbled on. 1971 would still be significant, though. It saw the release of Lennon's *Imagine* album and its iconic title track, and, more importantly for us, it saw John and Yoko reinvent the Christmas single.

The "WAR IS OVER!" peace campaign had been a mass media propaganda event, with press, TV and radio, print and global exposure. It had, however, missed a fairly obvious trick by not engaging John Lennon's most famous skill set. Another two years would pass before the couple finally got around to writing the accompanying song. It would be worth the wait. When it came, 'Happy Xmas (War is Over)' turned out to be a masterpiece, and one that quietly changed how Christmas pop songs were seen.

This modern, secular carol was recorded at New York's Record Plant at the tail end of October 1971, and was produced by Phil Spector, who'd handled all of Lennon's solo material since 1970's 'Instant Karma', including both the *John Lennon/Plastic Ono Band* and *Imagine* albums. Spector, of course, had some form with Christmas music.[6] His 1963 album, *A Christmas Gift For You,* had seen him marshal his stable of acts – the Ronettes, Darlene Love, Bob B. Soxx & the Blue Jeans and the Crystals – to record a revamped clutch of old-timey Americana Christmas songs: 'White Christmas', 'Frosty the Snowman', 'The Bells of Saint Mary', 'Sleigh Ride', 'Rudolph the Red Nosed Reindeer' and more, using his

---

[6] As with Harris, there is an elephant in the room here: Spector would die in prison in 2021, incarcerated for the 2003 murder of actress Lana Clarkson. Undoubtedly a genius who shaped how we think of pop music, he was also a murderer.

glorious, dense Wall of Sound (the technique also used elsewhere to devastating effect on classics like 'Be My Baby', 'You've Lost That Lovin' Feeling' and 'River Deep, Mountain High') and elevating what were by now fairly stale standards into mini pop masterpieces. Nestled among them was Darlene Love's 'Christmas (Baby Please Come Home)', an exhilarating combination of desperate seasonal misery and sugar-rush pop and the one original song on the record, co-written by Spector himself. For my money, it's one of the best Christmas songs ever put to tape.

Unfortunately, Spector's timing was horrible. The day it was released was also the day JFK was assassinated, after which America's appetite for upbeat Christmas pop evaporated. "On top of that," he told *Sounds* later, "it was the hottest Christmas in California in years." The album sank like a stone. Over the next decade, however, its legend grew among those in the know. In 1971 a retrospective review in *Rolling Stone* hailed the now extremely hard to come by album "an all out Christmas masterpiece" (ads in the music press for the subsequent reissue simply reprinted the *Rolling Stone* review in full). What tipped it over the edge was the patronage of the Beatles. All four mop tops were in awe of Spector's recording techniques and songwriting, to the point that he was later parachuted in to rescue the album that would become *Let It Be*, being let loose to do whatever he wanted with the scrappy recordings the band had made in early 1969. Since then, he'd produced both John Lennon and George Harrison's solo work, to great acclaim, and in 1972 the band's Apple label oversaw a reissue of *A Christmas Gift for You*, this time taking it into the US Top 10.

Spector's album is another of the building blocks in the pop-ular conception of Christmas music. His famous Wall of Sound, achieved by assembling orchestras of pop instruments (guitars, pianos, keyboards, electric bass, drum kits), then layering and mix-ing them to create artfully dense, lush atmospheres that punched through jukeboxes and transistor radios[7], lent itself perfectly to Christmas celebrations, again linking back to that spirit of riotous

---

[7] His best work was mixed in the era before stereo recording became the norm, and he always felt that mono was the best way to experience pop. He attended the "Happy Xmas" sessions wearing a "Back To Mono" pin badge on his

abundance that had always underpinned the season. Often, when we think of the sound of Christmas music, we're not thinking of the twinkly charm of 'Silent Night' or the smooth cosiness of 'The Christmas Song (Chestnuts Roasting on an Open Fire)', we're thinking of the big, messy, gorgeous party that is Spector's recordings of 'Marshmallow World' and 'Frosty the Snowman'. You can hear it on everything from Wizzard's 'I Wish It Could Be Christmas Everyday' (1973) to Shakin' Stevens' 'Merry Christmas Everyone' (1985) to Kelly Clarkson's 'Underneath the Tree' (2013). Tricks originating on Spector's album have become completely accepted as the norm: the *ring-a-ding-a-dinga-ding-dong-ding* backing vocals on the Ronettes' 'Sleigh Ride'? They're very much absent from the earlier versions by Bing Crosby, Andy Williams or the Andrews Sisters. Elongating the first *"Saaaaaaaaaanta"* on 'Santa Claus is Coming To Town'? That originates here with the Crystals and, thanks to Bruce Springsteen and the Jackson 5, is pretty much the standard for pop takes on the song. 'Christmas (Baby Please Come Home)', which incidentally has one of the best saxophone solos ever recorded, became the template for any number of ballsy festive anthems, not least of which is Mariah Carey's 1994 hit 'All I Want For Christmas Is You' – probably the last true Christmas pop classic.[8] For an album that flopped into obscurity for its first nine years of life, *A Christmas Gift For You* has a remarkable reach. It's Phil Spector that gave Christmas music its now standard maximalism.

It was a more restrained Spector than the giggling mad professor of the *Christmas Gift* album that had worked on Lennon's earlier

lapel, though the single itself was mixed in stereo. The following year, while promoting the *Christmas* reissue, he added a second badge: "Santa Lives!".

[8] In 1992 Darlene Love recorded a sequel to 'Christmas (Baby Please Come Home)' called 'All Alone on Christmas', backed by Bruce Springsteen's E Street Band, for the soundtrack of the film *Home Alone 2*. It's an attempt to once again capture that dense, brass-led soul that Spector had delivered 30 years earlier. The results don't raise quite as many goosebumps, but it's a decent stab all the same and includes a ripping sax solo from Clarence Clemons. Love gained a reputation as the Queen of Christmas, a title first given to her by TV host David Letterman in 1993, and was a little put out when Mariah Carey tried (unsuccessfully) to trademark the term back in 2022. The two divas have since made peace, which is only right and proper.

material, especially on *Plastic Ono Band* and 'Imagine' itself, where he allowed the raw songs space to breathe, and to great effect. On the new 'Happy Xmas (War Is Over)', however, John and Yoko were keen to let him do his thing. After all, as he was heard to mutter during the recording: "I know something about Christmas music, you know", (adding later, "How can we have a song called 'Happy Xmas' without bells?"[9]) He and Lennon built the song up through massed acoustic guitars and a double-tracked 30-piece children's choir. "It takes him about 10 seconds to get a sound which transforms the guitars from a happy rabble into a brilliant cutting wash of colour, and they aren't even miked properly yet," wrote Richard Williams in his biography *Phil Spector: Out of his Head*. "The Spector magic is again overwhelmingly apparent."

'Happy Xmas (War is Over)' has justly become a perennial; a true Christmas classic. Arguably it's the last truly great John Lennon song. The early '70s had seen him finally emerge from his wilfully obtuse period, no longer hiding behind the deliberately weird imagery of 'I Am the Walrus', the sonic art of 'Revolution 9' and the abstract experimental records he'd made with Yoko. Instead his solo albums were marked with a refreshing and elegant directness, through which Lennon was able to put his point over succinctly – whether that was stark and angry, as on 'Working Class Hero', shudderingly raw as on 'Mother', confessional as on 'Jealous Guy' or idealistic as on 'Imagine'. "Recently, I tried to make my songs uncomplicated so that people could understand them," he told *NME*'s Roy Carr in 1972, deadpanning "A Wop bop a loo bop … get outta Ireland".[10] With 'Imagine' he'd also learned that a spoonful of sugar really does help the medicine go down – there's a reason that something as idealistic as 'Imagine' sold dramatically better than his bleak 'Mother' or 'Cold Turkey' singles. 'Imagine' was, as John said in the same interview, "'Working Class Hero' with chocolate on."[11] On 'Happy

---

[9] As overheard by *Melody Maker*'s Richard Williams, researching a biography of the producer, during recording.

[10] "Now they're openly attacking me for simplistic lyrics!" he complained in the same interview.

[11] Or, as he wrote in a scathing open letter to Paul McCartney, published in *Melody Maker* that December, "'Working Class Hero' with sugar on it for conservatives like yourself." Ouch.

Xmas', the message wasn't just sugar-coated, but chocolate-topped, honey-dipped, strapped to a candy cane, brandy-braised, wrapped in tinsel and dropped down your chimney. The message of the song was as blunt as the poster that inspired it: "War is over, if you want it", but that candy cane delivery method was real pop confection.

In some ways 'Happy Xmas' is one of the least original Christmas songs you'll find. The musical palette has all the hallmarks of a Spector seasonal spectacular – sleigh bells, a children's choir (the 30-piece Harlem Community Choir) and a chorus that wishes you, literally, a "merry Christmas and a happy New Year". It combines the maximalist Spector sound of *A Christmas Gift For You* with the themes of peace and happiness found in traditional carols – a Greatest Hits of the season combined in one song. Not only that, the melody was a straight lift of an old folk number, 'Stewball' (sometimes called 'Skewball'), about a racehorse and dating roughly to the eighteenth century but rearranged in 1961 by New York bluegrass trio John Herald and the Greenbriar Boys – a version that the music obsessive Lennon would certainly have known.[12] Lennon took the stately waltz of their recording and built a series of key changes into its warm, circular chords, ramping up the exhilaration and sense of possibility as the song balloons and swells. During the recording Spector also noted that the melody of the opening line echoed the start of the Paris Sisters' 'I Love How You Love Me', an old Brill Building hit which he'd recorded in 1961.

For all of its borrowing and referencing, though, 'Happy Xmas' also does something novel. This is the first time in a generation that a contemporary British pop star had recorded a Christmas song in earnest. It was neither a novelty, nor a bit of fun, nor a cash-in. Lennon had written a hit single, knowing he was doing exactly that, and it didn't just *happen* to be released at Christmas, nor was the season tagged on as a gimmicky afterthought. This was a true Christmas song, written to mark the season itself. It was a song with a serious message and pop heart, penned by one of the most

---

[12] It had been covered in 1963 by the more palatable New York folkies Peter, Paul and Mary, and their version was easily the more well known – the fact that 'Happy Xmas' used the same mandolin-style guitar riffs as the Greenbriar Boys version, however, suggests that it was the earlier recording John was referencing.

respected songwriters of all time – a member of the band, in fact, that had defined British pop. It was a Christmas number that had been taken seriously as a pop song, and more than that, it was a pop song that proudly wore Christmas on its sleeve for the rockin' robins to peck at. Lennon knew exactly what he was doing when he brought in Phil Spector. In that sense it was revolutionary, at least for a British band. John and Yoko, two of the most artistically credible figures in the world, had said it was okay to take a Christmas pop song seriously. During recording, Lennon told visiting journalist Richard Williams that he was releasing the song merely "because I was sick of 'White Christmas'." Typical Lennon understatement. He fundamentally understood the power of Christmas pop. "I've always wanted to write something that would be a Christmas record that would last forever," he said later. "Every year you can play it and there's always war. There's always somebody being tortured or shot somewhere, so the lyrics stand in that respect." John, as usual, was trying to change the world. For the second time that year, he got pretty close.

Not that the record-buying British public noticed at first. A dispute over publishing rights meant the single didn't get a UK release that year. "A fucking shame," Lennon told *Melody Maker*, which ran the record's sleeve – John and Yoko surrounded by the children of the Harlem Community Choir – as the cover image for its 1971 Christmas issue.

It's a shame indeed. The Christmas chart that year could really have used it. The Christmas No. 1 was another novelty hit from a TV star – this time Benny Hill's 'Ernie (The Fastest Milkman in the West)', a dismal comic tale about a randy milkman and his arch nemesis, the local baker, sung by Hill in a Bristolian brogue and accompanied by a *Carry On*-style video promo.[13] The song hung on to the top spot until the second week of January and was eventually

---

[13] Backing vocals were provided by the Ladybirds, a trio of session singers who turned up on multiple hit records in the '60s and '70s. These shouldn't be confused with another contemporary Ladybirds, an all-girl rock band from California, whose main gimmick was performing topless. And *they* shouldn't be confused with the Ladybirds from Denmark, whose main gimmick was *also* performing topless. Astonishingly, all three bands were unaware of each other.

knocked off by the only slightly less nauseating 'I'd Like to Teach the World to Sing'– the New Seekers' attempt to spread international peace via a shared love of Coca-Cola.

The previous Christmas hadn't been much better. 1970's No. 1 had been Dave Edmunds' cover of the old R & B standard 'I Hear You Knocking'; it was one of those "just happened to be at No. 1 at the time" Christmas hits, and had been at the top for a month already. It's a decent enough record, but nothing to warm the cockles – it's been justly forgotten. That year's novelty horror had come from Clive Dunn, the *Dad's Army* actor (aged only 50 at the time), who had knocked out a queasy character piece called 'Grandad', singing it on *Top of the Pops* while rocking in a rocking chair, children at his knee. It would go to No. 1 a few weeks later, keeping T. Rex's breakthrough 'Ride A White Swan' at No. 2 and denying Marc Bolan his first No. 1, something he'd have comfortably achieved almost any other week. It was eventually knocked off by George Harrison's 'My Sweet Lord', but would still stay in the Top 40 for 22 weeks.[14]

It took until November 1972 for John and Yoko's 'Happy Xmas' to finally get a release on home soil. By this point, the idea that the Christmas chart would *ever* be something to be excited about seemed far-flung festive fiction. "Christmas is the time of year when music business heads get a screw loose and leap into the silly season feet first," wrote *NME*'s Julie Webb in a round-up of the seasonal hits of '72. "Records that would normally sell nought suddenly leap up the charts, established acts prostitute their singing by bringing out below standard songs about Yuletide – and there is, without fail, always one single that is so awful that you long for Spring." She was more or less right. Little Jimmy Osmond's punchably cute 'Long

Benny Hill, known for being chased around on TV by scantily clad women, ended up with the only Ladybirds that kept their clothes on.
[14] 'Grandad' had been co-written by Herbie Flowers, the respected session bass player who had played on David Bowie's 'Space Oddity', and who would create the iconic bassline on Lou Reed's 'Walk on the Wild Side', traverse the US with Bowie on the *Diamond Dogs* tour and join the final line-up of T. Rex in 1977 (presumably having been forgiven for denying Bolan to top spot back in 1971). Despite all that, 'Grandad' would have been the biggest earner of his career.

Haired Lover From Liverpool' took the Christmas No. 1, along with a still unbroken record for the youngest artist ever to top the UK charts. He headed up a chart that also included the Pipes & Drums & Military Band of the Royal Scots Dragoon Guards droning through 'Little Drummer Boy', Chuck Berry's absolutely rotten and, frankly, extremely creepy novelty hit 'My Ding-a-Ling' and Ken Dodd's 'Just Out of Reach (My Two Empty Arms)'.[15] Weirdo honky-tonk marching band Lieutenant Pigeon had two hits on the chart: 'Mouldy Old Dough', their deeply odd surprise No. 1 from earlier in the year, and its bloody awful follow-up 'Desperate Dan'. Business as usual then.

There was, however, a sign that things were changing. 'Happy Xmas (War Is Over)' peaked at No. 4 – not a No. 1, but a solid hit that was selling in huge numbers. It would go on to become a beloved perennial. There was, it turns out, an appetite for Christmas music that was both seasonally appropriate and actually worth a listeners' time. Christmas hits didn't have to be novelties, throwbacks, sickly ballads or accidents. They could be credible *and* festive and if you got the mix right, the public would buy them by the truckload. It had just taken a Beatle to prove it.[16] Things were looking up. It was time to look to the future ... it had, after all, only just begun.

---

[15] Though Dodd was best known as a comedian, he had a parallel career as a respectable crooner. Unlike Benny Hill or Rolf Harris there was absolutely no novelty aspect to Doddy's recordings; usually romantic ballads sung in a rich voice. He was a true all-round entertainer, and would usually have a song out for the Christmas market for the nans to lap up. Sir Ken Dodd died in 2018 at the age of 90, the last great performer of the music hall age. He was still doing two-hour stand up shows just a few months earlier.

[16] The other three Beatles would all attempt to have festive hits, with mixed results. Paul McCartney, predictably enough, was the most successful, managing both a Christmas No. 1 ('Mull Of Kintyre', 1977) and a bona fide *played every year* festive perennial with 'Wonderful Christmastime' (No. 6, 1979). Less well remembered is George Harrison's self-conscious attempt at a New Year's Eve song, 1974's 'Ding Dong Ding Dong', which barely scraped into the Top 40. Ringo, meanwhile, did a whole Christmas album – 1999's *I Wanna Be Santa Claus*. It's rather fun, but it sank without a trace.

Chapter 4
IT'S
CHRIIIIIIIIIIIIIIIIIIIIIIIIIISTMAAAAAAAAS!

Or how glam rock saved the season

On 12 December 1973 Conservative prime minister Edward Heath addressed the nation on television to declare a state of emergency, amid a growing coal shortage prompted by a miners' strike and astonishingly high oil prices following a war in the Middle East.[1] "A great emergency is now facing our country," he said, speaking from Downing Street. "Jobs will be in danger and take-home pay will be less … We shall have a harder Christmas than we have known since the war."

Though this wasn't the first official state of emergency faced by the public in recent years (in fact, it was the fifth since Heath's government came to power in 1970), it still promised a gloomy outlook for the coming Christmas. Street lighting was reduced. Offices and factories were banned from using electric heaters. Television was halted at 10.30 p.m., and periodic, rolling blackouts were scheduled across the country to limit the use of precious coal for the power stations. Even the lights on the Trafalgar Square Christmas tree in London were kept dark until Christmas Day itself. Anyone dreaming wistfully of a more Dickensian Christmas might suddenly have

---

[1] John and Yoko clearly hadn't put the work in.

been pondering the phrase before "*Be careful what you wish for*" It wasn't a happy picture – food prices had already risen by 3.3 per cent that October, and the government's plan to conserve power with a three-day working week was due to start as soon as the Christmas period was over. All in, it seemed the festivities of December 1973 were going to be a rather miserable affair. There was a desperate need for some sort of national injection of joy. Enter Slade.

On the very day of Heath's announcement, the *Kent Evening Post* ran a story about a new Christmas record that was selling out across the country. "'Merry Christmas everybody. Keep smiling. Things aren't as bad as they seem,'" it wrote, paraphrasing the lyrics. "To go around singing that in the middle of the energy crisis and strike threats, you have to be mad – or a member of the Slade pop group." The report goes on to call the new single by the rambunctious Wolverhampton rockers, titled with typical brevity 'Merry Xmas Everybody', "one of the bright spots in an otherwise gloomy December" that had led to "a stampede to the record shops by people looking for a bit of Christmas cheer". The paper noted that another disc, Wizzard's 'I Wish It Could Be Christmas Everyday', was also "adding to the festive mood" and flying off the shelves. The same scenes were repeating across the country. Noting the festive new records by Slade, Wizzard and Elton John, whose 'Step Into Christmas' was also out that week, the *Manchester Evening News'* Kevin Henry excitedly declared in his pop column that "there hasn't been such a groovy Christmas in years!"

'Merry Xmas Everybody' crashed straight in at No. 1 on 15 December following advance orders of half a million discs, with label Polydor having to ship an extra 30,000 copies a day from Germany to meet demand. It was, at that point, the fastest selling No. 1 single in British chart history (a record it would hold until a very different crisis produced another Christmas smash in 1984 – more on that in a few chapters). Some 300,000 sales later, and it was no surprise that the song was still at No. 1 come Christmas Day (and would stay there until mid-January). Across December 1973 and into 1974, 'Merry Xmas Everybody' sold over a million copies. This was a bona fide Christmas hit – the first UK No. 1 since 1957 to *actually be about Christmas*. And in this traditional annual dumping ground for one-hit wonders, novelty singles, unspeakably naff sentiment and oldies, it had come from one of the coolest, loudest bands in the country. The true era of the Christmas No. 1 had finally arrived.

The success of a bright, stomping and optimistic festive-themed record in a time of economic misery is not a coincidence. "December 1973 was the height of the 'Winter of Discontent'," wrote Slade's Noddy Holder in his memoir, *The World According to Noddy*.[2] "Money was tight and times were tough, everyone needed cheering up … It was a rowdy record and I made sure, from out of the economic gloom, the lyrics were upbeat and optimistic." "Everything was a downer," agreed guitarist Dave Hill in his own memoir, *So Here It Is*, the title of which is borrowed from the song's chorus. "So you looked forward to Christmas as a treat to get away from it. When Nod roared, '*It's Christmas!*' that was like a call to everybody to forget about everything and just enjoy the holiday … It was as if we were saying 'We've all survived the year, Slade and Britain, so let's celebrate!'."[3] According to a claim in *Look Wot I Dun – My Life In Slade*, a memoir cum biography of Slade drummer Don Powell, "on American national news, the single was proclaimed as the only good thing to come out of England during this period".[4] As the papers and the daily news broadcasts filled with doom and gloom, as the lights went out and the TV went dark, as belts were tightened and pennies pinched, the public had found the little piece of glitter and shine it so desperately needed.

---

[2] Nod's actually a bit confused here — the term *Winter of Discontent* is usually applied to the equally miserable winter of 1978/79. Though since this was winter and there was discontent, we may as well let him have this one.

[3] Dave Hill's autobiography is available on audiobook, narrated by Dave himself, and it's an utter joy – the most Black Country thing you've ever heard. He can't stop himself from adding little asides and chuckling at his memories. It's wonderful.

[4] I haven't been able to find a source for this claim. The record barely gets a mention in the US trades at the time. However, Powell's book, co-written with Lise Lyng Falkenberg, bases a lot of its information on a meticulous diary he kept in order to counter the amnesia he suffered following a near-fatal car crash earlier in the year, so there's every chance this is pretty reliable.

The Britain of the early 1970s has a justifiable reputation for misery, blighted as it was with strikes that had led to coal shortages, uncollected rubbish piling on the streets, raw sewage being pumped into the rivers and even undug graves. There was monstrously high unemployment, terror threats and bombings from the IRA; violence on the streets and the continual failure of England's football team to follow up its 1966 success.[5] An editorial in German magazine *Der Spiegel*, published in early 1974, cast a withering eye over the British capital: "The swinging London of the '60s has given way to a London as gloomy as the city described by Charles Dickens, with the once imperial avenues of the capital of a vast Empire now sparsely lighted like the slummy streets of a former British colonial township."

For a while it looked like Britain's music scene was as dour as its economy – album-oriented bands like Led Zeppelin, Genesis, Pink Floyd, Yes and more, upon which the music press bestowed a certain reverence, had sucked a lot of the spontaneous fun out of pop. The Beatles, the band that defined the '60s, had collapsed into bitching at each other in the press, poking each other in court and making solo records that, while often accomplished, were, even when they were Christmas-themed, rarely *fun*.[6] As indie stalwart turned pop historian Bob Stanley puts it, in his excellent *Yeah Yeah Yeah: The Story of Modern Pop*, Britain's charts were painting a picture of "a country of melancholic introspection, underachievement and lost idealism." The insipid and predictable Christmas charts of 1969 to 1972 are, as we've seen, testament to this dip in musical energy.

---

[5] Which sounds frivolous, but really was a factor – Labour prime minister Harold Wilson specifically scheduled the 1970 general election to take advantage of a national goodwill expected to come in the wake of that year's World Cup, for which defending champions England were firm favourites. After the team crashed out in the quarter-finals at the hands of old rivals West Germany, that bump of public joy never materialised and as the final whistle blew, both the England team and Wilson's government effectively ended their time as reigning champions.

[6] Aside from Ringo's brilliant 'It Don't Come Easy', a gem against which I will not hear a word said. Paul McCartney would finally start to cheer up in 1973 with 'Live and Let Die', 'Jet' and 'Band on the Run'.

Fortunately, pop music, like a student's bedroom carpet, abhors a vacuum. As the nation's woes increased, a lockstep movement of musical escapism sprang up alongside, rushing in like a glittering ocean to the fill the desolate gaps – loud, brash, Velcro-catchy, inspired by the primitive rock of the '50s, bolted to a knowing archness, spray-painted silver and sparkling like tinsel in firelight. Glam rock was on the rise, and it was as camp as, well, Christmas.

Glam had been threatening the Christmas charts for a couple of years. In 1971, T. Rex had the Christmas No. 2 spot with 'Jeepster', while Slade's 'Coz I Luv You', a former No. 1, was still hanging around the Top 20. By Christmas 1972, with the whiz-bang of glam in the ascendent, Marc Bolan and T. Rex were again in spitting distance of the No. 1 with 'Solid Gold Easy Action' – stranded at No. 3, sandwiched between Chuck Berry's 'My Ding-A-Ling' and John and Yoko's 'Happy Xmas'. Slade were there again, 'Gudbuy T'Jane' having slipped to No. 6, and glam-adjacent Elton John was at No. 7 with 'Crocodile Rock'; both records stuck behind the not-exactly-*un*-glam 'Crazy Horses' by the Osmonds at No. 5.[7] Lower down the chart, David Bowie's 'The Jean Genie' was at 16, starting a stinging assault that would peak at No. 2 a few weeks later, while Wizzards' 'Ballpark Incident' was at 29. The economically depressed British public, it seemed, were quite keen for the distraction of some glittering baubles.

There are a few different points that can mark the birth of the genre eventually known as glam rock. Some trace it back to 22 February 1970 when David Bowie and his band, the Hype, a proto-version of what would become the Spiders From Mars, played London's Roundhouse in elaborate costumes – though since hardly anyone was paying attention at the time and the costumes were soon discarded, calling that gig "the birth of glam rock", as a few have, feels a bit of a stretch. One person who apparently *was* present, though, was Bowie's friend Marc Bolan, the elfin frontman of cult folk duo Tyrannosaurus Rex. By the end of the year, he'd shortened his band's name to T. Rex, plugged in his electric guitar and written

---

[7] They may have been an insufferably clean-cut boy band, but 'Crazy Horses' is a *hell* of a song. An absolute all-time, glam-slam belter.

a '50s throwback rock and roll song called 'Ride a White Swan', a Christmas Top 10 hit that would peak at No. 2 a few weeks into 1971. It was Bolan who gave glam a far clearer year zero with his next single, another irresistible throwback called 'Hot Love' – the first of four No. 1s. Performing the song on *Top of the Pops*, he applied glitter make-up to his already pretty eyes. His slender frame meant he could wear women's shoes and clothes – satin trousers and fitted jackets – and he occasionally topped the whole thing off with a feather boa. Androgyny wasn't exactly new to pop music – Mick Jagger had been preening in satin shirts and frills and batting made-up eyes for a while now, and everyone was stealing from Little Richard and Elvis's '50s looks anyway. But Bolan did it with such a beguiling sweetness and against such accessibly catchy bops that it felt revolutionary. On his next single, 'Get It On', he leaned further into rock and roll, ripping off Chuck Berry's 'Little Queenie' and adding a mean guitar growl and a sexually charged vocal full of *ow!* and *yeah!*, over an irresistible groove. Combining that with the silver jacket, sequined shirt and glittery cheeks he wore on that year's *Top of the Pops* Christmas Day episode, he gave us a picture-perfect definition of the early glam template, cemented in the nation's consciousness and canonised over the turkey and trimmings.

As 1972 unfolded, those elements of bright colour, glitter and gender-bending fun started to surface everywhere, turbocharged when David Bowie emerged as Ziggy Stardust, blowing minds and changing lives when he performed 'Starman' on *Top of the Pops* in full sparkle-hard regalia. Maximalism became the name of the game in pop – the platform shoes got higher, the glitter got shinier, the camp got camper. The synergy of primitive, stomping rock and roll, OTT stage wear and the clashing of masculine and feminine styles proved to be pop chart gold. "Let's face it!" declared the *Daily Mirror* in September while interviewing Marc Bolan, "the world's No. 1 pop idol (and his drummer) prove that make up is no longer strictly for birds".

Established bands like Sweet and Slade now borrowed from Bowie and Bolan to sharpen their images to great effect, and though neither band would have considered themselves at first to be "glam" – or "glitter rock", as it was occasionally known in the press – both had one member (Sweet's Steve Priest, Slade's Dave Hill) who would consciously go full glam rock for their stage wear. If you track Slade's *Top of the Pops* appearances across 1972 and 73, you'll see Hill go from a simple silver, women's trench coat and a bit of make-up to golden, sci-fi armour with frills, huge platforms and a face that looks like it has been pasted with glue and rolled in a showgirl's knicker drawer.[8] Noddy Holder covered a Victorian stovepipe hat in mirrors so it would reflect beams of stage lights over the audience – and Dave Hill covered his entire outfit.

When Paul Gadd, an also-ran from the '60s, emerged as Gary Glitter with the monstrous 'Rock and Roll Parts 1 & 2' it was with a look entirely contrived around the glam formula – huge silver suits, big shoulders, high platforms and uncomfortable amounts of chest hair. That crystallised the scene. In the beat group era it had all been well-cut suits and sharp styles. In the hippie boom, it was flowers in the hair and floaty shirts. As 1972 ticked into 1973, the name of the game in pop was to go big, go camp or go home. *Top of the Pops*, with its huge audience of 18 million, including pretty much every teenager in the land, became the weekly battleground on which the glam princes tried to out-preen each other as, maybe for the first time in pop, the visual became as important as the song. Writer Mark Paytress quotes Gary Glitter in his book *Glam! When Superstars Rocked the World*: "We all tried to outdo each other. It was a healthy competition. We – Marc Bolan, David Bowie, myself, Slade and Sweet – were pre-video times but we tried to think like [a music] video. When we did *Top of the Pops* we'd try to create a video in one slot. I'd stand on moons, come up with motorbikes."[9]

Despite 1973 being the year that Bolan himself declared in the pages of *Melody Maker* that "Glam rock is dead", and that Bowie

---

[8] Slade bass player and co-songwriter Jim Lea *hated* Dave Hill's extravagant stage looks. Hill's response was always the same: "You write 'em, Jim, I'll sell 'em." For serious muso Lea, it was mortifying. He told the *Guardian* in 2006 that he remembered being asked by another band, "Have you seen the state of your guitarist? He looks like a metal nun!"

[9] In truth Bowie and Bolan, the true originators of the genre, felt themselves above these tricks, and the likes of Gary Glitter, Alvin Stardust and Sweet mildly embarrassed them. Both did their best to distance themselves, though both had some time for the ballsy rock of Slade.

killed off his Ziggy Stardust alter ego, the Christmas chart is suffused with glitter: Slade at No. 1, Gary Glitter at No. 2, Wizzard at No. 4, Alvin Stardust at 5, Leo Sayer at 7, David Essex at 8, Mott the Hoople at nine, Roxy Music at 10, Wizzard's Roy Wood with a solo hit at 11, T. Rex at 12, Mud at 22, Golden Earing at 25, Elton John at 26 and David Bowie at 32. All of which acts were, if not definitively glam rock, then polished by glam elements.

What also strikes you is how *Christmassy* the Christmas chart is that year. 1973 contained more explicitly seasonal records than had been seen on the hit parade since the 1950s. Slade and Wizzard, of course, but also Elton's 'Step Into Christmas', prog-folk group Steeleye Span's version of the ancient carol 'Gaudete' and Michael Ward's hymn 'Let There Be Peace on Earth'. While five songs doesn't sound much, that's a 70 per cent increase on the 1972 Christmas chart – and 1971 and 1970 didn't contain any Christmas-themed hits at all. In fact, 1973 was the most Christmassy Christmas chart since 1959 (and even then, two of the five records on the hit parade that year were different versions of 'Little Donkey'). That almost every act on *Top of the Pops* turned up dressed as a cross between a disco Dalek and a Christmas tree was the icing on the cake. Christmas was back.

Seasonal records had made their comeback at the exact point people had really started to write them off. "Rock 'n' roll's rise to 'art form' status can probably be blamed for the decline in the Santa music business," wrote the *New York Times* that December. "Rock is very much the premise of the young musician recording nothing but his own compositions, and your average, basic rocker is light-years away from the commercial sentimentality that makes up the bulk of the Christmas hits of the past." An anonymous producer who spoke to the *Reading Evening Post* that December claimed there was very little point in even bothering – "There's no way of doing 'White Christmas' any better," he told the paper's George Newton. "All the valid things about Christmas have been said and done." With some irony, that article, in which an apparently well-known anonymous producer dismissed Christmas pop records as over and done, is among the first times a British journalist used the phrase "Christmas

No. 1" in print.[10] The tide was changing, right there on that page. Still, some were slow to catch on. Interviewed for *Record Mirror* that December, hard rockers Stray were absolutely scathing about their glam rivals doing Christmas songs ("one expects Max Bygraves to do this sort of thing"). Curiously, such comments were all overlooking John and Yoko's 'Happy Xmas (War Is Over)', a huge hit just a year ago (and a modest one in the States the year before that) in which a definitively "cool" artist had recorded a consciously festive song and taken it into the Top 5. The hallowed Beatles walked a different path, apparently – the same rules didn't apply.

And yet the evidence that Lennon kicked the door open is pretty clear. Before 'Happy Xmas' you'd have to go back to the late '50s to find UK Christmas hits by credible, contemporary artists – Brenda Lee, Chuck Berry, Elvis, or the sole '60s effort, the Beach Boys' 'Little Saint Nick' (all American artists, incidentally). After that? Nothing. For a decade. Then, in 1972 John and Yoko had a proper hit, and the following year three of the biggest acts in the country – Slade, Wizzard and Elton John – all follow. That's no coincidence. And they're shamelessly Christmas songs too, gunning for the top spot. "We weren't sure it was the right thing to be doing, putting out a Christmas song," Slade's Noddy Holder told the BBC in 2023, finally admitting the obvious. "But Lennon had done it a year before, that's the only reason we thought it could be kosher to do."[11]

If anyone was going to lead the way, it would be Slade. By the end of 1973, the quartet's role as British pop's biggest dog was indisputable. Bolan got there first, Bowie has the greater legacy and

---

[10] The phrase *Christmas No. 1* is a surprisingly late entrant to its own mythology – it wouldn't be used regularly as a shorthand until well into the '80s. The *Guardian*, for example, didn't use it until 1990. This is the earliest use of the phrase I've been able to find in print – and the earliest one indexed in the millions of articles held by the British Newspaper Archive. The *Oxford English Dictionary* actually has *Billboard*, the US industry bible, using the phrase first, that very same year – though I've combed every issue of *Billboard* from 1973 and haven't been able to find it.

[11] Alright, *kosher* isn't exactly the most appropriate word to use when discussing Christmas hits, but we'll let Noddy have this one.

Elton would eventually sell more records than all of them put to-gether, but in 1973 Slade were untouchable. Formed in the late '60s in Wolverhampton and managed by former Animals bass player Chas Chandler (who, incidentally, had also managed Hendrix), the four-piece's no-nonsense, face-ripping rock and roll had, once it had got going, steamrollered the opposition. 'Merry Xmas Everybody' would be their fifth No. 1 in two years, and the third to go straight to the top – a feat previously achieved only by The Beatles. They wer-en't the prettiest, the cleverest or the most subtle band around, but they had bags of character. Very working class. Very Black Country. Very rock and roll. Not that this was dumb stuff – Noddy Holder had a real knack for smart, witty lyrics wrapped in killer choruses and delivered, as Bob Stanley rather brilliantly puts it, via "a voice like John Lennon screaming down the chimney of the QE2". He and bassist Jim Lea (who also played piano and violin, as deployed to great effect on their first No. 1, 'Coz I Luv You') made a slick songwriting partnership, while guitarist Dave Hill was the band's ridiculous, platinum-plated, tinselly showman.[12] Though they were capable of real subtlety – 'Coz I Luv You', which had an oddly mel-ancholic desperation to Holder's growling vocal, is a good example. Their dark 1974 film, *Slade in Flame*, in which they play a fictional Black Country glam rock band is, as the critic Mark Kermode has said several times, "the *Citizen Kane* of pop movies", but there's no doubt the band were at their best when they were blazingly raucous – 'Mama Weer All Crazee Now',[13] 'Gudbuy T'Jane' and, especially, instant classic 'Cum on Feel the Noize', probably the Slade song with the most longevity outside of 'Merry Xmas'. Even the idio-syncratic spelling was all part of a carefully calculated charm. Slade were a laugh: loud, funny, incredibly relatable, brightly coloured, slightly unhinged, shiny as anything, frequently drunk and oddly comforting in their classic Englishness. They were, in other words, what happens if you distilled the traditional, working class British

---

[12] My favourite Dave Hill story is that during Slade's peak he "accidentally" (he insists) bought a house next door to a private girls' school and had to wade through screaming, crying fans every day just to get his car out the drive.

[13] "Makes the Rolling Stones and even the Who sound like estate agents" as *Melody Maker*'s Chris Welch wrote in August 1972.

Christmas into a rock and roll band. Frankly they should never have needed John and Yoko's tacit permission to write a seasonal party anthem.

The band's record company, Polydor, had been pressuring Slade for a Christmas release for a few years, knowing that a hit in December meant even more gigantic sales from a band who delivered them in spades anyway. "Not a *Christmas* record, they didn't want that … they just wanted something to *release* at Christmas," Holder told the BBC's Mark Radcliffe. Unbeknown to their label, Christmas had genuinely been on Slade's collective mind. According to Jim Lea, interviewed by Birmingham's *Sunday Mercury* in 2016, manager Chas Chandler had told them that "the golden goose needs to lay a golden egg", challenging the band to be "No. 1 at Christmas". Being deprived the 1972 top spot by Little Jimmy Osmond pretending to be a lusciously locked Liverpool Lothario and Chuck Berry's ding-a-ling clearly stung. It's one of the first times a band had come out fighting with the specific aim of grabbing a Christmas No. 1.

The idea was put into bassist Jim Lea's head by Kathleen Ganner, his wife's mother, who in 1972 had pointed out over breakfast that, however big the band had gotten, Slade were never going to outdo 'White Christmas', and should try and write a perennial of their own. "I was furious," he later told *Uncut*. "I thought it was a stupid idea." Bands like Slade, after all, *didn't write Christmas songs*. A few months later, while pondering Chandler's "Christmas No. 1" challenge in the shower, his mother-in-law's words came back to him – and this time lightning struck. The melody to an old, unused Noddy Holder song called 'Buy Me A Rocking Chair' floated into his head, a tune dating back to 1967 and, incidentally, the first song Holder had ever written, though the rest of the band had rejected it. The words *Merry Christmas* fitted perfectly into the chorus.

After being presented with the idea, Holder got to work on the lyrics, which came out in a torrent during a Scotch-fuelled all-nighter, alone at his parents' house. "I began jotting down a list of things people associated with Christmas," he wrote in his first memoir, *Who's Crazee Now*. "I wanted it to be about a working class Christmas, not your picturebook snowflakes and reindeer job." The results were magnificent – an utter distillation of British seasonal celebration: panicking about room for the family, dealing with drunken relatives, all of that. You didn't get that stuff in the nostalgic, days of yore, Americana carols that had dominated the market since the war. The song is full of absolute pearls: "Does your granny always tell ya, that the old songs are the best" goes the conclusion to the second verse "Then she's up and rock 'n' rolling with the rest." Wonderful. Santa turns up, of course, but he's a Santa that needs to be kept "sober for the day". 'Merry Xmas Everybody' was a song that leapfrogged 30 years of Christmas schmaltz and plugged directly into the spirit of riotous mischief and full-bore partying that had defined Britain's festivities since before Britons actually knew what Christmas was. This was the Kalends of January, the Lords of Misrule, the wassailers and the waits. The spirit of all that and more had trickled down over the centuries, biding its time, until it found Slade. It's *such* a British record as well. It's sarcastic but it's also optimistic. It's a rattling rocker, but also oddly sentimental. It's completely irreverent and, crucially, it is *drunk*. And though knowing and a little sarcastic, it's a resolutely optimistic song that looks forwards rather than back. "Look to the future now", rather than "just like the ones I used to know". In 1973 it was a message Britain needed to hear – no wonder the song connected.

'Merry Xmas Everybody' was recorded in a suffocating heatwave that September, at New York City's Record Plant studios, during a break in John Lennon's *Mind Games* sessions (the intro features Lennon's own harmonium). The studio was set up in a building being used elsewhere as offices and, given the stifling New York heat and the elevators full of bemused businessmen, was as unlikely a location for the recording of a festive classic as you'll find anywhere. It was a challenging record to make, too. This was the first real sessions Slade had attempted since a car accident had left drummer Don Powell, who was lucky to survive at all, with rolling amnesia, frequently having to be reminded how his own songs went. The simple but effective, shuffle beat of 'Merry Xmas Everybody' was making a virtue out of a necessity – Powell was struggling to keep anything more complicated in his head. Slade's normal recording technique was to blast through a number exactly as it was played on stage, add a few overdubs and send it out into the shops. Powell's limitations meant a departure, with the song being built and layered in stages and the arrangements reworked on the hoof.

Though all four of Slade's members loved the song, there were still doubts, especially from Dave Hill, that a Christmas record was the right thing to do. Their management and label, however, knew a gold-plated smash when they heard one. When the band heard an early pressing, while on tour in Belgium that November, it was so immediately clear that 'Merry Xmas' was going to be a hit that the label broke out the champagne on the spot. At 10 a.m.

Risk? This was a no-brainer! It wasn't as if any of the UK's other glitter-adjacent rockers would be preparing a rowdy Christmas song of their own.

It was around this point that Slade appeared on ITV's pop show *Lift Off With Ayshea*, the commercial rival to *Top of the Pops* presented by actress and occasional pop star Ayshea Brough. The band were booked to perform their recent hit 'My Friend Stan' and were keeping their impending assault on the December chart close to their chests. Backstage, host Brough, who was dating Wizzard's Roy Wood at the time, casually dropped a bomb on them: "Ayshea came up to us and said 'Roy Wood and Wizzard have this Christmas song they're doing'," Dave Hill writes in *So Here It Is*. "'I think it'll be the No. 1 at Christmas' so we said, 'oh really? We've got one of them as well'." "I was mortified when I found out that everyone else was bringing Christmas songs out," Jim Lea told the *Guardian* in 2016. "I heard Elton's one, 'Step Into Christmas', but I thought: 'No competition.' Then I heard Roy Wood and Wizzard and the competition had arrived."

Slade had known Wood (affectionately known within the band as "Woody") for years. The two acts had emerged from the same West Midlands scene, alongside the Moody Blues, Black Sabbath, Jeff Lynn, the Spencer Davis Group, Robert Plant and more. Wood had found fame in the Move, the first band to ever be played on Radio 1, and by the early '70s he had formed ELO with Jeff Lynne, before quitting after just one album and embarking on a solo career while also putting together a new outfit, Wizzard. An unashamed showman, Wood had been doing glam rock before anyone had even put a name to it, appearing on *Top of the Pops* with the Move in 1970 performing the riff-heavy 'Brontosaurus' dressed as a harlequin, with brightly coloured stars painted all over his face, one shining in the middle of his forehead. He'd grown his hair out and teased it into a huge fright wig. He even appeared on the front cover of *Disc* that May, wearing sequins with silver lightning bolts drawn under his eyes. Whether Messrs Bowie and Bolan were paying attention is not recorded, but you can bet your bottom dollar neither of the pop-obsessed careerists ever missed an episode of *Top of the Pops* or failed to flick through the music press in John Menzies' every Wednesday. That said, one of the primary glam rock ingredients was camp, and there was little of that about Roy Wood, a plain-speaking Brummie made up to look like a space-age shaman.

He'd formed Wizzard to sound *huge* – double drummers, cellists, sax players, guitars … if he could have found a way for someone to play a kitchen sink, he probably would have. He was rebuilding Phil Spector's dense, glorious Wall of Sound, brick by sonic brick, and the effect was devastatingly successful. 'Ball Park Incident', the group's debut single, had made the Top 10 in November 1972. Their second, the brilliant, messy pop throwback 'See My Baby Jive', had gone to No. 1 in April 1973, as had its follow-up, 'Angel Fingers (A Teen Ballad)', that September, a '50s-flavour ballad powered by *boom ba boom tat* drums stolen from the Ronettes' 'Be My Baby'. Close listening revealed a chorus uncomfortably similar to 'See My Baby Jive', but no one seemed to mind. Like Slade, Wizzard were approaching Christmas following back-to-back No. 1s, bolstered by flamboyant stage presence and a massive live sound. Even the accents were the same.

Unlike Slade, though, Roy Wood had taken no convincing to record a Christmas song – it was an idea he'd been carrying around for years. The title came from Wizzard sax man Mike Burney, who after years of playing big band gigs was hugely enjoying his stint at the glam rock coal face, once remarking to Wood that it felt like "Christmas every day". Wood jotted the term down for future reference. It was May 1972 when the phrase *I wish it could be Christmas every day* popped into his head again. "I hadn't deliberately sat down to write a Christmas song," he told the *Birmingham Mail* in 2013. "But the more I think about it, I reflect that over the years there have only been novelty records out at Christmas … There's nothing rock and roll about Christmas at all. The only one I can remember before is Brenda Lee's 'Rocking Around the Christmas Tree'. Great. Time for a good rock and roll one, then." Like Noddy Holder, at roughly the same time, he jotted down everything he associated with Christmas and joined the dots into a lyric … snowmen, going to bed early the night before so Christmas comes quicker, singing children, rosy cheeks in the winter cold, cosy fires and melting icicles. The song was recorded that August, again in blazing heat, Wood blasting the studio with fans to create a wintery atmosphere for the song. As with all of Wizzard's hits, 'I Wish It Could Be Christmas Everyday' was a meticulously crafted studio creation, deliberately aping Phil Spector's techniques and building layer upon layer, everything double- or triple-tracked to create a thick, sledgehammer of Christmassy joy. The icing on the cake was a choir of Birmingham school children from Stockland Green Bilateral School ("Okay you lot! Take it!") and the jingling of sleigh bells.[14] The final cherry on top, and some welcome cynicism amid the seasonal fluff, was the sound of coins hitting an antique cash register.

Roy Wood and Wizzard, quite naturally, assumed they'd have the Christmas market to themselves, not realising they had competition until Slade's 'Merry Xmas Everybody' turned up on the radio one day. Both bands were a little stunned. "He'd obviously had the same idea as us from how Lennon had done it the year before made it cool," Noddy Holder told BBC 6 Music in 2023. "And of course, Elton John was doing the same thing." There was definitely something in the air. "I guess that for the last few years it's not been considered groovy to make Christmas records," wrote John Peel in

---

[14] When the band's label came to rerelease the song in 1981, it was found that the original mastertapes had been misplaced, meaning Wood had to rerecord everything from scratch for the re-pressing. According to Muff Murfin, the producer on the second version, almost every subsequent pressing of the record, on compilations, soundtracks and reissues, and thus the version most people will hear year on year, is the 1981 recording rather than the 1973 take. I have been listening to every version I can find, and I honestly couldn't tell you if this is true. I even sent them to an audio engineer I know, and he couldn't spot it either. If they did rerecord it, it was done so faithfully you can't spot the join. As my mate Jez said, "Fuck me! Roy Wood is a genius!"

his column in *Sounds* that December. "Therefore it's a pleasure to see that both Elton and Slade have followed the lead set by John and Yoko last year … it's even nicer that both [songs are] very fine indeed." Curiously, though he does review Roy Wood's solo single 'Forever' in the same issue, Peel overlooks Wizzard here in favour of Elton.[15] Elsewhere, however, Wizzard were getting solid write-ups. "An obvious hit, probably even if it wasn't Christmas," raved *Record Mirror*'s Pete Jones. "A busy, fuzzy, enthusiastic and energetic single." The *Daily Mirror*'s Deborah Thomas agreed, calling it a "fizzy, frosty, rocking sparkler", while damning Slade's 'Merry Xmas' as slow and lifeless, asking, "where has all the zazz gone, boys?" The *Notts Evening Post*, meanwhile, was Team Slade. "I think it's just about the best single they've done", writes James Belsey, smartly noting that 'I Wish It Could Be Christmas …' though enjoyable, was just "'See My Baby Jive' with some snowflakes on" – alas, an absolutely accurate critique.[16]

What's curious, given how mythologised the two records have become, is that any sense of their being a race or competition is largely absent from the music press and to be found nowhere at all in the mainstream media. The singles might be reviewed on the same page, but they're not pitted against each other directly, and fans weren't writing to *NME* or *Sounds* professing their support for one or the other. This wasn't a Blur vs Oasis situation. There was competition within the bands, certainly, but the public and the press weren't making much of it. "When I first heard it," said Slade's Jim Lea of 'I Wish It Could Be Christmas Everyday' "[I thought] it was so good that I remember joking: 'I hope Roy gets run over by a bus.'" "If it hadn't been for us," says Dave Hill in his memoir, "Roy

---

[15] Though mentioned in the music press that year as much as Slade and Wizzard, Elton's 'Step Into Christmas' didn't make much of a splash, peaking at 24. The song didn't really enter into the canon of festive perennials until it started cropping up as a space filler on Christmas compilations in the '80s.

[16] For someone with such a varied back catalogue and undoubted talent as Roy Wood, it's curious but undeniable that Wizzard's three big singles – 'See My Baby Jive', 'Angel Fingers' and 'I Wish It Could Be Christmas' – are, more or less, exactly the same song. It's a *very good* song, though.

would probably have been No. 1, but at the time nobody could compete with us."

Wood himself has always claimed that it wasn't a fair fight – his record was subject to a delay after manager Don Arden negotiated for the single to come out on the Warner Brothers label, who got as far as pressing it before it was pointed out that Wizzard were still technically under contract to EMI subsidiary Harvest, who insisted on releasing the record themselves. "It delayed the release of the record by two weeks," Wood told *Metro* in 2024. "So Slade had two weeks more than we did to get record sales, so consequently they got the No. 1." It's possible that 50 years' distance has muddled some details for Wood, however. Whatever was happening behind the scenes, 'I Wish It Could Be Christmas Everyday' made it into shops a week before 'Merry Xmas Everybody', charting at 19 on 8 December. Slade would gatecrash the chart at No. 1 the following week, with Wizzard jumping to 6, and then peaking at 6 in Christmas week itself. "Woody was blazing about it," Noddy Holder told Mark Radlicffe in 2023. "Soon afterwards, we were at a party at [Slade guitarist] Dave Hill's neighbours' and Roy was there," Jim Lea told the *Guardian*. "Eventually, he held out his hand and said: 'Put it there, the best man won.' We were still shaking hands when I looked up at him and said: 'Do you know what, Roy? I prefer your record.'" Wood's reply was "Me too." To this day Lea isn't sure if he was serious.

Wood, in fairness, had every right to a be a little bitter – it's very likely that had there not been two big records splitting the tinsel pound, particularly at a time of economic hardship when a family might only be able to justify one or the other, Wizzard could well have claimed their No. 1. 'I Wish It Could Be Christmas Everyday' is certainly good enough – just as big, raucous and fun as Slade's effort, if perhaps lyrically a little more sentimental. The two do have their differences – 'Merry Xmas' is a far leaner, more stripped-down beast, while 'I Wish It Could Be Christmas' goes all in on Spectorish, Disney maximalism. Neither sound like the classic idea of Christmas music as served by Nat King Cole and Bing Crosby. Both had an element of novelty simply as Christmas rock songs, but neither was the usual disposable dross the public was used to at that time of year. These were brilliant, buoyant songs at the exact moment such music was needed – and Britain responded.

Both records, tied together forever more, have had astonishing legacies that their writers could never have dreamed of at the time. Despite the *New York Times* claim of pop's elevation to art form, the charts were still disposable. Fads moved quickly. Records came and went. Both Slade and Wizzard were subject to extensive coverage in the music press that December, but surprisingly little of it focuses on their Christmas songs, usually covered in a few paragraphs with writers moving on to upcoming albums or tours. In 1974 music journalist George Tremlett published a biography, *The Slade Story*, and while it goes deep on their origins, their 1974 album *Old New Borrowed and Blue* and their excellent film, *Flame*, 'Merry Xmas Everybody' is largely glossed over. Slade and Wizzard were unwittingly cementing their legacies (and pensions) with these songs and, though no one realised it at the time, this was the biggest either band would ever be – neither would ever have a No. 1 again. In many ways both Wood and the members of Slade have spent the last half century in the shadow of December 1973, something that would have seemed absurd at the time. Contemporary writing views these songs as fun distractions, not legacy-defining game changers. "Whether their sales will equal the best-selling 'Mary's Boy Child' [the 1957 No. 1 from Harry Belanfonte] is doubtful," wrote *Record Mirror*'s Tony Jasper at the beginning of December. "Let alone compete with 'White Christmas'."

But compete with 'White Christmas' they did, at least in Britain. Though neither song has dented the American consciousness, it's impossible to imagine Christmas in the UK without Slade and Wizzard. The two songs, channelling rocking Christmases of yore but, crucially, with an optimism that looked to the future, would set a template for what a British festive hit should sound like. It should be BIG. It should be FUN. From the Darkness to Sam Ryder to Manic Street Preachers and beyond, whenever a rock band has a go at cracking the festive market, it's Slade and Wizzard they're echoing. The two hits also served as a proof of concept. Between them, they sold in the millions and would pop back up again every year. Even before the download and streaming market changed the business, both songs would regularly surface in the December charts. John and Yoko had given us the first hint that Christmas pop could be big business. That could have been a fluke, though. But Slade and Wizzard? That was mainstream. If *they* could have festive hits, then any pop star could have a go at a Christmas smash of their own. And by 1974, it seemed like every pop star was giving it a try.

Chapter 5
EYES FULL OF TINSEL AND FIRE

Being an account of the golden age of British Christmas singles

"CHRISTMAS HIT BATTLE!" – the front page of *Melody Maker*, 14 December, wasn't messing about, shouting in big, bold capital letters. With a week to go before the Christmas chart was announced, the venerable pop paper had just one story to tell: "CHRISTMAS CRAZY" went that week's leader. "The record market this year is swamped by Christmas singles – and two of them have already hit the *MM* chart." Specifically, the paper was referring to Mud's 'Lonely This Christmas' and Showaddywaddy's 'Hey Mister Christmas'. The two bands, styled as '50s throwbacks in brightly coloured suits, were part of the rock and roll revivalism that had grown out of glitter rock across 1974. It was still glam, certainly – still young men show-ponying in flashy clothes over stompy rock and roll (Mud's breakthrough, 'Dyna-mite', had been written for the Sweet, who rejected it) but it had, if anything, dumbed down further, swapping arch campiness for simpler thrills. With Bowie trekking across America, losing himself in milk and heroic amounts of cocaine, Bolan exploring a combination of soul music and fried chicken (and heroic amounts of cocaine) and Slade off making films, the stage had been left clear for their less subtle successors: Mud, Showaddywaddy, the Bay City Rollers, Alvin Stardust,

Gary Glitter, the Rubettes and, the pop surprise of the year, the Wombles. More of whom later. Most of those bands, and their record companies, had spent 1974 counting down to Christmas. It hadn't escaped anyone's notice that Slade had sold *a million* records with 'Merry Xmas Everybody' – and was still selling in the spring. Wizzard hadn't done half bad either. After years of politely ignoring the subject, Britain's pop machine had finally realised that singing about Christmas could pay off.

Mud were the latest beneficiaries of songwriting duo Nicky Chinn and Mike Chapman, aka Chinnichap (who also wrote for Sweet and Suzy Quatro). They had supplied their charges with a proper weepie – 'Lonely This Christmas'. The motivations behind it were pretty transparent: "Everybody wants to make a Christmas song because everybody wants to make money," Chapman told the *Daily Mirror*'s Deborah Thomas that December. "We decided to write a slowie with sentimental lyrics as a change from all the comedy records and up-tempo numbers you get at Christmas." Mud, like most of the glam crowd, had been knocking about since the late '60s without a great deal of success. They'd signed to pop kingmaker Mickie Most's RAK label in 1973, and the ever-canny Most had put them in matching Teddy Boy suits[1] and hooked them up with Chinn and Chapman. Within a year they'd had a hit with 'Dyna-mite' and their first No. 1 with the irresistible 'Tiger Feet'.

So far, the band had followed the Chinnichap formula – stompy, big, catchy, primitive, loud. For their festive effort, however, a gentler touch was required in order to utilise most effectively the band's secret weapon: singer Les Gray's uncannily accurate Elvis Presley impersonation. Gray was happy to switch to his Elvis voice at the slightest provocation; it was something of a party piece, and Chinn and Chapman had decided to lean fully in. 'Lonely This Christmas' was a song written specifically and shamelessly to sound like the latter-day, soulful, dewy-eyed balladeer Elvis; the one of 'Always on My Mind' and, more pertinently, his recent version of 'O Come All Ye Faithful'. They absolutely hit the bullseye. Whether it's a pastiche, a homage or a plain-old rip-off is left for the reader to

---

[1] Inspired, incidentally, by seeing Showaddywaddy on TV talent show *New Faces*.

decide for themselves, but either way it wears its big, soft, Graceland heart on a sleeve damp with tears. "I suppose it's a bit of a rip-off," Chapman admitted to the *Daily Mirror*, "but young kids today haven't heard that old Elvis sound. I think they'll like it." A genius move. The weenyboppers were going to buy a new Mud record anyway, but by channelling the King so perfectly, the band were able to appeal to the sort of record buyers unique to the Christmas window – kids, housewives and grannies. In other words, the actual public. It was a song about heartbreak, it was shamelessly retro, and – this cannot be stated enough – Les Gray really, *really* sounds like Elvis. A truly relatable, precision-targeted Christmas hit. Released late November, it went in at 36, was up to 15 on 7 December and shot up to No. 4 the following week. As Christmas approached it was selling 90,000 copies *a day*. "We're gonna be No. 1 at Christmas," Les Gray told *Melody Maker* that week. "At least we should be. Christ. I've never felt so nervous in my life".

Gray really shouldn't have been that nervous – 'Lonely This Christmas' was a nailed-on, dead cert for No. 1. Partly this is because it had got off to the right start, with a plum, attention-grabbing spot on *Top of the Pops* on 5 December, accounting for the 11-place chart leap; the band resplendent in white suits with red glittery trim, looking every inch the lounge-core festive balladeers. The record sleeve also had the frankly genius touch of a "To" and "From" label printed into its artwork, ready for Christmas gifting.[2] Mostly, though, 'Lonely This Christmas' succeeded because it was a really good Christmas ballad, an authentically weepie cracker. In pop, the simplest messages are always the best and it doesn't get much simpler than *I have lost you and I am lonely and it's Christmas and isn't that just awful*. While Slade and Wizzard had tapped into the anarchic side of the season, Chinn and Chapman had chosen the more wistful angle, the side established by Bing Crosby and Judy Garland – the evergreen, authentic and deeply effective trope of *Miserable Christmas,* in which the forced jollity and familial warmth highlighted the unhappiness of those left alone and without. A Christmas where your "tears could melt the snow" was also one, after all, where you "have

---

[2] You have to wonder how many bitter, recently jilted people sent it to their exes that year. The ultimate passive-aggressive present.

to muddle through somehow". *Of course* it was going to be a hit. By 21 December, 'Lonely This Christmas' was at No. 1, where it would stay well into January.[3] *Miserable Christmas* would become another enduring trope of the British Christmas charts, whether specifically seasonal like Wham!'s 'Last Christmas' (No. 2 in 1984 and No. 1 in 2023 *and* 2024) or simply well timed, as in East 17's 'Stay Another Day' (No. 1, 1994) and All Saints' 'Never Ever' (No. 4, 1997).

Mud, however, didn't have the Christmas chart to themselves. December 1974 saw most of that year's big guns chasing a lucrative December hit – the Faces, the Rubettes, Gary Glitter, Status Quo, Alvin Stardust, David Essex and Wizzard were all selling by the pallet load. One strong contender, and a well-timed, if not specifically seasonal, entry into the *Miserable Christmas* genre was 'Streets of London', the rather earnest tale of London's homeless by folk singer Ralph McTell, who'd had it kicking around for a decade but had held off on recording it for fear it was too depressing. This simple, warmly performed, finger-picked ditty eventually turned up on his 1969 album *Spiral Staircase* and was recorded again for his US debut the following year. It was a re-rerecorded version, however, done at McTell's manager's insistence, that was finally released as a single in December 1974, for the Christmas market. It was a smart move. As Charles Dickens had put it, Christmas was the "time of all others when Want is keenly felt" – reminders of those less fortunate were, oddly, a traditional contributor to Christmas cheer. 'Streets of London' sneaked into the top 40 at 39 on 7 December, earning McTell an all-important slot on the following week's *Top of the Pops*, where the song's gentle mood and maudlin message instantly connected. By the following week it was charting at 14. By Christmas week, it too was selling somewhere in the region of 90,000 copies a day, though in those days of gigantic singles sales, especially in the final weeks of December, that was still only enough to get it to No. 6. It would peak a few weeks into January at No. 2, and would stay on the charts for 11 weeks, eventually winning McTell a silver disc (for sales of over 250,000 sales) and an Ivor Novello Award.

---

[3] Exactly who buys Christmas singles in January is a baffling question, but clearly someone does – somehow, 'Lonely This Christmas' didn't fall off out of the Top 40 until 1 February.

It remains his only mainstream hit – a situation he says he's very comfortable with.

Mud's other challengers that year were all firmly in the Christmas camp. December 1974 was overwhelmingly awash with seasonal themed 7-inchers, to the point that the music press were getting serious festive fatigue. "The problem with reviewing records at Christmas," wrote *Record Mirror* editor Sue Byrom in her singles column, "is that you reach a stage when the strands of tinsel draped so attractively around your ears and record player starts to get just that touch tarnished." "Seasonal songs," sighed the music column in the *Grimsby Evening Standard,* "are reaching epidemic proportions." You can see their point. As well as Mud that year, there was the aforementioned Showaddywaddy's 'Hey Mister Christmas' and the Wombles' 'Wombling Merry Christmas'; there was the excruciating 'Father Christmas Do Not Touch Me' from comedy troupe the Goodies; and there were Gilbert O'Sullivan's 'Christmas Song', Bobbie McGee's 'It's Christmas', Mr Big's 'Christmas With Dickens', Andy Williams' 'Christmas Present', the Carpenters' 'Merry Christmas, Darling', Scaffold's 'Mummy Won't Be Home For Christmas', former miners Millican and Nesbitt with 'How I Wish It Was Christmas', Bert Jansch's 'In the Bleak Midwinter', Perry Como's 'Christmas Dream', Merle Haggard's 'If We Can Make It Through December', Young Tradition's rendition of the ancient 'The Boar's Head Carol' and George Harrison's 'Ding Dong, Ding Dong.'[4] Meanwhile, David Cassidy, the Partridge Family and the Pasedena Roof Orchestra had all covered 'White Christmas'.

---

[4] Alright, that last one is *technically* a New Year record. It performed abysmally for a Beatle, peaking at 38 and then dropping out of the Top 100 the following week. No one was very keen. "Ludicrous!" stormed a review in the *Evening Standard,* railing against a song it said had been forced on "an undeserving public" and noting with disbelief that Harrison had the cheek to "take advertisements out in the music press to reprint the lyrics, which merely confirmed their absurdity". To be honest, the song deserved its horrible reception – 'Ding Dong' is a pretty rotten cash-in, shamelessly grabbing for the festive season, and with a hint of unattractive bitterness beneath it as Harrison surveyed his crumbling marriage. He also, audibly, has a sore throat, making it an uncomfortable and unsatisfying record in all sorts of ways.

And that's before we get to the reissues – Harvest had put out 'I Wish It Could Be Christmas Every Day' again, to Roy Wood's immense irritation since it meant he was competing with his own biggest hit for the second year in a row, John & Yoko's 'Happy Xmas' was out for a second time ("It does tend to show up the rather inferior quality of the festive records we've had this year," said *Record Mirror*), Darlene Love's immortal 'Christmas (Baby Please Come Home)' was issued to promote yet another repressing of Phil Spector's Christmas album, Steeleye Span's 'Gaudete' was back and the traditional reissue of Bing's 'White Christmas' was getting an unusually big push to capitalise on the Christmas single mania. "We put it out each year and it always creates some interest," a spokesman for MCA records told *Melody Maker*, of the now 30-year-old classic. "It's incredible that there should be demand for it, but there always is. This year we're giving it a slight push, sending it out for review and sending it to radio stations, so it's doing very well again." For good measure, the Drifters' 1954 recording of the song was also reissued.

For years the assumption had been that, aside from a very, very few exceptions, Christmas records were a largely pointless and disposable project for a pop group, since they had shelf life of about three weeks in December, and would fall away for good come New Year. 'White Christmas' was thought an anomaly. 1973, however, had proven that, actually, if you could get the formula right, the potential was vast: a Christmas hit's appeal wasn't limited at all. Was, in fact, limit*less*. It could sell to every household in the country, and do so again, and again, and again, *every single year*. It's a lesson that would become clearer and clearer across the next decade as those disposable pop hits of 1973 and 1974, songs that Slade, Wizzard and Mud could barely be bothered to promote in interviews, resurfaced annually. When Mud's Les Gray joked to *Melody Maker*: "I don't care if they release it year after year. Maybe we'll make as much as Bing Crosby," he couldn't have imagined that his well-honed Presley impression would still be played on mainstream pop radio 50 years in the future. Bing had managed only 30 at that point. Unfortunately, if 1973 had proven that pop stars could make a feast out of Christmas, the lesson of 1974 was that dressing a tune up with mistletoe and holly wasn't necessarily a guarantee of success.

For every song that ascended to rarified perennial, there are dozens that never seem to get invited back to the party.

While Mud's approach to the Christmas market had been calculated and precise, Showaddywaddy's festive entry was altogether more spontaneous. The Leicester band were in the studio to record their next single, riding high after two hits in 1974, including the No. 2 'Hey Rock and Roll', when fate intervened. "It was very, very late on," recalls singer Dave Bartram. "We were due to record our third single, we'd got a couple of possible songs. And I think it was one of the engineers, the guy who maintained the equipment, he'd come in because we got an issue with one of the machines. And he said 'Oh, is it a Christmas song you're doing, lads?'" The casual comment sparked something. "We looked at the producer, and we all looked at each other and thought 'perhaps we *should* be doing a Christmas one'."

What followed was a rush of creativity that demonstrated just how quickly the rules of a Christmas single had become established. Within an hour, Bartram and guitarist Trevor Oakes had written two contenders, and producer Mike Hurst suggested combining elements from both. The title itself came from another passing comment – when they realised the original chorus, 'Hey, Merry Christmas', was a little too close to Slade's 'Merry Christmas Everybody': "somebody just walking by says, 'Oh, he thinks he's Mr. Christmas.' And that was it, literally it, you know, just a sort of slip of the tongue."

Once the basic track was laid down, the next step seemed obvious to everyone involved. "Someone said we need some kids' voices on it," remembers Bartram. "And I immediately said 'Yeah, children's choir!'" The Harpenden Children's School Choir were quickly located and brought in. Years later, Bartram would defend this decision against critics who suggested they'd "thrown in the kitchen sink". As he puts it, "it wasn't about that. It needed something to give it a sort of Christmasy appeal, and kids choirs go with Christmas."

By all rights it should have been a Top 5 record. Sure, it didn't sound like an instant classic in the way that 'Lonely This Christmas' did, and it didn't have that Elvis-aping crossover appeal either, but it's certainly not a *bad* record. It's a very bare bones, stripped down take, but that gives it a charm of its own. It's also delivered with the sort of nod-and-wink sauce the British have always appreciated in their festive fare (witness Bartram on *Top of the Pops* lifting his sunglasses and looking straight into the camera for a second after the line "Santa comes tonight."). Combine that with jingling bells, that kids choir and the band's teenybopper profile, and they should have been on to a winner. The similarly positioned Rubettes had just had a huge smash with an arguably more forgettable song and no seasonal advantage. Alas, the spontaneity that had birthed the record would ultimately work against it. "We had to do a rush release," says Bartram. "It came out a week later than we would have hoped." Even so, the sales were remarkable – while the song peaked at No. 13, the band received a silver disc for their efforts – "which for records that didn't make the top 10 is almost unheard of" – but Bartram remains convinced that with just one more week of sales, they "probably would have had a top three."

Meanwhile, at 18 on the Christmas week chart was Gilbert O'Sullivan's 'Christmas Song' – another specially recorded seasonal entry by a chart star of the time. By 1974, singer/songwriter O'Sullivan had two No. 1s under his belt, and though his star was on the wane (*A Stranger in My Own Backyard,* his album of that year, had peaked at 9, where his two previous efforts had charted at 1 and 2) he was still a big enough name for the *Daily Mirror*'s pop correspondent, Deborah Thomas, to declare him the favourite for the Christmas chart-topper. Like Showaddywaddy, he'd thrown in jingle bells and a kid's choir; like Mud the song had a maudlin mood; like John Lennon it was thinking of those worse off; and like Slade and Wizzard he started from the perspective of subverting the corny Christmas classics, in this case with a refrain of "I'm not dreaming of a white Christmas". The song just didn't catch. Even *Top of the Pops* came calling only once, and that was to show a rather boring pre-recorded video, with the song's children's choir bafflingly mimed by O'Sullivan's adult backing band. It's an oddly charmless piece, that nevertheless leapfrogged Showaddywaddy the week after Christmas to peak at 12, implying fairly gargantuan sales of its own – though within two weeks both had slipped quietly out of the Top

40, while Mud were still in the Top 10. Fifty years on, you rarely hear either song.[5]

The only other serious, festive-themed contender that year came from the Wombles and, in its own way, it was a perfect Christmas hit. The Wombles, for those not in the know, were small furry, litter-picking, recycling-obsessed creatures that lived on Wimbledon Common, busying themselves by "making good use of the things that we find".[6] The characters were the creation of children's author Elizabeth Beresford and had featured in a series of popular books, beginning with 1968's *The Wombles*. In 1973 they'd been adapted into a BBC television series, rendered as charming stop-motion puppets and narrated by the friendly tones of Bernard Cribbins. The show's catchy theme, 'The Wombling Song', had been composed by jobbing songwriter Mike Batt, who had rather over-delivered on the project, creating a melodically complex but, nevertheless, extremely accessible and ridiculously hummable piece in return for which he negotiated the rights to use the characters for musical projects. The song was released as a novelty single, but Batt had bigger ideas. Turning up in his record company office *literally dressed as a Womble*, he pitched "The Wombles" as a band in their own right, in which he'd write and sing the songs as well as lead a group of similarly costumed Wombles to promote the records on TV. It was a canny move that not only made 'The Wombling Song' into a huge hit, but allowed him to write follow-ups independently of the TV show and books (though Womble HQ insisted on okaying his lyrics). For good measure, the success of the song gave the BBC show itself the nudge it needed, generating a surge of Womblemania. By the beginning of 1974 the loveable characters had very much gone overground. Batt followed up his success with 'Remember You're a Womble', a light, glam-tinged rock record that lodged itself in the brain of anyone hearing it. It went to No. 2, with Batt and his Wombling chums making very good use of the *Top of the Pops* studio, as well as the studios of *Blue Peter* and *Crackerjack*, and even turning up as the interval entertainment of that year's

---

[5] A 50th anniversary reissue did put 'Hey Mister Christmas' at the top of the 7" single charts in November 2024, but it didn't make a dent in the Top 100.

[6] Readers of a certain age are already humming this.

UK-hosted Eurovision Song Contest. By Christmas, the Wombles had become the bestselling artists of 1974, at least in Britain, and the first act since the Beatles to have three singles in the Top 50 at the same time.

Naturally, a Christmas single was the obvious move, with Batt delivering the palatable 'Wombling Merry Christmas', a song that had everything going for it – novelty, chart momentum from previous hits, seasonal warmth, a built-in child audience and the fact that Batt prided himself on gorgeously produced pop records that were generally far better, and musically richer, than a spin-off from a kid's TV show had any right to be.[7] At one point 'Wombling Merry Christmas' was, according to Batt at least, outselling Mud's 'Lonely This Christmas' by two to one. The Christmas No. 1 was, surely, in the bag. Alas, some things aren't meant to be.

While Batt went above and beyond to make sure the Wombles' musical output could really stand on its own, including performing in high-quality costumes, hand-stitched by his own mother, the rest of the Wombling empire didn't have anything like that level of quality control. Rights holders were happy to slap the Womble brand on any product that would pay for it. With scenes that echoed the pop culture invasion of *Doctor Who* baddies the Daleks ten years earlier, the Wombles were suddenly everywhere, on lunch boxes, bubble bath, comics and sweets.[8] That winter it was decided that a Wombles Christmas Show should hit theatres around the country, not as a tour but as seven simultaneously running performances in different cities, including London, Glasgow, Liverpool and Belfast, with seven different casts, seven stage sets and seven sets of costumes. Against his better judgement, the protective Batt agreed to supervise the music. "It was a recipe for disaster," he wrote

---

[7] Batt was incredibly musically knowledgeable. An earlier Wombles single, 'Minuetto Allegretto', was based around the third movement of Mozart's Symphony No. 41, and featured elderly Womble adventurer Uncle Bulgaria remembering the days when he dreamed of being a classic composer. You didn't get *that* with the Rubettes.

[8] Had Dalekmania hit in 1973, rather than 1963, we probably would have gotten a Dalek Christmas single too. It's a tragedy that the British public were deprived.

in his memoir, *The Closest Thing to Crazy*.[9] "Everything about these shows, including the costumes was cheap and nasty … they stank of everything we Wombles, as a pop group, tried to avoid." A recipe for disaster indeed – reports soon emerged of children booing the inferior Womble shows and parents demanding their money back. In Liverpool 350 letters of protest were apparently handed in before the opening performance had finished ("Children were crying, over 500 people walked out," theatre manager Robert Lewis told the *Observer*, who ran the story on the front page). In Belfast there was a near riot, with kids rushing the stage. Reviews were disastrous ("the performers were inaudible with no attempt at characterisation" said the *Guardian*, "… the lack of any spark of real affection was deeply depressing."). Batt was furious, assuming his songs would be tarred by the same brush. And so it was – sales of 'Wombling Merry Christmas' plateaued almost immediately and the record went in at 21. Batt was forced to sit back and watch Mud sail past him to the top and stay there. Things rallied (the song would eventually peak at No. 2 and would remain on the chart for eight weeks) but the damage had been done. Though there were several more Wombling hits in 1975, Batt never got his No. 1, and 'Wombling Merry Christmas' never truly joined the pantheon of seasonal perennials.

Looking at Christmas 1974 and the years that followed in terms of pop music, we're struck by two unavoidable truths. Firstly, there were more seasonal-themed records out than any other time in the modern pop era. Secondly, barely any of them sold in significant numbers and of those that did, still fewer are especially remembered today. The music industry had woken up to the potential of the tinsel pound, and it's a lesson that would not be forgotten – but aiming at the Christmas market brought no guarantees, even for established names. The Scaffold had a Christmas No. 1 under their belt already (1968's 'Lily the Pink'), but 'Mummy Please Come Home This Christmas' sank without a trace, mostly because it was sentimental dross, as did Norman Wisdom's 'Do You Believe In Christmas' the following year for largely the same reason. Both of the Goodies' back-to-back Christmas singles – 'Father Christmas

---

[9] The title of which was borrowed from another Batt-penned hit: Katie Meluah's song of the same name, a Christmas hit in 2003.

Do Not Touch Me' (No. 7, 1974) and 'Make a Daft Noise for Christmas' (No. 20, 1975) – charted respectably, but neither have endured and both, frankly, have aged like milk.

By 1975, a peculiar cynicism about Christmas records had begun to settle in. "British record companies stand to lose a tremendous amount of money if most of us don't buy at least one dreadful Christmas record between now and December 25," wrote Martyn Sutton in the *Leicester Mercury* that December, tongue firmly in cheek. "It's [just] a shame that most of their products are abysmal." *Record Mirror*'s Wits End column went further, snarkily bemoaning the proliferation of novelty records as inappropriate for the still ever-present economic doom and gloom that hung like a smog over the UK ("this country's darkest hour") and calling, with magnificently overwrought sarcasm, for a return to the Dunkirk spirit and charts full of Gracie Fields and Vera Lynn. A year on from Mud's success, the 1975 Christmas chart was a lesson that popular bands singing about Santa didn't automatically get you the top spot: Queen's defining masterpiece 'Bohemian Rhapsody' became the first non-Christmassy Christmas No. 1 in three years, claiming the festive crown almost by accident – a complex, ambitious rock opera that had hit No. 1 mid-November and simply refused to budge.[10] The band hadn't aimed for the Christmas market at all; that slot was being eyed by the likes of Emerson, Lake & Palmer bass player Greg Lake; the Goodies with a return to the theme of Santa; and Judge Dread, the largely forgotten but massive at the time white reggae artist whose 'Christmas In Dreadland' lurked at No. 14.

Lake's 'I Believe in Father Christmas', which stalled behind Queen at No. 2, would have been a sure-fire tree-topper any other year. It was a song that was, at once, a twinkly ballad *and* a conscious critique of holiday commercialisation – both gorgeous and sophisticated. Like 'In Dulce Jubilo', a sprightly take on an old German carol released that same year by Mike *Tubular Bells* Oldfield, Lake's

---

[10] That said, a record that is so very, very *extra* does feel like something of an obvious Christmas hit. The opera sections smack of novelty, there's a sentimental bit, a raucous bit and the video has twinkly lights. It's all rather festive when you think about it. Well, aside from the murder confession in the first verse – though family Christmas arguments can, indeed, get quite out of hand.

song reflected a speedy evolution in British Christmas pop, as artists began to stretch themselves beyond party anthems and sentimental reflections. What began as just messing about with alternative tunings – Lake tuning his bottom string from E to D – would evolve into one of the most ambitious and stirring pop records ever made, a song that questions the magic of modern Christmas while celebrating its unrepentant joy. That Lake, moonlighting from his day job in prog giants ELP, manages to code those messages effectively into both the lyrics and the musical arrangement is quite the accomplishment. A descending acoustic guitar figure provides a gentle, almost lullaby-like foundation, but the song builds and builds, layering orchestration into something that, as the timpani drums beat and the horns and choir soars, becomes genuinely epic. And that's not a word to use lightly. The inclusion of a classical piece effectively serving as the chorus (Sergei Prokofiev's 'Troika', taken from his 1934 *Lieutenant Kijé* suite, included at the suggestion of ELP's Keith Emerson, who originally played the section on keyboards before being replaced by the London Philharmonic) becomes integral to the record's emotional journey, sweeping in like crisp winter air, bringing with it images of painted toy soldiers, nutcrackers and the sharp smell of snow. When the full orchestra and choir surge forward in the final third, it's genuinely heart-stopping.

The lyrics, by Lake and collaborator Pete Sinfield, are wonderfully constructed, moving from childhood wonder ("eyes full of tinsel and fire") to adult disillusionment ("they said there'd be snow at Christmas … but instead it just kept on raining") and back to a kind of weary hope ("Hallelujah, Noel/ be it heaven or hell/ The Christmas we get we deserve"). By the coda it has somehow made peace with its own contradictions; a rejection of empty Christmas sentiment and one of the most purely emotional Christmas records ever made – a philosophical Christmas cracker with a symphony orchestra inside.[11] Shortly before his death in 2016, Lake reflected to the *Guardian* on the song's origins: "It was about how Christmas had deteriorated and was in danger of becoming yet another victim

---

[11] You could argue that Roy Wood achieved something similar with the much simpler tactic of opening a Christmas celebration with the ringing of a cash register. That, right there, is the difference between glam and prog rock.

of crass corporate financial exploitation." The song, he insisted, was about something more profound than "12 pints of lager and a crate of Baileys. It's more important to make some spiritual human contact, or visit someone lonely."[12] Harking back to Dickens' view of the season, it's perhaps the only Christmas record, Roy Wood's cash register aside, that questions consumerism while being played in department stores full of Christmas shoppers, a quiet revolution in tinsel and fairy lights.

The novelty market was evolving too. Club DJ Chris Hill's 'Renta Santa' which peaked at No. 10 in 1975, began life as an in-house Christmas novelty for Phonogram Records employees. Hill, the resident DJ at the Goldmine discotheque on Canvey Island, had gathered friends to record amusing songs and skits for the company's annual conference. When word spread, Phonogram decided to release it properly. The record was something new for the UK, though the trick had been done in America many times – a record that spliced together snatches of other songs to create a comic narrative, linked with Hill himself doing a voiceover. Hill would follow it up with the similar 'Bionic Santa' (No. 10, 1976) but gave up on Christmas mash-ups after 1978's 'Disco Santa' didn't chart. Though Hill's 'Santa' records have been largely forgotten, they were, for their time, also pioneering, opening the way for future mash-up hits like Jive Bunny and normalising the idea of sampling on pop records. Hill's legacy was to put the DJ, rather than the artist, at the centre of the record, something we take for granted now. Christmas hits, as ever, were reflecting wider movements in pop culture with the growth of discotheques and clubs across the UK and the rise of Northern Soul in Manchester, Wigan, Stoke and Blackpool, where the guy picking the tunes was gaining as high a status as the records he was spinning.

---

[12] The recording sessions themselves were as dramatic as the song. Held in the sweltering August heat of 1975, Lake demanded a suitably festive atmosphere, leading to the installation of a 6-m (20-foot) Christmas tree with lights in the studio. Lake also wanted conductor Godfrey Salmon to do the session, despite the heat wave, in full Santa regalia (he refused). What followed was pure chaos involving a surprise performance by a stripper, a destroyed double bass as the orchestra surged forward to see, outraged choir members and, somehow, in the midst of it all, the perfect first take.

It had taken just five years for Christmas-themed records to go from something no mainstream pop artists would touch with a barge pole to a challenge every big act felt they should try, leading to a grating ubiquity as the market flooded, year after year, with seasonal product and no quality control. By the end of 1976, even the music press's Christmas coverage had developed a knowingly gothic edge. *Record Mirror*'s Barry Cain cast his singles review column as a horror story: a sinister stranger (revealed to be an *RM* reviewer driven mad by Christmas releases) torturing a family party with the unhinged December singles roster, including the Saints' Aussie punk classic 'I'm Stranded', cross-dressing music hall duo Hinge and Bracket's 'Cat Duet' and village folk singers the Woolpit Carollers' 'The Wind Is Blowing.' It's a snapshot of a peculiarly British moment – punk breaking through while light entertainment carried on regardless. The Christmas No. 1, meanwhile, was as traditional as it could possibly be: Johnny Mathis's soothing carol 'When a Child Is Born'. Mathis, the third bestselling artist of the twentieth century, was a Christmas veteran who'd already recorded three holiday albums, having released his first in 1958.[13] His latest single, as *Music Week* said at the time, was "the first new Christmas standard for years, probably since Mel Tormé's 'A Christmas Song' back in the Fifties." Though it felt like it could have topped the charts in 1956, the song was actually just three years old, written by Italian composer Ciro Dammicco under the pseudonym Zacar. By the time Mathis took it to No. 1 in Britain, it had already been a hit in Germany (although the German lyrics had an entirely different theme). Like many of the festive hits before and since, its success came from unlocking an audience that didn't typically buy singles: teenage and 20-something pop fans weren't buying Johnny Mathis, but just about everyone else was. It was, once again, the power of the granny market. The era of the credible festive-themed Christmas No. 1 had been short-lived.[14] 'When a Child Is Born' proved that a carefully positioned proper

---

[13] In 2023 he released *Christmas Time Is Here*, his eighth holiday album and his 71st in total. With the death of Tony Bennett, Mathis is, at the time of writing at least, the last of the great crooners, his chocolatey-smooth voice still doing the business.

[14] It lasted precisely one year – 1973.

song, of the sort grown-ups like, could clean up at Christmas, something underlined the following year when Bing's 'White Christmas' found itself in the Christmas Top 5 yet again, in the wake of the singer's death. While the music press was full of punk and New Wave[15] and while *Record Mirror*'s reviewers were writing horror stories about sinister salesmen torturing families with seasonal singles, Mathis's hit was shifting enormous quantities to an audience that likely neither knew nor cared about any of that. A recalibrating record biz was learning that audiences could be targeted with different approaches to Christmas – the season was big enough for everyone.

By the late '70s the Christmas market had settled down. The industry knew original Christmas songs could be winners but equally it now knew they could sink and, indeed, stink. The Christmas No. 1 now held real cachet, even if the phrase wasn't yet widely used, but the idea that it needed to be festive-themed was loosening its grip. A big record was still going to be a big record – 'Bohemian Rhapsody' was a hit that Christmas could only enhance, not derail. A December No. 1 wasn't the Baby Jesus-given preserve of the seasonal song, despite the fine work done by Slade and Mud. The novelty hits and comedy records of the '60s and early '70s were still in play, the oldies and weepies still had a shot, and the Christmas chart was still a different landscape to the rest of the year, where different rules applied – rules that were coming to be understood. The industry was beginning to realise that the No. 1 at Christmas, coming as it did with *huge* sales, could be achieved without taking risks and big swings. It didn't even, necessarily, have to be wrapped in tinsel and hung with baubles. In fact, as Johnny Mathis was showing, the best way to guarantee Christmas success might be to play it as safe as possible. This view was even confirmed algorithmically. In 1977, the Harlequin group of record shops used the data gathered from their stocktaking computers to mathematically predict the sort of song that would likely be a hit at any given time of the year. The results, as the *Guardian* reported, showed that "in the Winter the middle-of-the-road ballad wins".

---

[15] While Johnny Mathis was at No. 1, the Sex Pistols were sneaking into the chart at 38 with 'Anarchy in the UK' – a hint of the coming revolution.

Chapter 6
THE WINTER OF OUR DISCO TENT

Or how the Christmas charts got serious

1977 is often thought of as a year fizzing with innovation and right-eous musical fury, and for anyone invested in music culture that was largely true – it was the year of 'I Feel Love', *Marquee Moon*, *Never Mind the Bollocks*, the Buzzcocks' *Spiral Scratch* and David Bowie's *Low* and *Heroes*. At Christmas, though, teenagers could be forgiven for wondering if the biggest chart of the year had anything to offer them at all – unlike those of the '60s and, later, the '80s, the biggest pop hits of the mid to late '70s didn't really belong to the youth movements of the day. The singles charts were clogged with middle-of-the-road music – Barry Manilow, Brotherhood of Man, Olivia Newton-John, Kenny Rogers; while the heavy-hitting album charts, as approved by the music press, were dominated by the bloated dinosaurs of the previous pop generation – Yes, ELP, Pink Floyd, Genesis. By December, the British charts were once again au-dibly stagnating. Punk had happened, of course. Indeed, punk was *happening*. Across 1976 and 1977 the snottiest, most abrasive man-ifestation of rock so far had dominated the music press and, thanks to a succession of pearl-clutching horror stories, the mainstream press too. There had been a handful of all-time-great, firecracker singles (the Sex Pistols 'God Save the Queen', the Damned's 'New Rose', Buzzcocks' 'Orgasm Addict', The Adverts' 'Gary Gilmore's Eyes', The Jam's 'In the City'), but punk's commercial impact had been relatively limited outside of the music press and the *John Peel Show*. And while the growing scene of disco and dance music was taking off in the nightclubs, it was making only occasional forays into the charts.

In fact, Johnny Mathis's 1976 Christmas No. 1 seemed to herald the least punk musical era in a decade. 1977 got underway with the chart headed by a succession of light ballads that your mum might like. 'When A Child Is Born' was followed by David Soul's weepie 'Don't Give up on Us', then 'Don't Cry For Me Argentina' from the Lloyd-Webber musical *Evita*, Leo Sayer's *incredibly* drippy 'When I Need You' and a rare UK hit from the Manhattan Transfer, a cabaret throwback whose 'Chanson d'Amour' was a cover of an old French hit, popular in the '50s as an antidote to the incoming rock and roll. It was playing a similar role here. Even Rod Stewart, hard-drinking rocker that he was, had to go into balladeer mode to top the charts with 'I Don't Want to Talk About It'. Only in the summer was the spell broken, thanks to Giorgio Moroder and Donna Summer's pioneering electronic disco banger 'I Feel Love', one of the most extraordinary records ever made – but even that was something of a blip.

A depressed British public spent 1977 escaping into the soppy idealism of increasingly naff chart fodder or, at the younger end, rejecting that soppiness for either punk's primitive rock and roll resurgence or the euphoric pulse of disco. If all of this seems oddly familiar, it should – it was exactly the situation that had prompted the glam rock explosion earlier in the decade, and what are punk and disco if not the two facets of glam? One raw and rough, the other escapist, glittery and feel-good. Once again Britain, now back under a Labour government, was mired in economic crisis. Once again there were strikes, power cuts and uncollected rubbish piling in the streets. Inflation had been in double digits for four years in a row. Once again, the England football team were abysmal.[1] And once again, the charts seemed to be reflecting this entropy, filled

---

[1] Italy's 3-0 win against Luxembourg in early December '77 put England out of the running for the 1978 Argentina World Cup on goal difference – rotten luck, since they'd won all of their qualifiers. It was the second World Cup in a row for which the team had failed to qualify. 1966 felt a long time ago.

with anodyne European pop and Americana schmaltz. Just to sour the mood further, the back end of 1977 had seen the painfully premature deaths of two pop icons Elvis Presley (just 42) and Marc Bolan (not yet 30) plus, just in time to spoil Christmas, Bing Crosby and, on 25 December itself, Charlie Chaplin.[2]

The 1977 Christmas chart was perhaps the least inspiring and certainly the least festive since 1971, containing exactly one actual Christmas song – a commemorative reissue of Crosby's 'White Christmas' at No. 5. Much of the rest of the chart could have been a throwback to seven years earlier – there was a nice, safe instrumental at No. 2 (The Brighouse & Rastrick Brass Band with a colliery-approved instrumental version of the old folk song, 'The Floral Dance'[3]), some TV tie-in novelty (*The Muppet Show Music Hall* EP at No. 27), comedy (the Barron Knights at 32), reissued oldies (Bing, obviously, but also Dooley Wilson's 'As Time Goes By' at 23) and a bunch of pop big hitters (the Bee Gees' 'How Deep Is Your Love', Showaddywaddy's 'Dancin' Party', Queen's 'We Are the Champions') that would have been hits regardless of the date. *Record Mirror*'s annual mid-December rundown of Christmas singles genuinely struggled to find any proper festive releases to be snarky about, and instead rated non-seasonal songs on whether they were "likely to be a Christmas hit". Single of the week was awarded to an obscure, rough-voice comedy blues singer called Wounded John Scott Cree, simply for bothering to cover 'Rudolph the Red Nosed Reindeer'. "Whoever this loony is," says the paper's John Shearlaw,

---

[2] That's two living embodiments of rock and roll, the singer of the most famous Christmas song ever recorded and the most famous comic actor of all time. Bummer.

[3] Oddly, a second version of the song would chart a few weeks later. This time it had a vocal, provided by then ubiquitous BBC broadcaster Terry Wogan, who had taken to singing the original lyrics over the Brighouse & Rastrick version on his Radio 2 breakfast show. So popular was the item with listeners that London's Hanwell brass band were quickly rustled up to record a new cut of the song for Wogan to provide vocals for. Remarkably it stayed on the chart for 5 weeks, peaking at 21. Terry even got on *Top of the Pops*. Dreadful novelty records, it seems, like dogs and unpopular relatives, aren't *just* for Christmas after all.

"it doesn't matter." DJ Tony Blackburn apparently described it as the worst record of the year. It didn't chart.

The 1977 Christmas No. 1, meanwhile, was another of those unstoppable monsters that hit the charts and refused to budge for months. 'Mull of Kintyre', by Paul McCartney's post-Beatles outfit, Wings, went straight in at No. 5 at the end of November, bobbed to the top the following week and stayed there until February. It was McCartney's first post-Beatle No. 1 and would go on to break his former band's record for the bestselling single in British history[4] before it finally fell off the chart in early March, three months and two million sales later. For much of December it was selling 100,000 copies a day.

McCartney has always had unerringly popularist instincts – this was, after all, the man who had penned 'Let It Be', 'Hey Jude' and 'Yesterday', and who had the smarts to write a love song, 'She Loves You', in the second person in an era when everyone else was singing about themselves. His popular touch hadn't exactly deserted him since the break-up of the Beatles – Wings had been doing serious business as a live band and their albums were, more or less, critically acclaimed and sold well. His singles career was a little spottier, as all the former Beatles' had been, though he'd still had his fair share of proper hits, especially the cuts from the *Band on the Run* album – 'Jet' and the title track – and his James Bond theme, 'Live and Let Die'. What distanced Wings from the Beatles, though, was *cool*. The Beatles, from the very beginning to the very end, were the coolest band in the country. Maybe the world. They were on the cutting edge, first overtaking the zeitgeist and then coming to define it. The individual power of the Fab Four, however, had been dissipating gradually across the decade. John Lennon had managed to establish pop Christmas songs as a worthwhile pursuit, sure, but his most recent single, 1975's 'Ya Ya', hadn't charted. McCartney was faring better, but was scoring his biggest hits with his least interesting work. His best charting single with Wings had been 'Silly Love Songs', a No. 2 in 1976, ostensibly a defence of his reputation for sentimentality (largely levelled at him by John Lennon) but ultimately just a

---

[4] A record held by The Beatles' 'She Loves You' since 1963.

confirmation. All pretty weak sauce. It's a reputation that 'Mull of Kintyre' would do little to dissipate.

The Kintyre of the title refers to a peninsula in the south-west of Scotland, where McCartney had owned a farm since the late '60s, and the Mull was a hill at its south-westernmost tip. McCartney and his family spent much of their time there and had fallen in love with the place. Noting that Scottish pipe bands played any number of traditional songs – 'Scotland the Brave', 'Auld Lang Syne', 'St Mary's' (known these days as the melody for 'Amazing Grace'), 'The Hundred Pipers' – but seemed to have no new compositions to perform, McCartney went about writing a new Gaelic standard, a deeply romanticised tribute to his adopted home. It was recorded on his farm in the late summer of 1977, a simple two-chord ditty in waltz time, written purposefully to sound as old as the hills it depicted. On it, McCartney and guitarist and co-writer Denny Laine are joined by local bagpipers, the Campbeltown Pipe Band. The result was soppy, sentimental, cosy and possessed of about as much edge as a packet of shortbread. It did, however, feature a melody that genuinely felt like it had been kicking around for centuries (though penned by a man with no Scottish ancestry).

No record had ever sold two million copies in Britain before. Not Elvis, not the Beatles, certainly not Showaddywaddy. Not even 'White Christmas'. It's not an exciting song (despite McCartney throwing in one of those Little Richard whoops he does just before the fade out). It's not even especially beautiful. But it is, undeniably, comforting. That cosy, hummable melody, those warm acoustic guitars, that toffee-tin pipe band, those satisfying key changes. It's a warm bath of a song. And it seemed to be what people needed in that moment. Maybe it was a balm in a bleak economic landscape? Maybe it was an antidote to the unfamiliar and threatening shape of punk which, though not bothering the charts, was rarely out of the news? Maybe its portrait of highland life called to a nostalgia for a simpler time, one few in the UK had ever truly experienced? Whatever the reason, it quickly outsold the rest of the chart, and then every other pop record there had ever been, at least in the UK.[5]

---

[5] Though 'Mull of Kintyre' was a legitimate worldwide hit, especially in countries with British and Scottish ex-pat communities (McCartney still plays

It probably would have done spectacular business at any time of the year, but 'Mull of Kintyre' was especially suited to Christmas. It's a close cousin to the most famous Christmas song of them all; there wasn't a sleighbell or a snowflake in sight, but what were "smiles in the sunshine and tears in the rain" if not "where the treetops glisten and children listen" with a different weather report? Both songs were reaching back to something idealised, possibly even fictional, trading on a nostalgia for how things *should* be. Just like the ones we, at least in some vague memory, *used to know*. 'Mull of Kintyre' and 'White Christmas' are cut from the same cloth ... despite the fact that one was a paean to Scotland written by a Scouser and a Brummie, and the other a yearning for traditional rural Christmas written by a Russian-born Jewish New Yorker.[6]

Whatever the reason, the public embraced 'Mull of Kintyre' in all its plodding, super-traditional, hymnal glory. *Top of the Pops* aired the video for ten weeks in a row, it was played constantly on both Radio 1 and Radio 2, and it simply kept on selling. The band performed the song live on the *Mike Yarwood Show*'s Christmas Day special,[7] one of the most watched TV broadcasts of the '70s, pulling in over 21 million viewers and giving it a further springboard into the new year.[8] Even the most hardened cynic watching at home on Christmas Day, stuffed with turkey and roast potatoes, couldn't help

---

it live when he performs in Canada, Australia and New Zealand), and was an astonishing smash at home, it's one of the few McCartney hits to be utterly ignored in the United States, where radio completely passed over it. It was probably the bagpipes.

[6] You can argue that Paul McCartney, initially a pioneer, unashamedly popularist, hugely prolific and able to crystalise snapshots of real life in the most naggingly hummable form, is to the second half of the twentieth century what Irving Berlin was to the first.

[7] Yarwood was a popular comedian and impressionist and one of the biggest stars of the era, though as his routines were mostly topical his shows haven't aged brilliantly. Not many people today will get the jokes or recognise impressions of Dennis Healy and Edward Heath.

[8] Just a reminder: Britain in 1977 had just three TV channels and very little else to do but watch them, especially on Christmas day. Being on a show like Yarwood's or *Morecambe and Wise* meant being watched by half the population of the country, all at the same time. It's a staggering reach, achieved these days

but feel a little wistful when the dry ice parted and the Campbeltown Pipe Band strode out from behind silvery Christmas trees.

McCartney had been initially hesitant about putting it out at all; worried that a music press obsessed with the Sex Pistols and the Damned would be hostile and younger pop fans would reject it outright. Hedging his bets, he made the single a double A-side with a more upbeat rocker called 'Girls' School', which was felt to be a more modern and credible alternative to the trad ballad on the other side of the disc ... though in truth it sounds more like a second-rate Queen than a contemporary of the Clash and the Pistols. Radio barely touched it and McCartney's description – a "pornographic *St. Trinians*," he told the *Record Mirror* that November – has been justly forgotten. As it turns out, he needn't have worried. In his book *The Lyrics: 1956 to the Present*, he tells a story about being hailed by a punk in London when his car stopped at some lights, shortly after the song's release. Expecting to get a gobful of abuse, he heard instead: "Oi, Paul, you know that 'Mull of Kintyre'? It's fucking great!"

While its spiritual successor was breaking British records at No. 1, 'White Christmas' itself, the global bestselling record of all time, was making its debut in the Top 5.[9] Bing Crosby, of course, had finally groaned his last[10] a few months previously. A shame because Crosby was having an extremely good 1977, having just completed a UK tour, including a sold-out two week run at the London Palladium. During that visit he'd recorded his final album, *Seasons*, which included his final Christmas song, a recording of 'Sleigh Ride'. Not only did he score a Top 5 single that year, the album would peak at No. 25 in the Christmas week charts.

---

only by major sporting events and that time the Prime Minister told us to stay at home.

[9] Most of 'White Christmas's 30 million-odd sales were from the pre-chart era. Though Crosby's 1947 recording of the song (see page xx) was rereleased most years and sold respectably, it had yet to *officially* chart in the UK Top 40.

[10] Though you'll rarely hear it these days, Crosby was known affectionately as "Old Groaner", a nickname given to him by legendary jazz trombonist Tommy Dorsey back in the '20s.

A month before his death, Crosby was able to make one last, enduring contribution to the Christmas music canon, and indeed to the generational pop culture divide. That September he'd recorded a TV special in the UK, *Bing Crosby's Merrie Olde Christmas,* due to air just after Thanksgiving on CBS in the US and as part of ITV's Christmas Eve schedule in Britain. The show, a true old-fashioned TV special of the sort common in the days of light entertainment and variety, featured Crosby and his wife and teenage children visiting a fictional "distant relation", Sir Percival Crosby, in his manor house in England, and was mostly an excuse for some delightfully hammy sketches and duets with celebrity guests: British comedian Stanley Baxter,[11] actor Ron Moody (who plays Charles Dickens, and then a host of Dickens' most famous characters) and '60s model turned actor/singer Twiggy (who, in a bizarre turn, plays the Artful Dodger as Moody reprises his most famous role of Fagin from *Oliver!*). If that had been all there was to it, the special would be largely forgotten. There was, however, one more musical guest – David Bowie, who arrives fairly early in the show to play a little scene and duet with Old Groaner himself. A video clip of Bowie singing his current single, 'Heroes', is also featured as part of proceedings, recorded especially for the show, with Bowie performing against a plain black background, looking straight down the barrel of the camera, and throwing in a brief mime routine – something he'd been including in his act off and on since the '60s. A whole portion of the cosiest of Christmas specials is given over to what is, essentially, avant-garde, black box theatre.

Bowie's modernist masterpiece, one of his finest singles,[12] is bafflingly out of place on the show. It's a song of cold textures and desperate vocals, and its themes are obscure, even obtuse. The arty presentation only highlights the weirdness. The rest of the special is pure cornball, as comfortable and familiar as the cardigan Bing is wearing throughout. The 'Heroes' clip is wedged awkwardly in between Crosby and Twiggy's duet on 'Have Yourself a Merry Little

---

[11] Who would have been a familiar sight for British viewers but must have baffled the Americans.

[12] Arguably the best single Bowie ever wrote, and possibly the best single *anybody* ever wrote, to paraphrase Irving Berlin.

Christmas'[13] and a skit about writing Christmas card messages. It's like finding a copy of *1984* on a shelf of Enid Blytons. The juxtaposed tones couldn't highlight the difference between the two stars more – Crosby was one of the last links to the first flushes of pop, a man who'd been part of the texture of popular culture for so long that he practically defined old-school entertainment. He'd been there before Elvis. Before Sinatra, even. Hell, he'd been releasing singles since before *penicillin* was discovered. Your nan liked Bing Crosby. Your *great* nan probably liked Bing Crosby. Bowie, meanwhile, was as good a definition of modern pop as you could find – a cross-dressing, post-modern bisexual whose music evolved at lightning speed as he flipped from style to style. To some it was a passing of the torch from the first pop generation to the latest. To others it was just deeply, deeply odd. "Bowie's new song 'Heroes' is dropped on the show like a bomb," said the *Louisville Courier-Journal* across the pond, "If Bowie has a new image, this old-soft-shoe show wasn't the place to display it."[14]

As odd as Bowie's involvement seems, the pairing genuinely worked. He first appears in a short skit where the two singers get acquainted (Bowie: "Oh, you're the poor relation from America … you're the one that sings, right?" Crosby: "Well, right or wrong, I sing all the same," Bowie: "Well, I sing too") and a duet, 'Peace on Earth/Little Drummer Boy', a mash-up of the classic carol

---

[13] Twiggy, incidentally, appeared on the cover of Bowie's 1975 album *Pin Ups*, while Ron Moody was a close collaborator of one of Bowie's old '60s squeezes, Lionel Bart. Dame David's connection to Stanley Baxter is, as yet, unproven.

[14] Why would either Bowie or Bing agree to the collaboration? From Crosby's point of view, it was a matter of using a popular, newish act to bring in a different audience and some new-school kudos. Bowie, meanwhile, simply wanted to get his song in front of people. His previous album, *Low*, his artiest and least accessible so far, had been released with almost no promotion in terms of TV or live appearances and sales had been slow. For *Heroes*, its follow-up, and its gorgeous title track, Bowie was determined to put the work in and agreed to several live appearances, including on *Marc*, the late-afternoon teen show hosted by his old friend Marc Bolan, just two days before the Crosby taping. Prime-time ITV on Christmas Eve was absolutely worth a little weirdness. The special was also aired in the US, where Bowie was desperate to maintain his profile.

(Crosby providing the para-pa-pom-pomming) and a new, hastily written counterpoint piece by musical director Ian Fraser and co-writer Larry Grossman. Bowie, apparently, had bluntly refused to sing 'Little Drummer Boy', saying he'd always hated the song, and stormed off to his dressing room. The new section, Bowie's first and only foray into Christmas music, was written, arranged and rehearsed that afternoon. It absolutely shouldn't have worked, and yet somehow it's charming, Crosby's chocolatey baritone singing the old melody in counterpoint with Bowie's equally rich croon. Both men have fine voices and both, despite generational differences, are absolute pros who, when it gets down to it, know their job, and their vocals blend beautifully. "Oh, that's a lovely thing," says Crosby at one point. He's not wrong.

The two walked away with fairly different impressions of proceedings. Crosby had been impressed by the young singer – who, he assured fans, belied his wild man reputation. "It's a different kind of David Bowie, he's got no make-up, no beard, he's very clean-cut," he told the BBC's Pete Murray later that month. "I think he'll be a real fine contribution to the show." "You may think it's strange, David Bowie appearing with an ancient like me on a programme for Christmas," he says in a recorded message to his fan club. "David Bowie's always been known for rock, hard rock, whatever. The fact is, he's one of the best. In this show he appears clean-shaven, and I think he's just wonderful. A very nice young man."[15] Bowie, meanwhile, would later portray Crosby as doddering and confused. "The communication factor was very strange. He didn't know who I was. He couldn't remember my name," he told Conan O'Brian in 1997. "He just sat on a stool the whole day." Apparently Crosby had introduced himself to Bowie several times throughout proceedings, forgetting he'd already done so. "There was just nobody home at all, you know," Bowie told David Quantick in a 1999 interview for Q. "We were so out of touch with each other."

---

[15] Twice, Crosby makes a reference to Bowie's lack of a beard or stubble, as if proof of wholesome professionalism, perhaps unaware that Bowie hadn't yet sported a beard at any point in his career. Indeed, the calculated androgyny that had marked his star-making Ziggy Stardust period had taken *clean-shaven* to an extreme – not just beard and moustache, but eyebrows too.

Bing Crosby's Merrie Olde Christmas concludes with Crosby addressing the audience – "we wish you all the best of the season, and a dream to place under your pillow to see you through the cold nights. Until next time …", before launching into 'White Christmas', singing it alone. It's a more comfortable, relaxed version than that of 30 years previous, he sings it a little behind the beat and looking rather wistful, but he's in fine voice nonetheless. Of course there would be no next time. This was Bing's final performance of his most famous song, and he would die before it was screened.[16]

The broadcast itself came and went with little fanfare ("The mind boggles at the idea of Crosby and Bowie dueting 'Little Drummer Boy'," says the *Burnley Evening Star* in one of the few previews to bother commenting at all, "but it happens.") and the performance disappeared into legend, something of a curio in the careers of both singers, though it gained popularity for Bowie fans when bootlegs started doing the rounds. Eventually realising they had a cash cow on their hands, RCA, Bowie's label at the time, released the song as a single in 1982, going very much against the singer's wishes and further souring their relationship.[17] The release was no simple matter, either. The original 16-track studio masters had long been wiped and the recording had to be cobbled together from the audio captured by the live mics on the day. Despite this, it became one of Bowie's most successful singles, quickly selling 250,000 copies and peaking on the Christmas week chart at No. 3 – the highest charting festive song that year. It would go on to sell almost half a million. For Crosby this had been part of the plan all along. "They might release it as a record," he told the BBC just

---

[16] Bowie had recorded two duets in three days, one with Marc Bolan and one with Bing Crosby. Neither collaborator would live to see their performance broadcast, with Bolan dying in a car crash just days later. "I was getting seriously worried about whether I should appear on TV," Bowie later said. "Everyone I was going on with was kicking it the following week." (Quoted in Nicholas Pegg's *The Complete David Bowie*).

[17] Soon they'd be kicking themselves. The same month that 'Peace on Earth' was released, Bowie was busy recording *Let's Dance*, the album that would come out the following year on EMI and go on to be a global smash – his most successful record by quite some margin.

a few weeks before his death. "That could open up a new field for me, if I could get hooked up with David Bowie, that would be a big help." Poor Bing.

The national mood hadn't improved much by Christmas 1978, and a simmering undercurrent of resentment was threatening to boil over across Britain. By now, unemployment was at a post-war high of a million and a half (within five years it would be twice this), a baker's strike in November had led to bread shortages and the BBC Christmas schedule was put in serious doubt when strikes hit the corporation and took the whole network briefly off air, leading to an emergency schedule of films and repeats being prepared for the important Christmas period, though it wasn't needed in the end. Industrial action also took *The Times* out of circulation for almost a year. Gravediggers, lorry drivers and bin men were striking, too. As temperatures plunged to some of the lowest of the decades, a strike by oil tanker drivers meant some parts of the country were without central heating. Later, an editorial in the *Sun* gave the period a name that stuck: the Winter of Discontent. Pop music, meanwhile, had seen that *discontent* and collectively decided that only the first five letters were needed. Ignoring all the doom and gloom, it went clubbing.

That year's Christmas chart was stuffed with disco, with the Village People's 'YMCA' holding No. 2 and Rod Stewart's 'Do Ya Think I'm Sexy?' at No. 8, just ahead of a run of genuine dance-floor masterpieces: Chic's 'Le Freak' at 9, Chaka Khan's 'I'm Every Woman' at 14, and Funkadelic's 'One Nation Under A Groove – Part 1' at 27, among more floor fillers from Hot Chocolate, Earth, Wind & Fire and Sylvester. Even the punks had moved on to the twitchy, dancefloor-friendly phase of post-punk and New Wave (the Boomtown Rats' former No. 1 'Rat Trap' was at 15, Ian Dury's 'Hit Me With Your Rhythm Stick' at 13, Blondie's 'Hanging On the Telephone' at 17 and the Buzzcock's 'Promises' at 26). And the big stocking fillers of the year all came from the *Grease* soundtrack, which headed up the album chart while 'Greased Lightning' was at No. 11 on the singles Top 40 – 'Sandy', 'Hopelessly Devoted to You', 'Summer Nights' and 'You're the One That I Want' (with its sales of two million) had all slipped off the chart only recently. [18] It was, unusually for late December, a healthy, funky, and genuinely credible collection of songs. Compared to the previous year's, it was practically revolutionary. And right at the top of it, at No. 1, there was a Christmas carol.

Anglo-Caribbean funk machine Boney M. had enjoyed a pretty stellar 1978. Comprising three singers – Marcia Barrett, Liz Mitchell and Mazie Williams (only the first two appeared on the records) – and dancer Bobby Farrell, the band had been put together by German producer Frank Farian to front his productions, scoring their first UK hit in 1976 with the churning, bass-led brilliance of 'Daddy Cool'. They'd managed one of the biggest singles in British history in the spring of 1978 with the double A-side of 'Rivers of Babylon' and 'Brown Girl in the Ring' – sales of two million would have made it the bestselling UK record of all time had 'Mull of Kintyre' not pipped it four months earlier. Then, a month after its release, it was knocked into third place by 'You're the One That I Want' from *Grease*. That the three biggest singles in British pop history had all come out in the same 12-month period suggests that, whatever state the economy was in, music was a booming market. The band had followed it up with the completely bonkers but utterly fantastic 'Rasputin', a No. 2 hit in August that finally dropped out of the Top 40 on 2 December, the very day the group's next single, 'Mary's Boy Child/Oh My Lord' went straight in at No. 7, climbing to No. 1 the following week and staying there until the new year.

The song was based around Harry Belafonte's 1956 hit 'Mary's Boy Child', itself a Christmas No. 1 and the last festive song to hit the top of the charts before Slade revived the idea 17 years later. The older song was bolted on to a Farian original, 'Oh My Lord', to create a calypso mash-up. The whole thing had been put together in something of a hurry, with Farian having the idea in early November and summoning Marcia Barrett and Liz Mitchell, the band's singers, to a mammoth recording session in which the pair covered all of the song's vocals between them, while Farian did a spoken word

---

[18] I will not hear a *word* said against the *Grease* soundtrack. Not a word. Every spinner is a winner.

middle section to be mimed on stage by Bobby Farrell.[19] The short notice meant that label Hansa had to reach out to pressing plants in communist East Germany and Poland to meet orders, which itself led to an invitation for the band to perform a series of concerts in Moscow – the first Western pop group to do so. The single's sleeve and video were shot in Red Square.[20]

By the end of 1978 Boney M. were a huge name, rivalled in the charts only by the Bee Gees whose *Saturday Night Fever* soundtrack had become the bestselling album of all time.[21] The Gibb brothers already had a single lined up for the December market, the fairly lightweight 'Too Much Heaven', a safe, mid-paced ballad with none of the fizz of their other recent hits, 'Night Fever', 'Jive Talkin'' or 'Stayin' Alive'. As Boney M.'s Marcia Barrett says in her memoir, *Forward: My Life with and without Boney M.*, "back then competition for [the Christmas No. 1] was intense as so many of the big groups would put out a Christmas single." By now everyone knew that a Christmas hit meant huge sales, and one that was *actually about Christmas* could look forward to repeat business year on year.

---

[19] Farian made a habit of pulling this trick – in the '80s he had a global smash with Milli Vanilli, two beautiful male models who hadn't sung a note on their world-conquering debut album. It caused quite the hubbub at the time.

[20] In our age of instant digital distribution, where new music appears on streaming platforms worldwide and at the same time, it's worth remembering that getting records into shops in the 1970s was a massive logistical operation. Every single copy had to be physically pressed onto vinyl, packaged, shipped to warehouses, and then distributed to individual stores. A hit single might need millions of copies, each requiring hot vinyl to be stamped between metal plates. Labels typically used multiple pressing plants to meet demand, and if your regular plants were at capacity, you had to get creative. Sourcing pressings from behind the Iron Curtain, as Boney M.'s label did, shows just how desperate record companies could get when they thought they had a hit on their hands. It was particularly crucial for Christmas releases – you couldn't tell shops: "It'll be in next week" when next week would be too late for the Christmas market.

[21] It's often overlooked how staggeringly *big* Boney M. were. The band have two entries in the UK's Top 20 all-time bestsellers, equalling the Beatles. No other artist has made the chart twice, and of the two bands it's Boney M.'s two singles that have sold the most.

Like many contributors to British industry, Boney M. knew that this was the time to strike.

Farian's instincts were strong and his gamble on rushing out the single paid off in spades. Few records sound as immediately like a hit as 'Mary's Boy Child', which is naggingly hummable (it even contains a *whole humming section*) while having a genuinely great groove and the religious overtones to satisfy the granny market as well as the pop pickers. "It's expected to be THE Christmas single", said the *Daily Mirror*, while *Record Mirror* were equally confident of its smash potential: "If this isn't number one within a couple of weeks of release, I'll be greatly surprised," wrote Rosalind Russell in the paper's singles column. "Their delicate harmonies and light Jamaica coating has given this the Midas glow. You'll be sick of it by the time you're hanging up your pillow slip." The crossover potential was so obvious that, according to *Record Mirror*'s Juicy Luicy gossip column, a farmer in Colchester put in an order for 10,000 copies of the single to package with the Christmas veg. Pre-orders totalled half a million, putting the song comfortably into the Top 10 on release, and giving it a solid platform to bounce to No. 1 in the coming weeks. Mission accomplished.

'Mary's Boy Child' headed up a Christmas chart that was stuffed with modern classics but was resolutely un-Christmassy.[22] The post-Slade tinsel boom of the mid '70s seemed to have run its course, with only the very confident or the very clueless throwing their Santa hat in the ring. Boney M., comfortable with the golden ratio of being hugely popular already and having written an obvious hit, were always likely to hit a home run. The lack of festive cheer elsewhere in the chart, however, indicated pretty clearly that such songs were now outliers.

---

[22] The only other big festive tune in the charts was 'Christmas In Smurfland', a spin-off from the popular comics about tiny blue critters that had recently been turned into an animated film. As with the Wombles, a pop music incarnation was quickly created, fronted by a Dutch singer known as Father Abraham, aka muzak writer Pierre Kartner. Kartner was no Mike Batt, however, and unlike the Wombles, the Smurf songs were sickly sweet, verging on the putrid. 'Christmas In Smurfland' was no exception (the word *nauseating* crops up in almost every music press review). The single stalled at No. 19.

The following year's chart did little to restore confidence in the Christmas song. No. 1 that year, Pink Floyd's 'Another Brick in the Wall (Part 2)', might actually be, as the *Guardian* put it a few weeks later "the bleakest Christmas hit ever". It was certainly the least Christmassy Christmas No. 1 yet. John Lennon, Wizzard, Showaddywaddy and Gilbert O'Sullivan had all made good use of a children's choir to sprinkle some festive magic – Roger Water's cold, dystopian classic, a dark examination of such extremely seasonal themes as corporal punishment and child abuse in the school system, used one to add pure menace. It couldn't have been further from the cosy nostalgia, twee novelty or rowdy celebrations that had dominated the decade's early years. It did, however, sell by the bucketload.[23] The industry had settled into the idea that a truly massive band – and it's hard to think of many bigger than Pink Floyd – could absolutely capitalise on the Christmas market, but smaller acts knew enough to keep well clear unless they had something special.

"There's an old record company motto," wrote David Hepworth in *Smash Hits*, a magazine that had launched the previous year as a wry antidote to the increasingly dry and rather po-faced *NME*. "Never release anything in the month of December unless you really have to." You could probably add, "or you're confident sales are going to be through the ceiling anyway." It was no coincidence that ABBA, for example, had saved 'I Have a Dream', the syrupiest moment on their latest album and a song with *massive crossover hit* practically embossed into the grooves of the vinyl itself, for the Christmas market. Ditto the Police, following up their international mega-hit 'Message in a Bottle' with the jazzy 'Walking on the Moon'. These were singles released in full anticipation of being safe stocking

---

[23] In fairness to The Floyd, despite its miserable themes and angsty edge, 'Another Brick' is far from inaccessible. Producer Bob Ezrin had suggested the band add a disco groove, with Dave Gilmour chopping out some properly funky guitar over Walters' flowing, danceable bassline. It somehow added to, rather than detracted from, the song's menace (the best disco songs all have a slightly sinister edge), with the added bonus of making it ridiculously commercial. This was the first time in 11 years that Pink Floyd had bothered to release a single at all – you can absolutely see why they wanted to make this one an occasion.

fillers. Their confidence was rewarded with million-sellers. Even the novelty tunes and TV tie-ins were running scared that year, though folk band Fiddler's Dram got close to that territory with their Top 10 'Day Trip to Bangor (Didn't We Have a Lovely Time)'.

Britain itself was in the midst of seismic change. Margaret Thatcher's Conservative government, elected that May, had already begun its radical reshaping of the economy. Her first budget had seen VAT nearly doubled to 15% and public spending slashed by £3.5 billion, while interest rates hit 17% in a bid to curb inflation. The Prime Minister had declared there was no alternative to her free market reforms, and after the Winter of Discontent that had brought down James Callaghan's Labour government, there were those who seemed ready to believe her.

This brave new world of individualism and market forces was reflected in that year's Christmas chart. The communal, beery singalongs of Slade and Wizzard felt like relics of a different era, as did the cosy nostalgia of novelty singles and variety show veterans. More than anything, the 1979 Christmas chart suggested a growing sophistication in both the music business and record-buying public. There was proto hip-hop here in the Sugarhill Gang's 'Rapper's Delight', futuristic pop funk in Michael Jackson's 'Off the Wall', anthemic post punk in the Clash's 'London Calling', party ska with Madness' 'One Step Beyond' and gothy futurism in Gary Numan's 'Complex'. Even as employment fell and inflation rose, British pop wasn't retreating into comfort food.[24] Instead, the public seemed to be embracing change, even at Christmas – traditionally the most conservative moment in the pop calendar. Christmas hits might previously have been from comedians, novelties, calypso carols, trad folk songs or brash rock celebration, but they were rarely musically forward-looking. Even when Slade were "looking to the future" they were doing so while sounding like a yob Beatles. Innovation, as on 'Bohemian Rhapsody', had been the exception, not the rule. The coming 1980s would bring new approaches to the Christmas chart that would, for the most part, build on this growing sophistication.

---

[24] Well, yes, 'I Have A Dream' was at No. 2, but there's an exception to every rule, and ABBA, like the Beatles and Queen, operate in a rarefied field of their own where different laws apply.

The last Christmas chart of the '70s boasted pop music of great, futuristic depth and not a small amount of bleakness, reflecting a country exhausted by bitter hardship and at ideological war with itself. Only a particularly confident or completely delusional artist would try throwing a simple celebration of the season into an atmosphere like that … fortunately, Britain had a pop star knocking around who'd already had six Christmas No. 1s, including two of the bestselling singles in British history, and felt like giving it a go.

Just two years on from 'Mull of Kintyre', Paul McCartney was keen to get his reputation as an innovator back and had retreated to his farm that summer with a barn full of new toys to make a solo album – what would become *McCartney II*, released the following May. These were experimental sessions, in which the one-time Beatle, working without a backing band, engineer or producer and just his wife and foil Linda providing the odd vocal, built songs around arpeggiated synth patterns, working outwards from there and glorying in the pure creativity. It was in those sessions that he came up with 'Wonderful Christmastime', swapping the bagpipes and folk of his last Yuletide release for synthesisers and electronic textures. It's an odd song; deceptively simple and seemingly as insubstantial as smoke, especially if you focus on the lyrics ("The moon is right! The spirit's up!"). McCartney had never been big on subtext anyway. Here, he was writing his message in big, bright colours and simple terms, just as Lennon had done back in 1971. A message that wasn't quite as deep as "WAR IS OVER IF YOU WANT IT", though in its own way it was just as well meaning: "Have a great Christmas". Like Lennon he was also joined by a choir of children, which he summoned with the line "a choir of children sing their song". That choir then materialises to sing "ding-dong-ding-dong". Not particularly deep stuff. Musically, though, it's a different story. Even for the forward-looking 1979, its reliance on electronic instruments was comparatively rare. Britain may have been on the verge of the "new pop" synth revolution, with Gary Numan having hits already, while David Bowie dedicated a side on each of his recent albums to electronic experiments, but synth music was still for the most part the preserve of the arty and the oddball of either the buzzing, wurbling laboratory sessions of Throbbing Gristle and Cabaret Voltaire or the ponderous, topographical ocean-navigating of the big prog acts. McCartney harnessing all of that cold-wave technology, all of that twitchy power, just to make the lightest of Christmas confections was, in its own way, quietly revolutionary, and his lightness of touch as a songwriter masks something with quite a bit of melodic depth. Pouring all of that into something so simple and joyful is very McCartney. Not everyone was a fan ("nauseating," said *Smash Hits*' Dave Hepworth), but enough people enjoyed it for the song to jump into the chart at 31, rise ten places the following week, be in the Top 10 by Christmas and peak at No. 6. 'Mull of Kintyre' may have been the big seller, but it's 'Wonderful Christmastime' that has truly endured. That deliberate modernism would, ironically, help it become a perennial, played every Christmas for decades to come, while its reliance on electronic instrumentation and shallow but shiny messaging pointed the way to the pop hits of the coming decade. Yet again, it was a Beatle who pointed the way. The following Christmas chart would also be Beatle-dominated, though those circumstances would be very different indeed.

Chapter 7
WAR IS OVER?

A new decade and a new set of rules

Christmas 1980 was all set for the usual round of big hit pop and festive silliness. ABBA ('Super Trouper'), Queen ('Flash') and The Police ('De Do Do (De Do Do Do, De Da Da Da)') had all reserved safe bets for the lucrative December market, Slade had somewhat cheekily used a crowd singalong of 'Merry Xmas Everybody' from that year's Reading Festival as a new version of the song that morphed into a stompingly good fun take on the 'Okey Cokey' (it charted at No. 70), an appallingly twee children's choir were singing about how much they loved their grans and New Waver Jona Lewie had added to the Christmas canon with a tangentially festive existential crisis about war that was, musically, best described as "Salvation Army pop". But in a good way. More on these last two later.

By now, the media had started to frame the Christmas No. 1 season as a race – a prize to be had. "More runners have been announced this week in the Christmas chase for the number one spot" went the *Northern Echo*'s run down, going on to describe Kate Bush as a "classic filly" with "the best form" and pointing out that Steeleye Span were "familiar with the course". Christmas No. 1 had become, in the eyes of the press, a prize any pop star worth their stripes wanted in their trophy cabinet. Local and national papers were now regularly describing the Christmas chart-topper as "much-coveted", "sought-after" or, as the *Northern Echo* termed it, a

"coveted Christmas crown". It was painted as the lucrative and prestigious pinnacle of pop, and for a large chunk of the '70s that had
been absolutely true. For most of the previous decade the position
had been taken by record-breaking, even era-defining hits (Wings,
Queen, Pink Floyd) or modern Christmas celebrations that quickly
became perennials (Slade, Mud, Johnny Mathis, Boney M.). The era
of the laughable novelty, of little boys with wooden horses, milkmen
and Mormon urchins posing as folically gifted, amorous Scousers
felt, at this point, safely distant. As the polyester '70s slid onto the
Teflon-coated new decade, a hungry media with daily pages to fill
had finally clocked on to the idea that, since the prize seemed so
prestigious, the race to win it was worthy of comment. Chart races,
after all, appealed to a very British sensibility. As Bob Stanley puts it
in *Yeah Yeah Yeah*, "it meant competition, excitement in league-table
form, pop music as a sport ... fuel for a nation obsessed with train
numbers and cricket statistics." The media, which above all needs
content to fuel empty broadcast hours and blank column inches,
was happy to be complicit. Christmas No. 1 had become an annual
fixture, like the FA Cup final or *Eurovision*. A country that had endured four general elections in nine years was well primed for an annual popularity contest, and journalists were happy to fill space in a
traditionally slow news month by speculating on the winner ("Jona
Lewie," said the *Bristol Observer*; "St. Winifred's School Choir,"
predicted a slightly more realistic *Music Week*; "Elvis Costello's
'Clubland'," claimed a wildly optimistic *Widnes Weekly News*.)

The music industry itself had now grown comfortable with the
idea of the Christmas chart being decided by a race or a battle and
girded its loins accordingly. By 1980, industry paper *Music Week* was
outlining the runners and riders as early as October. Meanwhile, the
weekly, fan-facing music press had very much lost interest in uncool novelties that didn't reflect their readerships at all, and largely
ignored the crop of annual festive singles, except to dismiss them
sniffily: "Novelties, Christmas, goodwill, cheer, exploitation," said
Smash Hits' singles review column, covering 12 seasonal 7-inchers
in one sentence. *Record Mirror* was even more economical in its
dismissal: "What d'ya expect?" Those in the know acknowledged
this was all just a bit of fun. "Britain's record charts go haywire at
Christmas", Radio 1's Peter Powell told the *Daily Mirror*. "Where

else could you find St. Winifred's School Choir and AC/DC vying for the same chart position?" The public, for the most part, barely noticed the novelty Christmas tunes now, and the likes of former Steeleye Spanner John Kirkpatrick's 'Jogging Along With My Reindeer' (one of *Music Week*'s early tips, incidentally), the St Paul's Choristers' 'Captain Beaky's Christmas Carol' and Rocky Sharpe and the Replays' 'Christmas Crackers' have been lost to time, while seasonal offerings from cooler acts like the Damned ('There Ain't No Sanity Clause') and Kate Bush ('December Will Be Magic Again') became merely drops in the ocean of great careers. And while Elmo & Patsy's comedy number 'Grandma Got Run Over by a Reindeer' would become a future cult classic of sorts, thankfully no one was paying much attention to Jim Davidson's excruciating (and bluntly offensive) cover of 'White Christmas', delivered as cod reggae, in character as his "Black mate" 'Chalky White', a character that had been criticised as racist as early as 1977. It charted outside of the Top 40 and then dropped like a stone.

Only one of the new crop of seasonal-themed songs stuck that year – Jona Lewie's 'Stop the Cavalry'. It was a strange fish of a Christmas record, though an undoubtedly brilliant one – an oddball protest song by an even more oddball singer, released on the independent, punk-adjacent Stiff label. It wasn't an obvious smash by any means ("it has little chance of being a hit," sighed a dejected *Record Mirror* reviewing it that November). Lewie, aka singer/songwriter John Lewis, had been knocking around since the early '70s, first in blues band Brett Marvin and the Thunderbolts,[1] then as a solo act, before landing at Stiff, the label that had launched Elvis Costello, Ian Dury and Nick Lowe. His only previous hit had been that summer's 'You'll Always Find Me in the Kitchen at Parties', a deadpan New Wave novelty that had made the Top 20 thanks to a nagging chorus hook and a relatable lyric. Now, just as that song's momentum was starting to fade, Lewie had delivered something far more substantial.

His delivery, somewhere between Ian Dury's erudite music hall thug and Anthony Newley's weary theatricality, cut through a

---

[1] Also known as Terry Dactyl and the Dinosaurs for novelty-single purposes, as on their summer 1972 hit 'Seaside Shuffle'.

production that mixed mechanical, twitchy new wave synths with the warmth of a Salvation Army-style brass band.[2] The inclusion of the latter was a masterstroke – the sound of the Sally Army was woven into British Christmas; as familiar as the rattling of a charity collection tin outside Woolworths. Like the snippet of Prokofiev in Greg Lake's 'I Believe in Father Christmas' it was a direct injection of wintery delight, an immediate feeling of blowing on your hands and stamping your feet in the cold as you push on with the Christmas shopping. Under Lewie's direction it became something else, too – the eternal sound of Christmas twisted into the eternal sound of war. Those same brass bands had played soldiers to their doom in the trenches. And it was war, not Christmas, not really, that Lewie was writing about. "Basically, it's about this bloke at the front who misses his bird" was how Lewie nonchalantly dismissed it to the *Manchester Evening News* at the time, but it was more than that. It was about every soldier in every war, including the ones still being fought. The song starts in the Second World War, ducks back to the first, was inspired partly by the Crimean War, and ultimately leaps into the post-atomic combat of the future. Lewie had recently visited the eternal flame at the Tomb of the Unknown Soldier in Paris, an enduring monument to anyone fighting and dying in any war, and its symbolism runs all the way through his most famous hit.

'Stop the Cavalry' connected instantly. A generation haunted by IRA bomb scares in shopping centres and soldiers on the streets of Belfast, for whom Suez and Korea were on the edge of memory, whose parents or grandparents had fought on the beaches in France and slept in air-raid shelters, and whose great-grandparents might even remember the Somme and Passchendaele, understood implicitly what Lewie meant when he sang about fighting "throughout these centuries". The First World War setting of the promo video, all mud and barbed wire, might have pointed to the famous Christmas Day truce of 1914, but the public heard something more immediate in lines about nuclear fallout zones and soldiers missing their loved ones. The threat of the Cold War suddenly hotting up loomed

---

[2] Though it's unclear if this was an *actual* Sally Army band. In later interviews Lewie has always talked as if it was, but in a contemporary chat with *Record Mirror* he claimed he used Musician's Union session players.

large: a new, revised edition of the government's *Protect and Survive* pamphlet was made available that year, instructing the public on how to safeguard their families in the event of nuclear strike,[3] and a real war felt uncomfortably close. Only a year previously Anthony Blunt, the art historian in charge of the Royal Collection, had been stripped of his knighthood when he was revealed to have been a Soviet spy (the fourth man of the Cambridge Five). British soldiers were camped out in West Germany, peeping through the netting of the Iron Curtain. Meanwhile, there were substantial forces stationed in Northern Ireland fighting what was, in all but name, a civil war. The deceptively bright "dub-a-dubba-dum-dum" hook and warm brass arrangement of Lewie's song snuck all of that bleakness under the barbed wire – radio could focus on the Christmas elements if they chose while the song's anti-war sentiment hit home regardless. Some singles define their moment without meaning to. It would eventually peak at No. 3 in the chart – kept off the top by one extremely deserving record and one that was not – and continued to sell into the new year. And it was a hit on mainland Europe the following summer. For Britain, though, 'Stop the Cavalry' captured something in the air during those cold December weeks – a need for peace that felt increasingly urgent. That need could only be under-lined when, just two weeks after the song's release, an act of senseless violence sent shockwaves through the music world.

On 8 December 1980, at 10.50 p.m., John Lennon was fatally shot outside his home in New York City. His killer, Mark David Chapman, was a Beatles fan who had become obsessed with JD Salinger's novel *The Catcher in the Rye* and identified with its an-archist anti-hero, Holden Caulfield. Chapman felt that Lennon's lavish, millionaire lifestyle was a betrayal of the values espoused in songs like 'Imagine', and that by punishing that hypocrisy he could somehow step into the pages of Salinger's story. At least, that's what the voices in his head told him. It was the very definition of a senseless killing.

---

[3] According to Neil the hippie, played by Nigel Planer in the brilliant sitcom *The Young Ones*, this involved "painting yourself white to deflect the blast".

Now 40, Lennon was approaching Christmas in a good place, having recently returned to making music after five years off the scene. His record contract had elapsed in 1975 and, free of label obligations for the first time since 1962, he'd chosen not to seek another, instead becoming an early pioneer of the concept of the *house husband*, taking on the primary caregiving for his new baby son, Sean, surrendering himself happily into the role of bread-baking, stay-at-home dad, while his wife oversaw the couple's business portfolio.[4] With his son now five, and having eyed Paul McCartney's globe-spanning success with Wings, John had once again gotten the songwriting bug. That autumn he'd put out his first album in five years, *Double Fantasy*, a collection of homely rock and roll songs, if such a thing can exist, interspersed with artier Yoko Ono numbers, giving the album the feel of a conversation between the two. Reviews had been a little sniffy,[5] but sales had been healthy enough and the record had just gone gold, with its lead single, the Presley-ish '(Just Like) Starting Over' a Top 10 hit on both sides of the Atlantic. Plans were afoot for a follow-up, *Milk and Honey*, which was already partly recorded (it would eventually emerge in 1984), and the Ono-Lennons were making casual noises about touring in the new year.

On the final day of his life, John had gotten his hair cut in the old rockabilly style he'd sported during the Beatles' Hamburg days, done a shoot with the photographer Annie Leibowitz for *Rolling Stone*, a lengthy interview with the RKO Radio Network and spent the evening working on music at the Hit Factory studios. He'd returned home to say goodnight to his son. His killer had been waiting quietly for him all day among the small collection of fans who habitually camped out in front of the Dakota building, where the Ono-Lennons had their apartment. As John walked past him, Chapman called out: "Mr Lennon!", dropped to one knee and discharged all five rounds in his gun, in quick succession, into his

---

[4] The Ono-Lennons made more money in the second half of the '70s from buying and selling cattle than they did from music. Absolutely true.

[5] Which is unfair – *Double Fantasy* is as good an album as any Beatle had put out since about 1973. The John songs have real heart and warmth, while Yoko's contributions are quirky and creative and still sound contemporary now.

target's back, firing with both hands on his pistol. All five bullets found their mark. John continued a few steps before staggering and falling. He probably died immediately, though he wasn't formally declared dead until doctors had been unable to resuscitate him on arrival at the nearby Roosevelt Hospital. Chapman then sat quietly on the ground, waiting for the police, reading *Catcher in the Rye* and holding a copy of *Double Fantasy*, which Lennon had signed for him only that morning as he'd left for the studio. At the time of writing, 43 years later, Chapman is still in prison, having been denied parole consistently.

The death of a Beatle tore a hole in the world. Though Lennon himself had been relatively quiet since the mid '70s, his epoch-shaking role in popular culture had never been forgotten, and in many ways his legend had only grown in his absence from the limelight. The other Beatles were out there making noise, but John, known however unfairly as "the arty genius" of the band, had instead gone quiet ("The Beatle who became a recluse", as one paper put it). That's instant mystique, right there. His death would only amplify his silence and confirm his cultural sainthood. Coming as it did at the start of a new decade, it was almost impossible not to see the death of John Lennon as the final closing of pop's first great volume, especially coming just three years after that of Elvis Presley, that other great icon of early rock and roll.[6] The Beatles had, more than other band, ushered in the age of pop music as a dominant, permanent presence in the cultural landscape. They had established the pattern: the first group on the planet to ride out the notion of pop as a fad and represent it as a legitimate art form. Lennon had been key to that. And now he was gone.

That Lennon's death happened at Christmas added to the poignancy – one of his most enduring solo hits had, after all, been a Christmas song, and what's more one that had changed the game for

---

[6] The tragedy is that Lennon saw his new material as a renewal. On the day of his death he'd described his new music as a way of saying: "Here I am now, how are you? How's your relationship going? Did you get through it all? Weren't the Seventies a drag? Here we are, well, let's try to make the Eighties good, because it's still up to us to make what we can of it." One of his oft-repeated phrases at the time was "They say life begins at forty." Heartbreaking.

seasonal music in the UK. The Beatles, meanwhile, had dominated the December charts in the '60s. If you were in your twenties in 1980, you'd probably spent your formative teen years getting Beatle records for Christmas. Only a year previously, BBC 2 had screened a "Beatles At Christmas" season, showing the films *A Hard Day's Night* and *Help!*, the band's legendary Shea Stadium show, the *Let It Be* documentary, the animated *Yellow Submarine* and even the much-maligned *Magical Mystery Tour* – the film that had ruined Boxing Day for anyone who saw it without first taking quite a lot of acid when it was shown in 1967.[7]

As Beatley as the BBC had made Christmas 1979, 1980's would be much, much more so. Lennon's death triggered a huge wave of mourning and celebration of his work. *Double Fantasy* leapt to No. 2 on the album chart, with Lennon's new label, WEA, receiving 50,000 orders in 2 days. '(Just Like) Starting Over', which had been slipping off the Top 40, jumped straight to No. 1. Lennon's old label, EMI, took a few days to get its act together and ramp up production of his back catalogue, but by the week of the Christmas chart 'Starting Over' had been joined in the Top 10 by 'Happy Xmas (War is Over)' at No. 4 and 'Imagine' at No. 9.[8] Had Lennon's death occurred in the download or streaming era, both the album and singles chart would have been wall-to-wall Beatles/Lennon. In 1980, however, there were only so many records the public could lay their hands on at short notice and the sudden appetite for Lennon-related products was unprecedented. Only *Double Fantasy* and '(Just Like) Starting Over', as current releases, were stocked in anywhere close to the numbers that could meet demand. Catalogue titles were another matter. "The sheer size of that demand – and the way it rapidly widened to include, to varying degrees, every title ever released by himself and The Beatles – has totally disrupted this season's retail and wholesale patterns," reported *Music Week*. "Faced, within hours of the tragic announcement, with orders from all over the UK for

---

[7] This screening gave many people their first chance to see the Fab Four's psychedelic spectacular in colour, and it went over a little better than it had in the monochrome world of 1967.

[8] "*Number Nine. Number Nine. Number Nine. Number Nine.*" If you know, you know.

everything in the Beatles/Lennon catalogue, EMI admitted that it could not cope." 100,000 copies apiece of 'Happy Xmas' and 'Imagine' were ordered by British record stores, with the Beatles' 'The Ballad of John and Yoko' also in huge demand. BBC Radio 1 quickly put together a six-part series of hour-long shows dedicated to Lennon's career, to go out in early January. TV scrapped scheduled films to screen Beatle films and hastily assembled documentaries (ITV, handily, already had the 1979 TV film *Birth of the Beatles* on the slate) while tribute band the Bootleg Beatles found themselves in demand on television variety shows. The fresh surge of Beatlemania was so pervasive that *Daily Mirror* columnist Hilary Kinglsey ranted that "to switch on any radio or TV station … you'd have thought Lennon was Mozart, Shakespeare and President Kennedy all rolled into one".[9] *Music Week*'s Dooley column, meanwhile, called the media's ubiquitous Beatlemania "excessive", explaining his paper's minimal coverage of the tragedy with "we have no desire to add to some of the overblown verbiage being expounded."[10]

In a just world, all of that goodwill and certainly all of that coverage should have easily given Lennon a posthumous "coveted Christmas crown". Unfortunately, a world in which John Lennon is killed by a disturbed fan at Christmas is, by definition, not a just one. 'Imagine' would follow '(Just Like) Starting Over' to No. 1 on 3 January (with 'Happy Xmas' at No. 2), and would be knocked off the top spot by a reissue of another Lennon single, 'Woman', later in the month, which itself would enjoy two weeks at the top – three John Lennon songs occupying the No. 1 spot for seven

---

[9] "Perhaps," she went on to say, "to all of those 40-year-old producers with their hair still combed forward, he was." Ouch.

[10] This led to a furious letter in the following issue from *Melody Maker*'s editor-in-chief and future Beatle-biographer Ray Coleman, who had known the Beatles in the '60s. "Some of us who care about musicians and people of Lennon's calibre would say it is disgusting that *Music Week* failed to properly honour the memory of one of popular music's greatest composers with a thorough obituary." "Mr Coleman has sadly fallen into the journalists' trap of believing bigger is better," came the reply. "Some would say that it is disgusting the way in which certain sections of the media have graspingly cashed in on a bereavement, sensational or not."

weeks, a run that finally ended on 9 February.[11] Unfortunately there are *nine* weeks between 14 December and 9 February – which, if you're keeping track, means there was a fortnight's interruption in Lennon's chart dominance. In the week of Christmas itself and the week that followed it, the No. 1 single in the country was 'There's No One Quite like Grandma' by St. Winifred's School Choir. It sold over a million copies.

Though the Christmas charts had gained in both prestige and musical quality since the early '70s, the shadow of the novelty single had never quite lifted. Novelty songs rarely troubled the Top 10 and had been kept well away from the No. 1 spot since Little Jimmy Osmond's 'Long Haired Lover From Liverpool' in 1972, but labels looking for a Christmas cash-in still kept releasing them, and some poor souls were still finding them in their stockings come Christmas morning. It would ever be thus. Usually, as with 'The Sparrow' by the Ramblers from Abbey Hey Junior School (1979) or Father Abraham and the Smurfs (1978), such songs were Christmas-week flashes in the pan, slipping in and out of the charts quickly and leaving no traces. It had been a long time since something so slight had been a bona fide hit. 'There's No One Quite Like Grandma' was different. It's not a good song by any stretch of the imagination, but it was a smart one – as with Clive Dunn's 'Grandad' a decade before, children automatically bought it as a present for their dear old nanna.

The story of its success is pure Northern enterprise. Producer Peter Tattersall had serious form – he'd founded Stockport's legendary Strawberry Studios, worked with 10cc on classics like 'I'm Not in Love' and recorded the cream of Manchester's punk and post-punk scene, including Joy Division and the Buzzcocks. When his daughter Paula joined the respected choir at her school, St Winifred's, already an established musical unit which had appeared

---

[11] 'Woman' was dethroned by Joe Dolce's Greek-themed character comedy song 'Shaddap You Face'. When Dolce asked: "Why you look-a so sad?", the answer should have been pretty obvious. If it makes you feel any better, Dolce was replaced at No. 1 just two weeks later by Roxy Music's cover of Lennon's 'Jealous Guy'.

on the 1978 single 'Matchstick Men and Matchstick Cats and Dogs', he saw an opportunity to make an album they could sell to parents ... though those modest ambitions were expanded when he was sent 'There's No One Quite Like Grandma' for consideration. The song had been written by a jobbing songsmith, Gordon Lorenz, for the Queen Mother's 80th birthday earlier that year, but Tattersall recognised its potential as a Christmas release. The combination of a cute child soloist, Dawn Ralph, with pigtails and missing her front teeth, a simple keyboard backing from, of all people, prog legend Rick Wakeman, and a choir of well-behaved Stockport schoolkids proved irresistible.[12]

The Music For Pleasure label, an imprint of EMI better known for budget compilations, took the song on and by December it was shifting in astonishing numbers. After Terry Wogan played it on the Radio 2 breakfast show, it achieved silver disc status (250,000 sales) by lunchtime and had gone gold (500,000) by evening of the same day. '... Grandma' became one of the fastest sellers of the year, eventually picking up an Ivor Novello Award for bestselling single of 1980 – causing titters in the room as it beat both the Police and Barbra Streisand. The choir would go on to perform with ABBA and meet Margaret Thatcher.

This was a peculiarly British success story: a Northern school choir singing about their grans, shifting 2.3 million copies globally and using the proceeds to buy new carpets and library books, with their headmistress, Sister Aquinas,[13] waiting patiently each week for a phone call from the record label and an update on sales. Among the members of that choir was a seven-year-old Sally Lindsay, who would later find fame as an actress, playing barmaid Shelley Unwin in *Coronation Street*. "I was only seven so it's not really my fault we knocked John Lennon off No. 1," she told the *Daily Record* years later. "It's something I can't get away from at this time of year. It's always on programmes about 'TV Hell' or 'rubbish Christmas

---

[12] Wakeman had played on David Bowie's 'Space Oddity' in 1969, alongside bass player Herbie Flowers, the man who'd written the very-similar fogie-loving, school kid-featuring novelty nightmare 'Grandad' back in 1970. A gig is a gig, alright?

[13] A nun, though I'll admit her name does make her sound like a pop star.

number ones of all time'." On another occasion Linsday was less calmly accepting of her first role in popular culture. "We knocked John Lennon off number one the week after he was shot dead," she said. "How fucking shit is that?"[14]

St Winifred's was, fortunately, something of a last hurrah for a certain kind of novelty hit – more of a throwback to the pre-Slade days than any kind of resurgence. Once the '80s properly got underway the Christmas charts would gradually get more credible, at least in the upper reaches, and songs like 'There's No One Quite Like Grandma' would get increasingly short shrift (with inevitable exceptions). The reasons for that were partly cultural, partly economic. Radio 1 DJ Simon Bates, no stranger to audio slush himself, was fairly blunt when he told the *Evening Standard* that the year's Christmas-themed crop was "dreadful ... worse than ever before". He also noted, cannily, that the economic strife of the early Thatcher years wasn't playing in the favour of novelty hits. "There isn't as much money around," he explained, "so people are buying slushy records by Julio Iglesias, ABBA and Cliff Richard rather than shelling out on something they will play twice and then forget."

It wasn't *just* safe slush the public was buying, though. They were also happy to shell out for great pop. Exhibit A: the Human League. The Sheffield synth band began life as an arty electronic project, but a schism over musical direction led to singer Phil Oakey rebuilding his group from the ground up, recruiting two local teenage girls, Joanne Catherall and Susan Sulley, alongside some seasoned session pros and setting about the task of writing razor-sharp pop bangers. The resulting album, *Dare*, topped most of the music press Album of the Year polls. By the end of 1981 they were massive. They hadn't set out to conquer Christmas that year, but it belonged to them all the same and despite a chart that was full of "new pop" big hitters (Madness, Adam and the Ants, Soft Cell, Kim Wilde) and hardy chart perennials (ABBA, Cliff and Rod Stewart), it was the Human League's machine-driven tale of love gone sour that was dominating the nation's turntables; the first Christmas No. 1 to come from the new school of synth bands that were injecting a very British form of escapism and colour into the charts.

---

[14] Quoted by Alwyn W. Turner in his history of the 1980s, *Rejoice! Rejoice!*

The band's label, Virgin Records, was still something of an out-sider in the industry, built on prog rock oddities like Mike Oldfield's *Tubular Bells* and Tangerine Dream (plus a willingness to take on the Sex Pistols when no one else had the bottle) and hits were almost accidental. "We weren't like the majors," recalls Jon Webster, then Virgin's sales manager. "They would be killing for a Christmas num-ber one because of the kudos. We were slightly different. When I was a sales manager, our ethos was 'hang on – have we made any money out of this? Can we make a profit?'" 'Don't You Want Me' changed everything. "I remember the day after it first went to number one," Webster recalls, "we sold 132,000 copies out of the warehouse". The major retailers knew they had a guaranteed Christmas smash on their hands. Webster took the figures to Virgin's head of production who went ashen-faced. "We haven't got 132,000," came the reply. "You better go make some," said Webster. 'Don't You Want Me', the fourth single taken from the album and held back for big December bucks,[15] was as near perfect a piece of dramatic pop as you will find, a song apparently built entirely of choruses and hooks – and its success was a reminder that, even at Christmas, music fans will always respond to great records. For the first time since the '60s, this was a Christmas No. 1 with no novelty, seasonal or calculated cross-market appeal at all. This was just fantastic pop: a dance floor filler that still sounds fresh and futuristic. Go to any nightclub, anywhere in the Western world, get the DJ to drop 'Don't You Want Me' and watch the place explode.

Meanwhile, the freshness and originality of punk, New Wave and synth pop, which had been building in music since the late '70s, was finally infecting Christmas-themed releases. A perfect ex-ample, though not one that sold particularly well at first, was New York-based ZE Records' compilation *A Christmas Record*, assembled by ex-Westminster schoolboy, "heir to the Mothercare fortune" and unlikely record executive Michael Zilkha. Where Phil Spector had declared his intention to "take the great Christmas music and give it the sound of American music today", Zilkha wanted original

---

[15] Several reviews at the time expressed some surprise. "A suitable step in the right direction [of taking over the world]," said *Smash Hits*, "... assuming there's anyone out there who hasn't already got the LP."

125

songs – Christmas seen "through thoroughly modern eyes", as he told the *Daily Telegraph* in 1981. The result was arguably the best new compilation of original seasonal songs in 20 years, and the first ever "indie" festive compilation. Was (Not Was) contributed 'Christmas Time in the Motor City', a bleak tale of Santa shaving his beard to improve his job prospects, while Alan Vega's 'No More Christmas Blues' was so arty, minimalist and modern as to sound like it had been beamed from outer space. The album's standout was the Waitresses' 'Christmas Wrapping'– a witty, New Wave tale of romance in an all-night grocery store, bubbling and funky and shot through with a cool-as-hell, disinterested, gum-chewing vocal from Patty Donahue and a word count that itself showed how far Christmas music had come since Bing Crosby.[16] The music press, already losing their minds over indie-pop like Altered Images and Orange Juice gushed, with *NME* running a feature on the label and *Record Mirror* declaring, "if it doesn't get the airplay to make it a hit, then there ain't no justice." Such an oddball single breaking big wasn't as impossible as it seemed: no one had thought that Jona Lewie was going to have 1980's standout new Christmas song. Alas, as has already been discussed, there really "ain't no justice". It was ignored by radio and didn't chart, though a reissue of the single did sneak in at 45 in 1982. The song's reputation has very much grown over the years, however, as it's picked up annual radio play and new generations of fans. In the streaming era, it hits the Top 40 every year and you'll find it on most decent Christmas compilations.

Back in 1981, the music industry was adapting to a British economy that felt no more stable under Thatcher's Tories than it had under the Labour governments of the late '70s. Money was tight, and for the first time music piracy was taking a noticeable bite out of sales, as better home stereos and cheaper cassette tapes made it incredibly easy to make a free copy of an album. Home taping was estimated to be costing the industry £200 million annually, with the British Phonographic Industry (BPI) and Musician's Union constantly attempting to litigate against anyone seen to be encouraging

---

[16] 'Christmas Wrapping' runs to 426 words. 'White Christmas' has 54.

the practice – mostly unsuccessfully.[17] 1981 saw the launch of the "Home Taping Is Killing Music" campaign, with its famous logo featuring crossed bones under a cassette. The rise of Sony's Walkman and other personal tape players didn't help, since they encouraged listeners to switch to cheaper, easily duplicated cassettes over vinyl. Sales of LPs, the bedrock of the music industry, had fallen from 85 to 65 million between 1979 and 1981, and though the singles market was still healthy, belts were being tightened. Labels used to flood the Christmas market with festive products in the hope something might catch light, but by 1981 they were becoming more selective. "In the past, record companies have issued five or six Christmas records apiece," a spokesperson for the Bonaparte Records chain told the *Evening Standard*, "but this year they're limiting them to one or two." Even that felt optimistic – most of the majors were concentrating on keeping their current hits in stock rather than taking risks on seasonal fare. The days of every label throwing novelty records at the wall to see what stuck were fading.

Thankfully, there were always a few outliers willing to give it a go. Stiff records, emboldened by their success with Jona Lewie, had hastily assembled a band called the Snowmen, the identity of which was kept secret, who effectively photocopied Slade's cover of 'Okey Cokey' (here titled 'Hokey Cokey'), complete with a promotional video of dancing snowmen that looked like it had been filmed for a tenner in someone's garden. It couldn't scrape into the top half of the chart, despite the band appearing on *Top of the Pops*, wearing full-body snowman costumes, including masks.[18] Similarly under-

---

[17] In 1981 the BPI and MU lobbied the government to add a levy of £1 to £3 on sales of blank cassettes and £17 on stereos with tape recorders, which would then be passed on to the industry. The proposal was ultimately rejected as inflationary, unenforceable and, since it would make stereo equipment unaffordable to the industry's vital teenage market, kind of dumb.

[18] This is because the band that appeared on the show was entirely made up of Stiff records office staff. The original single had been recorded by session player Martin Kershaw, doing an Ian Dury impression, with the secrecy around the project leading to speculation that it was Dury himself, who had recently quit Stiff. Hilariously, the snowmen costumes were just floor-length cloth tubes, making it impossible for the wearer to put his or her right or left leg "in" or "out" or, indeed, noticeably "shake it all about".

performing were Cockney superstars Chas & Dave with 'Stars Over 45', a medley of old music hall classics belted out around the "old Joanna". Holly and the Ivys, a supergroup featuring Pink Floyd's Dave Gilmour playing a medley of old carols, fared even worse – their 'Christmas on 45' tickled the bottom of the Top 40 and then disappeared. The music press was typically scathing – "This week there's not much more than a handful of records by people I've never even heard of," sniffed *Record Mirror's* singles reviewer Sunie, "so the Waitresses' little gem is extra welcome." Even novelty records needed to show some sophistication.

1982 bought little that was new to the party. That year's Christmas No. 1 was Renée & Renato's 'Save Your Love', and while it was objectively *dreadful* it wasn't really a novelty hit in the way previous Christmas No. 1s had been and its success was genuine rather than gimmicky. Renato Pagliari was a tiny (1.65 m / 5' 5"), rotund, former singing-waiter turned nightclub singer, who'd been on the ITV talent show *New Faces* (judge Noel Edmonds told him he'd "never be a pop star") before signing to the miniscule Hollywood label (not to be confused with the US label Hollywood Records) and being paired with Renée, actually a session singer called Hilary Lester. Championed, as 'Grandma' had been in 1980, by Terry Wogan on Radio 2, 'Save Your Love' was one of those godawful throwback ballads bought largely by older people who wouldn't be seen in a record shop at any other time of year, but turned up in their tens of thousands every once in a while to buy Cliff Richard or Ken Dodd tunes. The song was a huge hit – a million seller, knocking the final single by the Jam from the top spot and outselling some the biggest names of the time (including the combined star power of David Bowie and Bing Crosby, whose 'Peace On Earth/Little Drummer Boy' was finally released that year). It was mercilessly parodied on TV comedy shows, most notably by Kenny Everett, and totally ignored by most of the mainstream press (literally the only mention in *Smash Hits* was a parody sent into the letters page[19]).

And yet, 'Save Your Love' *was* a sincere hit. The people turning up to buy the disc genuinely did so because they enjoyed the song

---

[19] "Darling I am wide as I am tall/my mouth is big, my piggy eyes are small." The magazine awarded the writer a £5 record token.

... though what they saw in it is difficult to imagine – it would have sounded dated in *1962*, let alone 1982. It was the duo's only success, a true one-hit wonder. It was also, in its own way, quietly historic. No single released on a fully independent label had ever reached No. 1 before[20] – an example of the peculiarly democratic nature of the Christmas charts, in which the right record can leapfrog major label products with huge marketing budgets. 'Save Your Love' might have felt incredibly out of step with an increasingly sophisticated pop landscape, one dominated by the synth-driven New Romantics – Duran Duran, Spandau Ballet, Soft Cell – and the shock and awe of pure pop in the form of Culture Club, Wham! and the latest incarnation of David Bowie, but it did show that there was always room at the top for the right song with the right champion, in this case Wogan, to connect it with an underserved portion of the public. Thankfully, it would be another decade before something quite so unexpected and categorically naff would top the biggest chart of the year again. There were a lot of Christmas classics to get through before that happened.

---

[20] Incidentally, Hollywood records boss Johnny Edward, who wrote the song with his wife, had once played guitar in the Mannish Boys, a long-forgotten '60s R & B act fronted by a pre-fame David Bowie. He was also the creator of '80s children's TV fave Metal Mickey. Edward, that is, not Bowie.

Chapter 8
WE'LL BE BACK AT CHRISTMASTIME

In which history repeats itself, the Pretenders are perfect and the pop video is king

There's a theory that says pop music works in decade-long cycles; 1960 was dull, and so was 1970, 1980 and 1990. 1956, meanwhile, was a corker – as was 1966, 1976 and 1986. The theory has a lot of holes in it, and there's any number of examples you can cite to push the phrase *the exception that proves the rule* way beyond breaking point. That said, there is a certain rhythm to the charts, an ebb and flow of boom and bust, creativity and stagnation. The Christmases of 1983 and 1984 weren't *exactly* reruns of '73 and '74 but, well … there are similarities. Even the mainstream press noticed. "Pop music stood still in 1983," said the *Daily Mirror*, noting the success of David Bowie, Elton John, Rod Stewart, the Rolling Stones, the Who and Paul McCartney across the year – all of whom had been superstars a decade earlier. The Christmas season only amplified that sense. Elton John, for example, found himself just the wrong side of the Top 20 with a song with the word *Christmas* in the title, something he had only done once before, in 1973. The fact that 'Cold as Christmas (In the Middle of the Year)' was, as the name suggests, *not actually about Christmas at all* is neither here nor there.[1] Other

---

[1] Though a fine song, this tale of a couple breaking up on a Caribbean holiday didn't exactly scream "festive season", and its release was a little bit of lazy

returning acts from a decade previous included Rod Stewart, Cliff Richard and Paul McCartney (the latter two underlining the *pop moves in ten year cycles* theory by also being refugees from the *1963* Christmas chart). Out in the real world, the parallels between 1973 and 1983 were there if you looked for them; England, Scotland, Wales and Northern Ireland had all, yet again, failed to qualify for a major football tournament, there was a miner's strike on the horizon and a spate of IRA bombings kept the country on edge.[2] 1973 had low unemployment but high inflation. By 1983 inflation had been brought under control, but unemployment had spiked to record levels. Neither year was a picture of social and economic stability. Following a divisive general election, which had seen Thatcher's Conservatives trounce an opposition riven by infighting, the mood in the country felt combative and sour, with tensions high, confidence low and the divide between the well-off and the struggling, north and south, "them" and "us", feeling sharply pronounced. It wasn't a cheerful year. Just like it had a decade earlier, what the country needed now, more than ever, was Slade.

The originators of the whole concept of a Christmas No. 1 had hit the December charts a few times over the previous decade, with inevitable reissues of 'Merry Xmas Everybody' hanging around the nether regions of the Top 40. The band would then dutifully

---

opportunism on behalf of Elton's label. Its low chart position also had a lot to do with the fact it was the fourth single from an incredibly successful album – *Too Low For Zero,* a sparkling return to form that saw him reunite with the backing band from his mid '70s prime as well as lyricist Bernie Taupin – which, of course, meant a lot of people already owned that song and had no need to buy it again. Elton, after a few fallow years, was very much back at full strength and had hit big earlier in 1983 with all-time classics 'I Guess That's Why They Call It the Blues' and 'I'm Still Standing'. A Christmas No. 1 would have been a nice cap to the year. As it was, he'd have to wait another 30 years or so for that honour – and when it came, as we shall see, it wasn't much to shout about.
[2] A particularly nasty incident in December 1983 had seen the IRA detonate a bomb outside Harrods department store in London at rush hour. Police had cleared the area after receiving the organisation's customary early warning, though four people who had ignored the police cordon were injured. It wasn't the first time terrorists had targeted Harrods – the IRA had set off firebombs in 1973 and 1974.

go through the motions of miming the song on *Top of the Pops*, to the point that their appearances became a semi-annual tradition ("It wouldn't be Christmas without them!" said Peter Powell introducing Slade in 1984). For its tenth anniversary, 'Merry Xmas Everybody' had charted at a very respectable 20, which isn't bad for a decade-old song. Something far more interesting, though, was happening at the top end of the chart, where the band's new single, 'My Oh My', had become comfortably their biggest hit since 1974 and given them their first visit to the Top 10 almost a decade.

The back end of the '70s had been rough for Slade. Though no one could have foreseen it at the time, Christmas 1973 had been their peak and it had been a slow decline since then, with the band all privately considering throwing in the towel as the decade came to an end. A last-minute, unbilled appearance at the 1980 Reading Festival changed that. Had that particular field in Middlesex had a roof, then Slade – always a tremendous live act – would have ripped it off with a flourish. As it was, they detonated like an atom bomb. The set climaxed in a mass singalong of 'Merry Xmas Everybody' – despite the fact that, it being August, the band hadn't actually played the song. It turned out the nation had kept Noddy and chums in their hearts all along, and the reaction gave the band a boost which launched them into the '80s with enough momentum for another three years of successful touring and a trio of well-received albums. Alas, though, the hit singles hadn't come.

Then, in 1983, Jim Lea and Noddy Holder delivered 'My Oh My', a huge-sounding power ballad that was essentially one long chorus, consciously following the cyclical pattern of Rod Stewart's massive hit 'Sailing'. 'My Oh My' started gently, had slamming drums coming in about two thirds of the way through and ramped up to a big guitar solo from Dave Hill and a mass, chanted singalong at the end. The words were easy to pick up, lighters were automatically held aloft and fans were encouraged to wave football scarves from side to side, both arms raised in the air. The song was rush-released for Christmas, a time of year Slade had practically trademarked by now, and it quickly ascended the charts, powered by affection for the band tied to a genuinely anthemic song that created communal moments wherever it was played, arms thrown around shoulders and pints held aloft. It was a perfect pub jukebox record as Christmas approached. Britain, you see, still really cherished the Wolves foursome. They were good for the soul. The communal nature of the song wasn't lost on reviewers – "Noddy and the lads attempt to out-chant Queen's 'We Are the Champions' and might very well succeed," said heavy metal bible *Kerrang!*. "[It] builds nicely to a rousing finale that should have them waving their scarves on the terraces by Christmas." "It must be a hit with all those terrace rowdies that are forced to sit down and be nice to their wives this time of year," proclaimed *Sounds*. "Surely destined to be a football terrace anthem for decades to come," said *Melody Maker*. The bubblegum pop market was wooed, too: "I think it'll be a boozy Christmas hit," said Bananarama's Keren Woodward when the band were invited to review the week's singles in *Record Mirror*. "But is the world ready for it?" replied future goth legend Siobhan Fahey. "Anyway, we all love Slade." The song was even a minor hit in the US, peaking at 37 on the Hot 100. "A tuneful, love-your-fellow-man anthem, awash in power chords,", said *Billboard*, "the irrepressibly cheerful Noddy Holder joined by what sounds like a whole football team of singalong choristers".[3]

Had the universe any sense of poetic justice, 'My Oh My' would have been Christmas No. 1 that year, no question. That's how the story was always meant to go. Unfortunately, surprise disappointments were a hallmark of Thatcher's Britain. Not only did 'My Oh My' stall at No. 2, despite selling a very respectable 500,000 copies (it did give them a No. 1 in Sweden and Norway), it's also been largely forgotten. At least, it's not a song that's made it onto the merry-go-round of Christmas-adjacent classics. A shame. It really should be spoken about in the same breath as 'Sailing' and 'We Are the Champions'. It really *should* have been a terrace anthem remembered for decades. Alas, it came and went, and ultimately it was a last hurrah for the band, who never bothered the Top 5 again (though the following year's surprisingly contemporary sounding 'Run Runaway' did get to No. 7, and an impressive 20 in the US). Slade

---

[3] After nearly 20 years of work, Slade were finally making inroads in the USA. Quiet Riot, a young LA metal band currently tearing up the scene, had scored a huge hit with a cover of 'Cum on Feel the Noize', opening up a new stateside audience for Wolverhampton's most beloved sons.

were forced to cancel a lengthy American tour with Ozzy Osbourne after hepatitis put Jim Lea out of action for months, essentially missing their window to capitalise on recent successes and consolidate their new-found Stateside popularity. It knocked the wind out of everyone's sails. Holder, going through a divorce and burned out from 20 years on the road, decided to opt out of playing live and the original band never toured again. They had a crack at another anthem for Christmas '84 with 'All Join Hands', which was decent enough but very much a retread of 'My Oh My'[4]; it did respectably but stalled at No. 15, and by Christmas week it had dropped down to 27. A whole Christmas album, *Crackers*, was released in 1985, featuring some by-the-numbers retreads of classics (photocopying Springsteen's 'Santa Claus Is Comin' to Town', rerecording their own 'Cum on Feel the Noize', butchering 'Do They Know It's Christmas?') but it sparked very little interest. They limped along as a studio act into the '90s scoring the occasional minor hit, the last of which was the rather good 'Radio Wall of Sound' in 1991, but the spark wasn't there anymore and without live gigs to sustain interest, all but the hardcore of their audience withered away. Holder and Lea both left the band in 1992, bored of infighting and the constant disappointing returns. Don Powell and Dave Hill kept going as Slade II, later changing their name back to just Slade, promoting themselves mostly as an oldies act and sustained by annual Christmas tours. Holder says he doesn't mind his bandmates making a living off the name – he and Lea, after all, as the writers of 'Merry Xmas Everybody', had their pensions secured already. Every year the band's biggest song is inescapable. Every year Noddy Holder, who went on to a respectable TV and radio career, is paid a small fortune to shout "IT'S CHRIIIIIIIIIIIIIIIIIIIIIIIIISTMAAAAAAAAAAAAAAS"

---

[4] A reference to singing 'Auld Lang Syne' in the lyrics underlined something that had already been discovered by George Harrison with 'Ding Dong Ding Dong' and ABBA with 'Happy New Year' – New Year's songs rarely connect. It's an oddity of pop that Christmas songs are so popular, but New Year's songs aren't. Possibly it's because, on New Year's Eve, we tend to be looking back only at the previous year, and looking ahead to the next one, rather than being pinned to the moment itself. Maybe someone will crack it one day.

somewhere or other. And who can begrudge him that? Slade – national treasures, always.

The No. 1 song that Christmas, keeping Noddy and friends from a much-deserved second coming, was rather an oddity – a mostly a cappella cover of Yazoo's 1981 synthpop ballad 'Only You'. This new version, by a quartet of left-wing actors going by the name the Flying Pickets, stripped the song down, replacing the already minimal instrumentation with beautifully harmonising male voices and giving the UK its first a capella chart-topper.[5] The band had all been members of the 7:84 theatre group, an agitprop troupe founded by socialist playwright John McGrath (its name was a reference to oft-quoted statistic of the time – that 7% of the population owned 84% of the country's wealth[6]), and had been touring a play about colliery bands during the 1974 miner's strike called *One Big Blow*. Arranging a cappella cover songs was something they'd been doing in the van to pass time on the road, performing them in pubs between shows as a party piece. The reactions were so good that when the tour eventually wound down, the group decided to focus on the singing instead, quickly gaining a reputation on the cabaret and club circuit and doing a successful run at the Edinburgh Fringe. The name 'The Flying Pickets' was a reference to a favourite tactic of the unions, in which supporters were bussed over to bolster the picket lines wherever a key strike was taking place. Two of the band had been miners during the historic industrial action a decade earlier.

---

[5] This isn't *strictly* true. If you listen carefully there's a quiet, ghostly choral effect underpinning everything and a very subtle hiss and thump of an electronic hi-hat and kick drum, achieved using the new-fangled Fairlight synthesiser, a state-of-the-art bit of kit which back then retailed at a cool £12,000. Most people were happy to look the other way, although *Music Week*'s singles reviewer Tony Jasper found it decidedly iffy. "I'm not sure whether I want back-ups 'gonging' away in simulation game" was his verdict at the time, though what he meant isn't entirely clear. "But otherwise this is well vocalised even if slowish and against sometimes unnecessary backcloth."

[6] It would be nice to say that things had improved a lot, but data from 2022 suggests that the top 1% still holds a quarter of the nation's money. The gap between the richest and poorest sectors of the British public is the second largest in the developed world, with only the USA ahead.

The phrase would once again enter the public lexicon during the miner's strike of 1984, but in the meantime its political connotations went unnoticed.[7]

Having already self-released a live album, the group landed a distribution deal for 'Only You', their debut single, with Virgin's new 10 Records imprint. The label's radio plugger was able to get them on the Radio 1 playlist and things took off from there. The song went straight in at No. 9 on 3 December and was at No. 1 the following week, where it sat for the rest of the year. The group themselves were unlikely popstars: a mismatched six-piece who all looked as if they were in different bands and were, as pop magazine *No.1* put it, "almost as old as the Rolling Stones".[8] It would be nice to say that the avowedly left-wing band's political inclinations caught the public mood, but that's hard to substantiate – certainly little of the press coverage they were getting at the time focused on their politics. This was more a case of a genuinely lovely version of an already very good, melancholy pop song connecting with listeners. 'Only You' is sighing and wistful, the Pickets' recording is warm and soothing, and Britain, as we have seen, has an occasional tendency to gravitate to songs about heartbreak at Christmas time – it's another song about longing for something you no longer have. About thinking about a time when you were happiest at a time when you are not. That sort of thing always catches on in the dark, cold nights when loneliness is magnified. *Miserable Christmas* is always a winner. Despite strong competition from Slade, current flavours of the month Culture Club (whose soul ballad 'Victims' was at No. 3) and Paul Young (whose slightly nauseating cod calypso 'Love of the Common People' was at 4), it was six socialist theatre actors, ageing

---

[7] According to a story doing the rounds at the time, the Flying Pickets version of 'Only You' was one of Margaret Thatcher's favourite songs. There are three possible explanations for this. One, that someone made this story up for laughs. Two, that it's true and the reference in the group's name went entirely over her head. Or, possibly, three, that she had more of a sense of humour than people think.

[8] True. Both the Rolling Stones and the Flying Pickets were composed, at that point, of men in their mid to late thirties – ancient indeed – with the exception of the Stones' Charlie Watts, who was a positively geriatric 42.

and unpretty, who closed out the Christmas Day edition of *Top of the Pops* that year, resplendent, as the fake snow fell, in matching donkey jackets.

Meanwhile, Paul McCartney, now 20 years into a career as one of the most successful songwriters of all time, was making another play for a Christmas classic with 'Pipes of Peace', the title track of his recent solo album. No other artist had managed more than a solitary Christmas No. 1 at this point – Paul McCartney had five under his belt, two of which, 'She Loves You' and 'Mull of Kintyre', were in the Top 5 bestselling songs in British music history. Since 'Wonderful Christmastime' had missed the mark back in 1979, he clearly felt it was worth another go.

McCartney was enjoying what would turn out to be his last run of proper pop hits, having just had a US No. 1 and UK No. 2 with 'Say, Say, Say', the best of three duets he'd recorded that year with Michael Jackson.[9] That had followed the previous year's 'Ebony and Ivory', a well-meaning if somewhat on-the-nose duet with Stevie Wonder that had hit the top spot on both sides of the Atlantic. Now 41, McCartney was clinging on to his era as a credible singles artist by his fingertips, resisting the slide into heritage oldies act as best he could. It wouldn't be long before *Smash Hits* would endearingly dub him "Fab Macca Wacky Thumbs Aloft" and he would move into a new role, as the affable elder statesman of rock.[10] Cast an eye over his chart career, and what's notable is that he had never had a solo UK No. 1 single. All of them had been collaborations – with

[9] 'Say Say Say' was recorded for McCartney's *Pipes of Peace* album, while another co-written duet, 'The Girl Is Mine', would appear on Jackson's *Thriller* – indeed it was the first single to be released from that record. Which, when you consider that the album had 'Wanna Be Startin' Somethin'', 'Beat It', 'Billie Jean' and the title track, is one of the weirdest decisions in music history. It goes without saying that *Thriller* is a better album than *Pipes of Peace*, but 'Say Say Say' is degrees of magnitude a better song than the tepid 'The Girl Is Mine', which is the only blight on Jackson's otherwise unimpeachable masterpiece.

[10] A role he still inhabits, and one which glosses over his tendency to be quite calculating and cynical when it comes to his career, as many of his collaborators, not least the other Beatles, will tell you. It's a similar story with Dave Grohl.

John Lennon in the Beatles, with Denny Laine in Wings, and most recently with Stevie Wonder. His Christmas release of 1983 could be seen as a straightforward attempt to correct this. 'Pipes of Peace' is probably the most Beatley song he'd recorded in years, helped enormously by his old band's collaborator, George Martin behind the mixing desk. And while it wasn't a Christmas song *per se*, it did have all of the hallmarks of one: a children's choir, a plea for peace on Earth and goodwill to all men and, well, the fact it was by Paul McCartney, who post 'Mull of Kintyre' and 'Wonderful Christmastime' had become almost as synonymous with December hits as Slade.

In truth, 'Pipes of Peace' was a new phenomenon in the pantheon of seasonal music. It wasn't overtly festive, but became Christmas *adjacent* thanks to its video – a trick that would be pulled many times in the future, most successfully a decade later by East 17. By 1983 the "pop promo" had become an absolutely fundamental part of the hit single playbook, something that McCartney had seen first-hand – 'Say Say Say' had been underperforming until *Top of the Pops* screened the video, a brilliant clip which saw McCartney and Jackson playing vaudeville entertainers and travelling snake oil salesmen, pulling scams in old-timey America. Following its *Top of the Pops* premiere it bounced straight up to No. 3, going up a place the following week. Jackson himself was the modern master of the art form, having won an Emmy for the 'Beat It' promo and then topped both 'Say Say Say' and 'Beat It' with *Thriller*, a 15-minute mini-movie directed by horror supremo John Landis, costing just shy of $1 million. It changed the game for music videos forever, particularly in the US where the relatively recent launch of MTV had immediately boosted the value of a good promo clip. McCartney was clearly taking notes.[11] Like 'Say Say Say', and unlike many of

---

[11] To be fair to Macca, it was the Beatles who had, at least in part, pioneered the idea of music videos back in the '60s, creating clips for 'We Can Work It Out' and 'Day Tripper' (Christmas No. 1 in 1965) to meet an otherwise unworkable demand for TV appearances. Subsequently they'd do it for all of their singles, and the clips got increasingly conceptual. By the time of 'Strawberry Fields Forever', 'Penny Lane' and 'Hello, Goodbye', they were making short films that contained all the grammar of the music videos we'd recognise today.

the more image-focused or performance-based videos around at the time, 'Pipes of Peace' was impressively staged and shot, with a large cast and detailed sets. It was essentially a short film, re-enacting the famous 1914 Christmas truce that had broken out spontaneously in the trenches of the First World War, football match and all. In the clip McCartney plays both a British Tommy and his German counterpart, who exchange pictures of their loved ones in the middle of a freezing, muddy no man's land. It was one of the most ambitious commercial music videos a British artist had made at the time, beautifully shot with meticulous attention to period costuming and setting. While it didn't redefine the medium, and pretty much followed the path already set by Michael Jackson, it was a striking example of the cinematic potential of music videos in the early 1980s. Arguably, it marked one of McCartney's final moments as a leading innovator in British pop.

If Macca truly wanted a Christmas hit, though, he'd left it too late. 'Pipes of Peace' entered the Top 40 on Christmas Eve at No. 22, unable to compete in the crowded marketplace. Reviews were hardly ecstatic either. For the music press, McCartney simply wasn't cool anymore. "A final, late, and I'd say, unsuccessful bid for the Christmas No. 1 spot from the greying heart-throb," said *Sounds*, "it's no 'Mull of Kintyre'." "Turgid, unashamed mush" was Maureen Rice's verdict in *No.1*. *Smash Hits* didn't even bother to review the single, though it did print the lyrics. Even a *Top of the Pops* screening of the video on 15 December wasn't enough of a boost to send the single stratospheric on a Christmas chart that was already very strong. The single just didn't have the lead-up time. 'Pipes of Peace' would eventually top the charts a few weeks into January, giving Fab Macca Wacky Thumbs Aloft his first and only true solo No. 1 and, effectively, closing the door on the chart-topping singles career of the most extraordinary musical force Britain had ever seen – it had been 20 years since the Beatles first UK No. 1. They wouldn't have another, as solo artists or as a band, until 'Now and Then', a warmed-over song John Lennon had left behind and which was worked on by his bandmates and finally released in 2024.

Despite the appealing terrace racket of Slade, the soothing lilt of socialist harmonies from the Flying Pickets and the pipe-playing trench antics of Paul McCartney, the best and most enduring

Christmas song of 1983 was found a little further down the chart. In fact, it never got higher than No. 15. And, no, it's not the 'Singalong-A-Santa (Medley)' by Santa Claus and the Christmas Trees.[12] Nor is it 'Rat Rapping' by popular TV puppet Roland Rat, despite dozens of local press reviews calling it a "dead-cert for Christmas No. 1" (it peaked at No. 14 in January – one of the few recorded instances of seasonal good taste by the British public). No. The best Christmas record of 1983 – in fact, arguably one of the very best records of any sort that year, was the Pretenders' gorgeous '2000 Miles'. Gary Crowley in *Record Mirror* had it right: "As those cold winter nights draw in, millions of souls and Dansettes across the country are screaming out for boss waxings[13] like this … a slice of pure yuletide joy." And it absolutely is.

That the Pretenders had new material at all is testimony to singer Chrissie Hynde's workhorse, *pay your dues* punk ethic. Though originally from the US, Hynde had found her musical home in London during the punk explosion of '76, working at Malcolm McLaren and Vivienne Westwood's SEX boutique, bouncing between early incarnations of the Damned and the Clash and hanging out with the Sex Pistols before forming the Pretenders in 1978. Their self-titled debut album and its follow-up, *Pretenders II,* had established them as one of the brightest bands of the new decade, moving punk and New Wave forward with classic songwriting. In truth Hynde had more in common with Bruce Springsteen than she did with Sid Vicious – that same devotion to rock's fundamentals, that same clear-eyed chronicling of real lives, that same instinct that a musician's place was on a stage, anytime, anywhere. By 1983 the band had rather been through the wringer. First founding bass player Pete Farndon had been fired after an escalating heroin habit had gotten way out of hand. Two days later, guitarist James Honeyman-Scott died after taking cocaine. Farndon himself would pass away within a year, drowning in the bath after shooting up. It would be enough

---

[12] A Chas & Dave style knees up medley put together by Polydor A&R Dennis Munday in a shameless cash-in attempt inspired by the previous years 'Hokey Cokey' by the Snowmen. It peaked at 28 – enough to get them a *Top of the Pops* appearance.

[13] This is '80s pop magazine-speak for "good records".

to finish off most bands. Giving up, however, is not in Chrissie Hynde's genetic make-up. She and drummer Martin Chambers made the decision to push forward. As Hynde later recalled in the liner notes to the band's *Pirate Radio* box set collection, "We were going to be miserable either way, so we decided we might as well be miserable in the studio. So we just carried on."

'2000 Miles', a snow-swept ballad with chiming guitars that twinkle like icicles, was captured at London's AIR Studios, George Martin's facility perched above Oxford Street's bustling shopping district where a reconstituted Pretenders – now featuring guitarist Robbie McIntosh and bassist Malcolm Foster – worked with producer Chris Thomas to shape what would become their third album, *Learning to Crawl*. The view from the studio fed directly into the song. "When we were sitting in AIR Studios looking down on the Christmas lights in Oxford Street, above Oxford Circus, they had these twinkling lights," Hynde said in those same liner notes, "and '2000 Miles' really does sound exactly how that Christmas looked." Even while admitting her own ambivalence about the holiday season ("I can do without Christmas myself... the commercial aspect is grotesque"), she couldn't deny how perfectly the moment and the music had aligned.

'2000 Miles' is a song that juxtaposes the bitter and the sweet as well as any you'll find. On the one hand it has an undeniably Christmassy glow, inspired by those London Christmas lights shining in the frost. Its guitars shimmer and glisten, and Hynde's voice rings clear and true like a silver bell. On the other hand, it's a lyric full of distance and loneliness and longing. When pressed about the song's meaning on Dutch television's *Countdown*, Hynde's response was awkward and uncomfortable: "I wish you hadn't asked me that," she said, before deflecting: "let's just say it's about Father Christmas." The pain was still raw, the loss too near. Later, she would acknowledge that the song's sense of distance was channelling the loss of Honeyman-Scott, influenced by Otis Redding's 'Thousand Miles Away' – "another thing I thought everyone would pick up on, and of course no one even knows that song."

Speaking to *Sound On Sound* in 2005, engineer Steve Churchyard remembered how the recording captured the essence of the band: "Invariably, when we'd get to guitars, everything would be layered. It's a sound that Jimmy [Honeyman-Scott] had created, along with the great live feel of Martin's drums and having Chrissie's vocal really loud in the mix, leaving no doubt that she's in control of the song." That vocal prominence was deliberate – as Churchyard noted, "It was very much in the tradition of all that early British pop where the vocals were so far out front. That would never fly today."

And perhaps that's what makes '2000 Miles' such a perfect Christmas record – it's a song that wears its heart on its sleeve, even as its singer tries to guard hers. While Hynde might have deflected questions about its meaning, the truth twinkles just beneath the surface. In becoming a Christmas standard, '2000 Miles' transformed private grief into public comfort, personal distance into universal closeness. Four decades on, it's a reminder that the best Christmas songs sync with a full spectrum of human emotion that lies beneath all that tinsel and snow. Christmas can be, at once, magical and miserable. You can feel utterly alone in the bosom of your family. Once again it's a song about something *missing*. That's very Christmas.

'2000 Miles' wasn't released as a single in the US, where it remained a B-side. That says a lot. Even in the ultra-commercial early '80s, cool American bands didn't do Christmas – it wasn't punk, it wasn't New Wave, it wasn't cool. It was merely cold. The British market, however, where Christmas records were cherished, and miserable ones above all, was a perfect home for this pretty much perfect song. It's a song that's endured. You'll rarely get through December without hearing it. Quite right, too.

Chapter 9
1984 PART ONE –
GIVE IT TO SOMEONE SPECIAL

Welcome to the silver age of the British Christmas single

Here's an interesting exercise. Buy any British Christmas compilation and divide the songs by year. 1974 will have maybe two, 1973 possibly three. Most years will have one or none. 1984, though? 1984 will likely have five or six ... and two of them are arguably the most iconic British Christmas pop songs of all. They're among the most iconic pop songs of *any* sort, really. That one year is the single biggest contributor to the Christmas canon, and one of pop's absolute finest.

British pop was having quite the moment – Duran Duran, Eurythmics, Spandau Ballet, Wham!, Culture Club and Frankie Goes To Hollywood were each experiencing a Beatlemania all of their own, garnering smash hit after smash hit. Despite being lumped with the sarcastic tag of "English haircut bands", they were all massive in America, too. This was what *NME* had taken to calling "The New Pop" – bright and flashy. Androgyny and futuristic sounds. Glamour and decadence. Boys in make-up driven by synths and funky bass. Like the glam rock of a decade previously, pop had exploded into colour and camp and those institutes dedicated to the aesthetic of pure pop were thriving. Over ten million tuned in to watch *Top of the Pops'* host a school disco in your living room every week, an explosion of eyeliner, arts and crafts creativity and awkward teen dancing. *Smash Hits,* with its bold, full-colour covers, pull-out posters and printed lyrics sold half a million copies of wry, pop-focused musical fun every fortnight. The music industry, despite its fears about home taping, was booming – a hit single could sell 400,000 copies and *still* not get to No. 1. This was British pop in its pomp.

And like a decade previously, the pure, aspirational escapism of the pop scene thrived because there was so much in Thatcher's Britain that people needed to escape. The winter of 1984 saw the country arguably more divided than at any point since the war. The miners' strike, which had begun in March, was becoming increasingly bitter as Christmas approached. Over 140,000 miners were still out, their families surviving on union handouts, fundraising drives and soup kitchens. Violence had broken out repeatedly between pickets and police, most notably at the Battle of Orgreave that June, where mounted police had charged the picket line with truncheons and shields. The Prime Minister had labelled the striking miners "the enemy within", while National Union of Miners leader Arthur Scargill compared the police to a "Latin American state". Lessons had been learned from the 1974 miner's strike – a great victory for the unions who had been able to withhold the means of producing power for the country. Another clash was always going to happen; it was inevitable. This time, though, the government had been ready. Thatcher had done her research. The Electricity and Gas boards had long been stockpiling coal and gas, and preparing alternative means of transporting it. The NUM didn't have the same leverage and the feud was bitter and increasingly ideological: a battle for the heart of the country. Naturally, the strike became a huge cause célèbre for British pop's left wing. As Christmas approached, Paul Weller's Style Council had collaborated on a benefit single, 'Soul Deep', under the name 'Council Collective', intended to raise money for striking miners' families. Sometimes it felt like *NME* talked more about Arthur Scargill than it did about David Bowie or New Order.

It wasn't just about the miners, though. As the year drew to a close, the economy told two different stories depending on where you lived. In the south-east, a new affluence was emerging: the stamp duty threshold on house purchases had been raised to £30,000, credit was becoming more readily available, and a culture of aspiration and consumption was taking hold. "Thatcher's children," as they would later be known, were revelling in money and success. Meanwhile, manufacturing regions, particularly in the north, Wales and Scotland, were experiencing record unemployment. Over three million people were out of work – more than at any point since the 1930s.

The musical form variously known as New Pop, synth-pop and New Romantics reflected this by being either very aspirational or completely escapist, depending on your perspective. Many acts went the other way, leaning into the problems. While Duran sang about champagne and yachts and Spandau literally had a song called 'Gold', benefit gigs for striking miners were becoming regular occurrences, with everyone from Bronski Beat to the Smiths to Wham! playing fundraisers. The underground music scene was overwhelmingly and overtly political, and every serious young band was required to take a stand. The tension spilled occasionally onto the hallowed ground of *Top of the Pops* itself – Paul Weller had performed 'Soul Deep' wearing a NUM support T-shirt, while Billy Bragg used his appearance singing 'Between the Wars' to pledge his performance fee to the miners. Pop had rarely felt as politically charged as it did in 1984.

It was against this backdrop that the music industry positioned itself for the annual Christmas rush; a period that would generate 40% of the profits for the entire year. The big players all knew the importance of a festive hit, and with an eye on a public in need of distraction from the miserable scenes dominating the front pages, more of the year's big players went with Christmas-themed records than at any point since the mid '70s.

The chart year had been dominated in particular by two young pop acts, both with a run of No. 1s that soaked up headlines and airtime; and both were looking for the ultimate capstone to their year. In the red corner was Frankie Goes To Hollywood, the overtly queer Liverpool funk band whose first singles, 'Relax' and 'Two Tribes', had raised endless controversies but also shifted in astonishing numbers, both hitting No. 1. 'The Power of Love', the third single from their No. 1 album *Welcome to the Pleasuredome*, had been earmarked for the Christmas market – a dramatic ballad and a complete departure from the floor-filling bangers they had made their name with thus far.

In the blue corner were Wham!, the poptastic dreamboat duo of George Michael and Andrew Ridgeley. They'd already enjoyed three No. 1s that year: 'Wake Me Up Before You Go-Go', 'Careless Whisper'[1] and 'Freedom', all brilliant plastic soul bops that sent young hearts fluttering the world over. Their second album, *Make It Big*, had also hit the top spot. George Michael dearly wanted that fourth consecutive No. 1. He'd put together a weepie titled 'Last Christmas', Velcro-catchy, thoroughly emotional and maudlin as anything. The band and their entourage had spent a fortune getting tipsy in the Swiss Alps for the video. The smart money would be on Wham! to take the Christmas crown that year – or at least it would be if anyone was yet publishing the odds. They weren't – though 1984, a year which pushed the profile of the Christmas charts higher than ever before, would change that. Thanks partly to Wham!, partly to Frankie and mostly to a charity single that would redraw the map.

Not that the chart triple of Wham!, Frankie and Band Aid had the festive landscape to themselves. The rock establishment was always ready for an assault on the December charts. There was Queen, for a start. Almost a decade on from 'Bohemian Rhapsody', Freddie and co were ready to have another crack at a Christmas No. 1, this time with the rather more on-the-nose 'Thank God It's Christmas', a yearning, if rather safe mid-pacer, that ticked a lot of boxes without really managing to exist outside of any of them. By Queen's towering standards it's a fairly ordinary pop song, though in the hands of almost anyone else it would be far worse – 'Thank God It's Christmas' sinks or swims on Freddie Mercury's character-istically soaring, emotive vocal and those killer Queen harmonies. When Freddie implores us to literally "let it be Christmas", adding "Thank God it's Christmas", he's not saying much of any note … essentially the theme of the song is *Christmas is pretty great, huh?* A Freddie Mercury vocal, though, is never anything but committed,

[1] Technically 'Careless Whisper' is a George Michael solo release, though ironically it was the only one of three singles to be co-written by both members of Wham!. More on that later.

and while the theme might be rather shrug-worthy, the delivery is anything but. Sincerity beams from every note. Not that it made much of a splash – the song went in low and peaked at 21 the week before Christmas. Queen didn't even bother to put it on their next greatest hits compilation, though it would finally get a look in when *Greatest Hits III* turned up in the '90s to mop up the leftovers of the catalogue. Fundamentally though, it's still Queen, and Queen songs endure. They sit in their own space and obey their own rules. Automatic graduation to festive compilations has ensured 'Thank God It's Christmas' has stood the test of time, and while it's a hard song to adore, it's a difficult one to dislike. The music press, of course, were utterly nonplussed. "Maybe Paul McCartney's been giving him [Freddie] secret tuition in the art of mercenary melancholy?" mused *Melody Maker*. Worse came from *No.1* magazine, who turned the single reviews over to British Eurovision stars Bucks Fizz, an act so banal they make ABBA look like the Prodigy. Freddie and the boys may have been able to shrug off *Melody Maker*'s sniffiness, but Mike from Bucks Fizz saying, "If even Queen can't come up with a good Christmas song, then no one can"? That's going to sting.

A bigger hit at the time was Gary Glitter's 'Another Rock and Roll Christmas', which peaked at No. 7 in Christmas week. In the decade since his chart peak, Glitter had very much settled into the role of faintly embarrassing oldies act, and this unashamed throwback would be his last real hit. There's not a great deal to say about it – it's built around the descending scale that opens Slade's 'Merry Xmas Everybody' played at triple the speed and goes downhill from there; catchy, but absolutely by the numbers in its glam racket. Glitter was far from fashionable in 1984 and the song received short shrift in the music press. "Preposterous, predictably and lamentably inept," said *NME*. "As overbearingly theatrical as a parish pantomime," said *Smash Hits*. "Another pathetic record for him to mime during his numerous TV appearances," said *Record Mirror*. Nevertheless, 'Another Rock and Roll Christmas' did decent numbers at the time, powered by silvered nostalgia and some sort of knee-jerk positive response to festive glam rock. Glitter, of course, is quite rightly a pariah these days, and though some of his earlier hits have survived as separate entities to their creator, there's not enough substance here to keep this one afloat.

Firmly in the oldies camp, and this should come as no surprise by this point, there was, inevitably, Paul McCartney. Having already tried trad folk, quirky synth-pop and Beatley ballads, he was back with another of the Christmas chart chestnuts – the children's song. Back in 1970, McCartney had announced that he was working on an animated film based on the beloved British children's staple *Rupert Bear*, the adventures of a yellow-trousered young bruin created by Alfred Bestall for a comic strip in the *Daily Express* and a huge favourite of the baby boomer generation growing up after the war. McCartney had begun writing and recording songs for the project that year. Across the next decade he would dip in and out of Rupert's world as he attempted to get the film off the ground – it had been a Rupert-themed song he'd been working on with George Martin on that bleak day in 1980 when the news of John Lennon's death reached London. The fruits of that long-gestated film, and indeed of those 1980 studio sessions, were finally introduced to the world in 1984 in the shape of *Rupert and the Frog Song*, a 13-minute animated short that went out in cinemas alongside McCartney's much derided live-action film project *Give My Regards To Broad Street*.[2] The supporting feature was substantially better received (it won the BAFTA for best animated short the following year), and its centrepiece musical number, 'We All Stand Together', was a legitimate hit for Paul McCartney and the Frog Chorus, peaking at No. 3 in Christmas week behind Wham! and Band Aid. People sneered when the song was released, but you count Paul McCartney out at your peril.

Over the years 'The Frog Song', as it's often inaccurately referred to, has become totemic of McCartney's most twee tendencies. Accepted wisdom has it as the nadir in his canon; syrupy, unforgivably naff and musically irredeemable. A song that makes 'Mull of Kintyre' sound like Kraftwerk. Upon the week of its release, *Smash Hits* called it "one of the worst singles in living memory" and it's

---

[2] A musical written, composed and produced by the former Beatle, and in which he starred – and which was ripped to shreds by critics that December. "Humourless, unwritten, unperformed, undirected, witless … the worst excuse for a movie we've seen all year," said the *LA Times*. That was one of the kinder ones.

served as a punchline to McCartney's career ever since. Accepted wisdom, however, has it dead wrong. Yes, of course, 'We All Stand Together' is no 'Helter Skelter'; hell, it's barely an 'Ob-La-Di, Ob-La-Da'. But those are unfair yardsticks. It's closer to 'Yellow Submarine'. This is a *children's song*, absolutely and unashamedly. It's intended as the soundtrack to the adventures of a cartoon bear. To judge it as anything else is to miss the point, because honestly 'We All Stand Together', when assessed on its own terms, is marvellous. Children absolutely loved it at the time. McCartney and producer George Martin created something sumptuous and quite lovely. Criticising 'We All Stand Together' for being childish and twee is like criticising *Teletubbies* for treating its audience like babies. It's *meant* to be childish and twee. The sales speak for themselves – a Top 3 hit during Christmas week in the early '80s can only be achieved with fairly astonishing business over the counter. Any other year it would have given McCartney his sixth Christmas No. 1.

For all of McCartney's success, alas, Christmas 1984 wasn't going to be remembered for a cartoon novelty, and it certainly wasn't going to be remembered for the embarrassing embers of glam rock or a C-list Queen single. 1984 belonged to bands with youth on their side and far, *far* better hair. It was Frankie Goes To Hollywood that were first off the blocks: 'The Power of Love'[3] followed its parent album, the 18-track *Welcome to the Pleasuredome* into stores at the tail end of November with immediate impact. It was a smart move. Keeping a ballad back for the third single and putting it out at Christmas was hardly an original tactic – ABBA had been doing it since the '70s – but 'The Power of Love' was *so* different to the band's previous hits that it couldn't help but raise eyebrows.

Frankie had already been knocking around for a few years, and their success in 1984 must have seemed a faraway dream just a year earlier when the band were signing on and watching their debut single fail to break into the Top 40 at all. Singer Holly Johnson had been one of those faces about town on the Liverpool scene who

---

[3] Not to be confused with the *other* 'Power of Love', made famous by both Céline Dion and Jennifer Rush, or the other *other* 'Power of Love' by Huey Lewis and the News.

151

seemed to know everyone. He'd been in post-punk pathfinders Big In Japan alongside Julian Cope (later of the Teardrop Explodes), Ian Broudie (later of the Lightning Seeds) and Bill Drummond (later of the KLF), and when that band failed to be big *anywhere*, let alone Japan, he'd put together Frankie with Paul Rutherford, whom he knew from the local gay scene. Frankie Goes to Hollywood, you see, were deliciously, pioneeringly and very overtly gay. It was pretty much the crux of their image – though in truth only Johnson and Rutherford were *actually* homosexual. The band's rhythm section was all straight. Not that anyone noticed them. You were too distracted by Rutherford and Johnson looking so very, *very* gay. Which is exactly the way they wanted it: Rutherford, all handlebar moustache and leather daddy styling; Johnson cuter, dressed sharper but with a fetish club twist. Johnson would later describe the band's image in his memoir, *A Bone in My Flute*, as "post-apocalypse S&M punk", which pretty much hits the nail on the head. Their debut single, 'Relax', was a solid gold dance floor classic that had knocked Paul McCartney's 'Pipes of Peace' from the No. 1 spot at the beginning of the year and squatted at the top of the charts for six weeks despite being banned by the BBC after Radio 1's Mike Reid had clocked what the lyrics were actually about and clutched his pearls so hard they'd fossilised. They'd followed it up with another floor-filling classic, 'Two Tribes', about a Third World War, which spent *nine* weeks at No. 1. Few bands sold as many records as Frankie Goes To Hollywood that year.

'The Power of Love', though, was something else – a genuine ballad. Producer Trevor Horn built the whole thing around a swelling orchestra and Johnson's powerful, incredibly soulful voice.[4] The song was swooping and dramatic, not a love song to a specific person but a celebration of love itself, stirring and gorgeous and beautifully arranged, full of perfect little touches. The moment Johnson staggers his final delivery of "love … with tongues of *fi-er*", leaving

---

[4] Horn had rarely required the services of the rest of Frankie Goes To Hollywood in the studio, and had largely built the backing tracks up himself using synths, drum machines and session players. Though the sound of all five jumping into a swimming pool does appear on 'Relax'.

a little hiccuping half-beat before the final line, could raise goose-bumps on a cooked sausage.

On the surface, 'The Power of Love' had none of the controversial furniture of its two predecessors. It's a song you could play to your nan at Christmas dinner without having to answer awkward questions (like, "When he says: 'Don't do it', what's he talking about?"). The band's label, ZTT, however, felt a little spice was needed. "I'd always had a little pattern that I'd wanted to pursue," ZTT's head propagandist Paul Morley, who also happened to be an *NME* writer, told the *Guardian* in 2022. "The first three singles would be: sex, then war, then religion." 'Relax', obviously, was the sex; 'Two Tribes' was the war; 'The Power of Love', then, was the religion. Though the song itself is secular, giving it a religious twist wasn't hard. It already sounded grand and churchlike and highly gothic, with its talk of keeping "the vampire from your door" and "death-defying love" – though "the hooded claw" is almost certainly a knowingly camp reference to the cartoon *Penelope Pitstop*. Tom Watkins, the future Pet Shop Boys/Bros/East 17 manager who was working as a graphic designer for the label at the time, has it right in his memoir when he describes the song as sounding "like it was booming out of the world's biggest, grandest cathedral."[5] ZTT, without bothering to consult the band, simply pointed the video in that direction. The clip, by pop promo pioneers Godley & Creme, was a beautifully shot and straight telling of the traditional Nativity story, done so faithfully that it was literally filmed in rural Palestine using a local cast. Suddenly the song ticked all the boxes for a Christmas hit. After all, what's more Christmassy than the birth of Christ? The video gave 'The Power of Love' an editorial context it hadn't previously had, taking Holly Johnson's themes of love and devotion and magnifying them through the lens of Christianity. Wise men kneel, shepherds cower[6] and the little lord Jesus lays down his sweet head. It's an incredibly effective video, and it tied Frankie's best song irrevocably to Christmas, for evermore a seasonal single; much to

---

[5] Watkins' cattily entertaining book, by the way, has one of the most brilliantly knowing titles in literature: *Let's Make Lots of Money: Secrets of a Rich, Fat, Gay, Lucky Bastard.*

[6] The shepherds in the video were literally Palestinian shepherds.

the annoyance of its creator, who never conceived it as anything of the kind.

It was an obvious hit. Frankie were one of those rare bands that covered all bases. The music press had, by now, largely split into two camps – *NME*, *Sounds* and *Melody Maker* considered themselves the voice of authentic "real" music, favouring indie labels, pseudo-intellectual deep dives and arguments about the miner's strike, while *Smash Hits* and *No.1* were pure pop, proudly disposable and with tongue usually in cheek. (*Record Mirror*, meanwhile, attempted to straddle both camps while, where possible, printing as many pictures of topless women as they could get away with.) All were capable of brilliant writing: while *NME* could be preachy and a little pretentious, it could also be incisive and smart; and while *Smash Hits* might come off as shallow, its writers were more than capable of nuance, sharpness and not a small amount of wit. You were unlikely to find much coverage of Kajagoogoo or Dollar in *Sounds*, but equally you'd rarely get the Birthday Party or the Fall in *No.1*. Both sides of the music press, though, loved Frankie Goes To Hollywood. As December rolled around the Frankies, on tour in the US, found themselves on the cover of *Smash Hits*, *NME*, *Record Mirror*, *Melody Maker* and *No.1* in the span of two weeks, almost a clean sweep, while receiving substantial column inches from the *Daily Mirror* and the *Sun* as well. The song appealed to audiences of both Radio 1 and Radio 2, and got plenty of play on both; the video courted surprisingly little of the controversy people were expecting and ZTT had presumably hoped for ("I watched the 'Power Of Love' video the other night," said Duran Duran's John Taylor in *No.1*. "It was designed purely to make people talk about them. That's blatant."[7]) In fact, so literally faithful was its depiction, and so perfectly matched to the song, that it tended to be taken at face value.[8] "I'm sure the Frankie Goes to Hollywood video will have

---

[7] Duran Duran, of course, were known for their understated *art for art's sake* videos.

[8] A letter in *NME* provided a rare dissenting voice: "It's bad enough that Christmas is so commercialised and money grabbing but to make a video of the birth of Jesus and the Star Of Bethlehem (it would have been okay if it had been Cliff) is going too far," ranted one Nancy Perry of Hoddesdon, Herts.

an influence," an infant school teacher who had been writing that year's Nativity play told the *Cheshire Observer*. "At least it's about the Christmas story."[9]

'The Power of Love' went straight in at No. 3 on 1 December, helped hugely by a showing of the video on the previous week's *Top of the Pops* – a rare honour, since the show hardly ever screened videos or performances of songs before they charted. Such was the power of Frankie that the rules were bent. The following week it rose two places to No. 1, making Frankie Goes To Hollywood the first band to have their first three singles top the chart since Gerry and the Pacemakers in 1963. Though it stayed at the top for only one week, it hung around the charts for nine and capped a remarkable year for the band – one they ultimately would never better.

Their closest rivals for the crown, at least their closest rivals that weren't a cartoon bear or a charity collective, had dominated 1984 as much as Frankie had, though without the latter's *NME*-approved hipness.[10] Wham! had enjoyed a couple of hits the previous year, particularly the sun-kissed 'Club Tropicana', but had supercharged their career with their second album, *Make It Big*. George Michael and Andrew Ridgeley, two lower middle-class kids from suburban

---

"Come on Frankies, I know you're talentless, we all know you're talentless, but this! A porno vid would have been an improvement."

[9] The band themselves were only added at the last minute after ZTT got cold feet about having a Frankie Goes to Hollywood video without Frankie Goes To Hollywood. A gilt frame was hastily added, featuring the band as cherubs and with Holly Johnson at the bottom of the image, singing upwards, his eyes turned toward God as in a Renaissance painting. The whole thing, without really trying, ends up being satisfyingly camp.

[10] Actually, that's not entirely true: when they'd emerged in 1983 with 'Wham Rap!' and 'Young Guns (Go For It)', songs about being young and on the dole in Thatcher's Britain, the music press had taken them at face value as socially aware and political. However, though the songs were sincere, that's not who Wham! wanted to be, and they set about consciously repositioning themselves into the *Smash Hits* camp. Once 'Club Tropicana' with its budgie-smuggling holiday video came along the pseuds over at *NME* and *Melody Maker* got very sniffy indeed. As did their readers – when *Melody Maker* ran an interview with George Michael in 1984 the paper was flooded with letters of complaint. Wham! were pure pop and proud of it.

Essex, both the children of first-generation immigrants, had met at school and bonded over a shared love of Queen and Elton John. Ridgeley, the better looking, more outgoing and more charismatic of the pair, had been the driving force to begin with, talking his friend (whom he affectionately nicknamed "Yog" after struggling to pronounce his Greek birthname – Georgios Panayiotou) into forming a band and pushing into the big time. By 1984, though, it was clear who was the major talent in Wham!. George had blossomed magnificently as a singer and a songwriter, had grown well and truly into his looks and positively glowed with pop star charisma. Wham! were pure pop – two good-looking boys in their early twenties who loved music and clubbing. Their songs, from their debut 'Wham Rap!' onwards were *about*, targeted *at*, and powered *by* the energy of youth. As such the duo had known from the start that their band had a built-in obsolescence. Wham! was not a unit either could picture themselves in at 30. That was never the point. It would be betraying the whole feel and purpose. Wham! *only* made sense while its members were carefree, rambunctious 20-somethings. What became clear, as George's potential bloomed, was that the group's real purpose, aside from a party pop machine in itself, was as a launch pad for a future global superstar. Andrew Ridgeley, with commendable grace, realised the best thing he could do for his friend was to get out of his way. He had bowed out of the songwriting altogether, knowing they weren't operating on the same level anymore, and his voice and guitar are hardly noticeable, if they're present at all, on the band's biggest hits.[11]

It had been a banner year for the duo. Three No. 1s in a row: 'Wake Me Up Before You Go-Go', 'Careless Whisper', 'Freedom'.

---

[11] That year's 'Careless Whisper' had, in the UK at least, been marketed as a George Michael solo single, essentially a water-testing soft launch for his post-Wham! career. A persistent urban legend has it that a grateful George gave his partner a songwriting credit as a thank you. Ridgeley has every right to be annoyed – the aching, poignant 'Careless Whisper' is a legitimate co-write between the two. In fact, it was one of the first things they'd written together. With some irony, his only co-writing credit in the most successful year of his life was on a song he doesn't appear on. As we shall see, it was a later Wham! single that truly deserved the title of solo hit.

Screaming fans and huge venues, massive success in the US, Australia, Japan, even communist China where they would shortly become the first Western pop artist to tour. Magazine covers, tabloids, shiny discs on the wall … the whole popstar shebang. The ambitious George, though, knew there was a piece missing. A year like that had only one cap. "It would be impossible to consider yourself the biggest success in the music business," Wham!'s manager, Simon Napier-Bell told the BBC in 2024, "without having a No. 1 at Christmas. Every major artist always seemed to have that No. 1. It became obsessively important to people."[12] George Michael obviously agreed, and pursued the perfect Christmas pop song with a thoroughness that might have seemed calculating if it hadn't come so easily to him.

The melody to what would become 'Last Christmas' had popped into his head one Sunday afternoon while he and Ridgeley had been watching football at the Panayiotous' house (both members of Wham! were, rather sweetly, still living with their parents). With no interest in football anyway, George had excused himself and headed up to his bedroom and the four-track portable studio and Roland synthesiser he'd recently acquired. It took him just an hour to throw together a sketch of the song, which he was able to play to his bandmate straight away. "He was in a state of high excitement," Ridgeley told the BBC. "*Oh my god*, I thought. *That's it. He's absolutely nailed it. A bafflingly brilliant work of genius.*" He elaborated in his memoir of the period, *Wham! George & Me*: "I listened to a basic track that had been recorded on his synthesiser, its instantly memorable chorus hummed over the top, and beamed. George had captured the very heartbeat of Christmas, framing its lyrics within the pain of a broken romance." The demo was fleshed out into a full studio version a few weeks later, George producing the song, as he had all of their recent singles, with the help of engineer Chris Porter "translating his ideas with the technology". The label in the middle of the disc may have said "Wham!", but 'Last Christmas' was the most purely solo effort of George Michael's entire career. An absolute perfectionist about his music, he played every instrument

---

[12] This isn't *quite* true. It's something of a myth that's been repeated so many times that people who should know better started to believe it.

on the admittedly quite minimal track: bass guitar, synthesiser, the distinctive sound of a LinnDrum drum machine (which was very much the sound of early '80s pop) and, of course, sleigh bells. Not that 'Last Christmas' sounds in any way plastic or artificial. How could it when, at its heart, it is one of pop's most achingly pure vocal performances?

It's hard to think of another Christmas pop song as perfect as Wham!'s 'Last Christmas'.[13] George Michael knew what he was about. For a start, George *loved* Christmas. Every year, for the rest of his life, he would gather his close circle of friends around him for Christmas parties, dinner, even door-to-door carol singing (though he'd hang back in the group when that happened, since the sight of one of the most famous artists in the world gleefully singing 'Once In Royal David's City' on the doorstep tended to raise eyebrows). "December gave him the opportunity to do all of his favourite things," said Wham! backing singer Helen "Pepsi" DeMacque in the book she wrote with fellow Whamette, Shirlie Kemp,[14] "throwing parties, buying presents for people, decorating and dressing up … Christmas brought out George's best sides – his boyish enthusiasm and his legendary generosity." You can see that spirit in the video to the song, which saw the boys and their entourage decamping to Saas-Fee in Switzerland for what amounted to a boozy Alpine holiday that just happened to be filmed. Pepsi & Shirlie, alongside

---

[13] And that includes Barry Manilow's 'Can't Smile Without You', a song similar enough that Manilow took the band to court. The case was thrown out when the band's legal team found a musicologist to present dozens of other songs from all eras with a similar chord sequence and melody. Since all proceeds from 'Last Christmas' ended up going to Ethiopian famine relief anyway, Manilow's attempt to grab a slice of the pie seems particularly cynical.

[14] Pepsi & Shirlie, as they became known, were a huge part of Wham!. Shirlie had been at school with George and Andrew, and had briefly dated the latter. When the band started to happen she was roped in, along with another singer, Dee C. Lee, to help pad out the group's stage act. When Lee left to join Style Council ("I don't like [Wham!'s] music *at all*, but they know that," she told *Smash Hits* in 1985), Pepsi – a professional singer – was drafted in as her replacement and the quartet became firm friends. As cool as they looked on stage and as important as their vocals were, Pepsi & Shirlie's biggest contribution to Wham! was camaraderie and company.

several other old friends, had formed a protective ring around the duo which had solidified into a tight circle as their fame started to rise to ridiculous levels, so the enthusiasm and warmth on display in the video were absolutely genuine. Only Kathy Hill, the model employed to play George's love interest (and, indeed, Andrew's, such was the plot) came from outside of the group, though she was quickly adopted into it. The song, of course, is classic Christmas melancholy, something which is emphasised by the closeness and familiarity of the gang on-screen. George, a connoisseur of Christmas, absolutely knew that projecting loneliness into the heart of warmth was part of the secret recipe.

'Last Christmas' is probably the best example of what we've been calling *Miserable Christmas*. Like 'White Christmas', a song that's definitely somewhere in its DNA, and especially like Elvis Presley's 'Blue Christmas' (which had itself been a minor hit for Welsh rocking throwback Shakin' Stevens the previous year) and Mud's 'Lonely This Christmas', it has a timeless, winning narrative. *Once upon a time, Christmas was happy. Then my heart was broken and now it's just a reminder of what I've lost.* As someone from a close family, with close friends who *loved* Christmas more than any other time of year, George had a fundamental understanding of the season's warmth, which made it easy for him to flip the coin and show its worst aspect. The fact that the season is *so* magical, *so* warm and *so* concerned with closeness and love makes the loneliness and the hurt of betrayal so very much sharper.

There's also some fairly clear subtext in the song's straightforward *boy meets girl, boy loses girl* narrative. George Michael was gay, and though he was open about that with those closest to him, he was still closeted as far as the wider public was concerned. There's traces of that double identity here. For starters, there's nothing in the song itself to indicate that George isn't talking about a man – though he never suggested publicly that the lyric was based on any real situation. In this context though, the key line comes in the second verse, where he describes himself as "a man undercover". There's certainly some autobiography there. He felt his image as a teen heartthrob, available to millions of swooning schoolgirls, was too important to his brand and that news of his sexuality getting out would harm his career. Matching him with a good-looking woman to moon over in the video was a necessary misdirection. A man undercover, indeed. That subtext leaks into the poignancy of the song – how could it not? That Christmas he gave everyone his heart. It's there on every note.

'Last Christmas' wasn't the Christmas No. 1 that year – prevented by a unique set of circumstances. It certainly *would* have been, though. Any other year. Released as a double A-side with the soulful, sophisticated 'Everything She Wants' – the clearest hint yet of the direction of George's solo career – the single went straight in at No. 2 on the week of 15 December and stayed at No. 2 for five straight weeks. It was, until recently, the biggest selling British single to never get to No. 1, a statistic that was spoiled in 2021... not because it was outsold, but because it disqualified itself by finally topping the chart in the week after Christmas. The song is the very definition of a Christmas classic, probably more ubiquitous in December than any other British pop single. So ubiquitous, in fact, that in 2015 an internet meme started to circulate called Whamageddon, in which people were challenged to go from 1 December to Christmas Eve without hearing 'Last Christmas' out in the wild, making a charity donation when they were inevitably caught out. It's become something of an annual tradition.

Streaming and downloads have ensured that 'Last Christmas' enters the Top 5 every year and in 2023 George Michael's wish finally came true: 'Last Christmas' became the Christmas No. 1, a feat it repeated the following year for its 40th anniversary. It won't be the last time. If you're reading this book in December, there's every chance it's No. 1 even now. George and his song are now inexorably wound up with the season, especially in the UK. This was double underlined on Christmas day, 2016, when millions of Christmas dinners were interrupted by the awful news of the death of George Michael, aged just 53. Depending on your perspective, the date was either very fitting or an extremely bitter irony.

Back in 1984, there was no chance of Wham! bagging the Christmas top spot, something that even a month before seemed an absolute certainty. And it wasn't any single by an iconic 80s artist that blocked their way. It was *all* of them. All at once. Because unbeknown to Wham!, Frankie, McCartney and the rest, the world was about to change.

Chapter 10
1984 PART TWO –
IN OUR WORLD OF PLENTY

In which pop music tries to feed the world,
and shifts it on its axis

Bob Geldof, lead singer of the Irish new wave band the Boomtown Rats, was not having a particularly great 1984. The Rats had been a big deal; in 1978, the brilliant R & B of their hit 'Rat Trap', with its breathless, tumbling vocal and dirty, ripped saxophone hook, became the first song by an Irish band to top the UK charts. A year later Geldof had written his masterpiece, 'I Don't Like Mondays', a sort of modern pop murder ballad inspired by a real-life school shooting; stark and emotive and arresting. It was a remarkable record, lyrically nuanced and built around a rippling piano that lodged in the brain, and it was a deserved global hit, even reaching the US *Billboard* chart. The song stayed at No. 1 in the UK for four weeks. Alas, it had been diminishing returns ever since and the '80s had not been kind. By 1984, the band found themselves relegated to the university circuit when once they could command theatres, and their sixth album, *In the Long Grass* and next two singles all failed to make the Top 40.

Geldof, a man for whom the phrase *the gift of the gab* could have been coined, was refusing to give in to despair and had taken over a desk at his label, Phonogram, so he could act as his own PR and record plugger, working the phones and his contacts to try to breathe some life into the campaign for his latest single, 'Dave', a tribute to the band's sax player, whose wife had been found dead. It was a great song – Geldof still thinks of it as one of his best. The public, alas, ignored it completely. As gifted a lyricist and as charismatic a frontman as Geldof was, as brilliant as his band could be, it was clear to anyone paying attention that his was a career on the slide. If history was looking for a pop star to make a record that would save millions of lives and shift pop culture, just slightly, on its axis, it would presumably have flipped quite far through its Rolodex before settling on the name "Bob Geldof". Still … cometh the hour, cometh the man.

On the evening of 23 October, while Frankie Goes to Holly-wood and Wham! were readying their assaults on the festive chart, a despondent Geldof trudged home to the house he shared with his wife, Paula Yates – a journalist for *Record Mirror* and the co-host of Channel 4's alternative pop show *The Tube*, and their baby daughter, Fifi Trixibelle. That night they did the same thing that millions of families across the country did – they switched on the television and watched the news. What they saw would change Geldof's life forever. It would also change British culture.

The BBC's Michael Buerk was reporting from Ethiopia, where a brutal famine following years of drought exacerbated by over-farming, an exploding population and government corruption had swollen into a humanitarian catastrophe of horrifying proportions. Five million people were at risk of death from starvation. It was, as Burke said in his report, a "biblical famine". No one who has seen that report will ever forget it. This was humanity pushed to the very edge of survival, captured on film for the world to see. Indeed, many were pushed *beyond* survival. What Buerk found, and filmed, in a camp established at the small Ethiopian town of Korem, what families across Britain saw that night, was death.

"Dawn, and as the sun breaks through the piercing chill of night on the plains outside Korem, it lights up a biblical famine, now, in the twentieth century," his report began. "This place, say workers here, is the closest thing to hell on earth." Women and men and children, dead or dying. Bodies skeletal or unnaturally distended. Clouds of flies. Utter helplessness. What Geldof later called in his book *Tales of Boomtown Glory* "the horrifying pornography of starving human beings". In the camp, Buerk said, in tones of horror and pity and barely contained anger, someone, an adult or a child, dies every 20 minutes. A starving three-year old girl perishes in her mother's arms. A man, his skin stretched across his skeleton, fleshless, age indeterminate, offers up the corpse of his emaciated child to be counted. A young nurse, Claire, an aid worker, is forced to choose who to give food and water to, knowing she was condemning to death those she didn't pick. Sixty tons of food, which Ethiopia didn't have, was needed every month to halt starvation on an unprecedented level in the modern world. It was heartbreaking. Inhuman. And made more so because it was happening in a time of so much abundance.

News stories in the UK that year had talked about a record harvest, with grain surpluses, food stockpiles and "butter mountains" taking up warehouse space across the country thanks to generous farming subsidies. Mining families hit by the strike might be struggling, but communities had rallied round to help. Pop stars played benefit shows. It was hard, but people were surviving. All that was put into perspective on the television that autumn night. In the late twentieth century, when humanity prided itself on having come so far, on putting man on the moon, on developing supersonic travel and creating weapons that could wipe out cities in seconds, in a world of computers and satellites where it felt like the future had arrived … babies were starving to death. And nobody was helping. As Geldof wrote in his autobiography, *Is That It?*, a few years later, "a horror like this could not occur today without our consent." Droughts were natural disasters, but famines? A famine in 1984's world of plenty could only be created by mankind's neglect.

It's not that people hadn't been aware that this horrible event was happening. Back in July an ITV documentary, *Seeds of Despair*, had shown similar scenes to those Buerk captured, exploring the sociopolitical landscape that had led to the current catastrophe and noting the farmers who had to choose between using their seeds as food, meaning no harvest and probably starvation in the future, or saving those seeds for next year's crop and risking death now. The piece was powerful enough to kick the British government into action, and an aid programme had been hastily put together. Since then, Ethiopia had been a consistent newspaper story but it had rarely made the big headlines. People were aware that *something* was going on, and that it was pretty bad; there were already benefits and fundraisers being organised. It was small stuff, but every little helped. Still, the geopolitical background tended to cloud things. Ethiopia was a communist country engaged in a civil war and backed militarily by the Soviet Union, which made Western governments queasy about getting involved. There were also reports that grain and aid weren't getting to the right people. Such complications can often dull the public's interest until, eventually, they stop paying attention. The BBC report, so vivid and so stark and so horrible, brought it back to the surface.

The response was immediate. The BBC switchboard was jammed, almost before the report ended, with members of the public asking how they could help and where they could send money. Major relief agencies like Oxfam found themselves manning their phones into the small hours as donations flooded in. The next day, the newspapers were all carrying the story. The *Daily Mirror* launched a national campaign for donations and its billionaire owner, Robert Maxwell, funded planes to get food where it was needed. The famine in Ethiopia seemed to put everything else into perspective, including the current pet concerns of the pop intelligentsia. "The miner's strike is voluntary," one letter to *Smash Hits* went. "The horrific tragedy of the Ethiopian famine is not. But do we hear of the people clambering to the aid of Oxfam and other worthy charities with donations, benefit gigs etc to attempt to even *begin* putting this right? No ... I'm sure Duran Duran could spare a few bob, and if the Ethiopians were paid up members of the Labour Party maybe Paul Weller, Heaven 17 and Billy Bragg could see their way to care?" Another letter was even more direct: "With children dying of starvation in Ethiopia and various charitable organisations desperately in need of funds, I would like to tell George Michael that his squandering of £50,000 on videos ... is a prime example of his thoughtless selfish vanity." The target may have been Wham!, but it could have been directed at any of Britain's pop stars. In a divided Britain, the images of Ethiopia's catastrophe had united people around one very simple, very direct question: *What can we do?* And by extension: *Why aren't you doing anything?*

That night, Bob Geldof found he couldn't sleep. He was unable to shake the images of the death and the flies and the dying babies from his head, desperate and driven to help in some way. He briefly considered donating the proceeds from a Boomtown Rats single to Oxfam but was realistic enough to know what a drop in the ocean that would be, especially given his band's fading profile – something that suddenly seemed unimportant. Back at his desk the next day, he found he couldn't focus on promoting his single. People were dying. Nothing else mattered. Everyone in the office was talking about the BBC report, and Geldof's suggestion of a record to raise money was met with enthusiasm – meaning that he would at least have the support of a label. And since no one would bother about a Boomtown Rats charity single, the obvious move was to bring someone else in. Someone substantially more famous. That night he phoned his wife, who was on set of *The Tube*, Channel 4's edgier response to *Top of the Pops*, and told her about his plan, asking: "Who's on the show this week?" "Ultravox," she replied, and put Midge Ure on the phone.

Jim "Midge" Ure had a career that mapped itself completely onto the British music scene of the last decade. In the mid '70s he'd been in a post-glam bubblegum band called Slik who'd even had a No. 1, 1976's 'Forever and Ever'. After that band's demise he'd been swept along by punk, playing in the Rich Kids with former Sex Pistol Glen Matlock, had a spell playing guitar in Thin Lizzy and got involved in London's Blitz Kid scene: the arty, decadent gang of exhibitionist ex-punk Bowie obsessives who centred their lives around a weekly night at the Blitz Club in Covent Garden and between them managed to create a year zero for a lot of '80s pop culture. He'd formed Visage with fellow Rich Kid Rusty Egan and local scenesters Steve Strange and Billy Currie, and their 1980 single 'Fade To Grey' became one of the first big hits of the synth-pop era, helping to establish the cultural dominance of what would become known as the New Romantics – synth-driven groups born out of that intense London scene of make-up and escapism that also birthed Spandau Ballet and Culture Club, alongside a generation of young creatives working across the arts, and influencing concurrent scenes up and down the country from which would spring Duran

Duran, Heaven 17, Soft Cell and the Human League. It was Currie who dragged Ure into his other band, Ultravox, to replace departed frontman John Foxx. Ure completely revitalised them, pushing the group into gloomy synth-pop, resulting in their massive 1980 single 'Vienna', a UK No. 2 and a huge hit around the world. By 1984 Midge Ure was part of British pop's big league – a career that had ticked up just as Bob Geldof's had ticked down. He was a singer, songwriter, guitarist, keyboard player, producer and studio engineer – an extremely useful pop Swiss Army Knife.

Dropping into Paula Yates' dressing room after that evening's *Tube* recording, he found a telephone thrust in his face with Bob Geldof on the other end, ranting about Ethiopia and saying he wanted to make a record to raise money. Ure quickly agreed to help. He hadn't yet seen the BBC report, but that didn't matter. "You don't," he said later, "say 'No' to Bob." A few days later the pair met to discuss their options. Covering an old classic was out of the question, since that would mean giving up almost half of the earnings through royalties. No, the clear path was to write an original song. Geldof felt he had something they could work with already, a rough tune called 'It's My World' that could be retooled, but he was uncharacteristically nervous about putting it forward. His confidence in that department had been shaken by his band's descent through pop's ranks. Geldof's hesitancy surprised and rather irked his friend – Ure was a busy man, and he had no time to deal with Bob Geldof feeling sorry for himself. "I kicked him up the backside," he later wrote, telling him, "You are a songwriter; just write a song." And so Geldof did.

Swiss Army Midge was an important first call. Not only was he a capable songwriter and producer in his own right, he was also a hit machine. Ultravox were a big deal at the time, and their last four albums had all gone Top 5. Just that year they'd enjoyed a Top 3 hit with the rather good 'Dancing With Tears in My Eyes'. Midge Ure's involvement meant this couldn't be seen as a niche project by a washed-up star – it would be contemporary. *Smash Hits* and the tabloids could get involved. This was the boost Geldof needed to kick things up a gear. He wasn't just phoning people to say: "I'm doing a song, are you in?". He was able to say: "Midge Ure is writing it with me." It meant people listened.

His next call was to Sting, currently on a hiatus from the Police[1] and in the process of launching a solo career. He agreed straight-away. Emboldened, Geldof moved on to Duran Duran's Simon le Bon. "Who's involved?" "I've got Midge Ure and Sting." "We'll do it."[2] Suddenly they had three huge names. After that, everyone else fell like dominoes. No one wanted to miss out on something every-one else was doing. As an insider, albeit one who hadn't had a hit in years, Geldof could call artists directly and not worry about man-agers acting as gatekeepers. On the same day that Sting and Le Bon had been cornered, Gary Kemp, guitarist and musical driving force in Spandau Ballet, was looking at antiques in a shop on the Kings Road in Chelsea, haggling over the price of a hanging lamp, when a frantic hammering broke out against the window. It was Bob Geldof – who happened to be walking past and had spotted a pop star. A few minutes later, Spandau were on board, double underlined when Geldof ran into Kemp's brother Martin, Spandau's bass player, at a party that night. Each door seemed to open another, and the re-markable thing was that almost everyone wanted to help.[3] U2. Paul Weller. Wham!. Culture Club. Those who weren't available found other ways to support the project – Frankie Goes to Hollywood and Paul McCartney were abroad but agreed to send messages that could be used on the B-side, as did Eurythmics and David Bowie, who agreed to record an intro for the video. Trevor Horn, Frankie's won-der producer, donated a day in his SARM studios in West London.[4]

---

[1] As it turned out, quite a *long* hiatus. The band got back together for Live Aid the following year, tried and failed to make a new album in 1986 and then stayed out of each other's way until 2007.

[2] For weeks Le Bon assumed the song would be a duet between him and Sting, not realising Geldof was approaching everyone.

[3] Geldof has been cagey over the years about the few acts that turned him down, generously sparing their blushes. All, apparently, were a result of approaching management rather than artists directly. One such was certainly Human League, whose manager apparently pitched it to them as "Do you want to make a record with Bob Geldof?" – in the autumn of 1984, that was hardly a compelling offer.

[4] Horn was originally approached to produce, which made sense since he was probably the country's hottest producer at the time. He claimed he'd need six weeks to record and mix a single. Since they wanted to get it done in 24 hours

Still the names came. Phil Collins. Paul Young. Bananarama. The label agreed to waive all fees. Geldof called the major record retailers and asked them to give up their profits on the single, telling each one that their rival outlets had already agreed. Status Quo. Kool & the Gang. Heaven 17. Peter Blake, the artist responsible for the iconic cover to the Beatles' album *Sgt. Pepper's Lonely Hearts Club Band,* agreed to do the artwork.

The music press offered advertising space for free. The *Daily Mirror* gave them a front page exclusive.[5] The Musician's Union agreed to waive its royalties. The pressing plants offered to work overnight for free. The ladies who packed record sleeves did unpaid overtime. "Even those mysterious characters who put up fly posters are doing it for nothing," Geldof told *Music Week*. Eventually he was able to order, harangue, bluster and bully the entire record industry into giving up its profits and donating its costs – from the moment Midge Ure pressed record on the mixing desk at SARM to the moment someone ran a 7" single through the till at Woolworths, almost every penny would go to Ethiopia. A remarkable feat. After all, he had the ultimate trump card: people were *dying*. The only sticking point was the VAT – on which Her Majesty's Government was immovable.

Bringing in Midge Ure, someone who could help write the song and quickly and throw together a recording was important, but it was Geldof who made the whole thing happen. His talent wasn't recording or producing, it wasn't even songwriting, *per se*. Geldof's talent was *words*. The power of them. He could talk the birds out of the trees. He was possessed of a particularly intense charisma and had the rare ability to channel passion into articulacy. When he had the bit between his teeth, he was unstoppable. "His was a genius of vocabulary and communication," U2's Bono said in his book *Songs*

---

or so, it was decided that Midge Ure would produce. Horn ended up doing the 12" mix.

[5] Originally Geldof had been told that the song wasn't important enough for the front page. He had then pointed out that *his* story involved all of the biggest pop stars in Britain and would literally save lives, while the cover of that day's issue was the back of the Princess of Wales' head. In the end he called Robert Maxwell directly.

of Surrender. "Words would do anything for him. It was as if the words knew how much respect he had for them and decided to give him special permission to improvise." It was as Midge Ure had said – nobody says no to Bob. Later, *Life* magazine would ponder why Bob Geldof, a washed-up Irish pop star who couldn't get arrested six months earlier, had been the one to achieve all of this. "Did God knock at the wrong door by mistake," pondered the article, "and when it was opened by this scruffy Irishman, think 'Oh, what the hell – He'll do.'?"

Geldof wasn't divinely chosen, accidentally or otherwise. He was simply the perfect person in the perfect place. Most useful was his utter inability to take no for answer, no matter what the excuse. "To Geldof it didn't matter," wrote Midge Ure in his memoir. "He was electric, impassioned, utterly driven by what he believed in … if [anyone] tried to wriggle out of it, Bob had no conscience – he resorted to intimidation and blackmail. 'I'll tell the world that you've fucking turned it down because you can't be arsed.'"

Next the project needed a name. *Band Aid* came from someone in the Phonogram office, and stuck mostly because nobody could think of anything better. Also considered were Food For Thought and The Bloody Do Gooders, neither of which inspired much excitement, mostly because both were terrible. Band Aid was not much better, though Geldof liked it. It's a serviceable pun – his group of stars would be, literally, a band, providing aid, and also attempting to put a sticking plaster on a gaping wound. The name would do. More important was the song itself, although Geldof has often said otherwise. No one needed to listen to it. They just needed to *buy* it "Even if you hate the song," Bob Geldof said in one interview, "buy it and throw it away."

Still, beneath the bluster Ure and Geldof had their pride. The song needed to be good enough to hook people. Geldof had worked his earlier sketch into a ramshackle, acoustic demo and rewritten the lyrics, which were corny but also had a certain urgency. It worked, just about. Working in his home studio, Ure then did the mother of all polishing jobs, neatening the whole thing up, adding an instrumental keyboard hook,[6] changing the key and generally turning a

---

[6] "It sounds like *Z Cars*," remarked Geldof, referring to the jaunty theme tune to the classic '60s police show. It does, rather.

scrappy tape that sounded like a drunk Bob Dylan improvising a sea shanty, into something relatively tight. He also worked on the lyrics a little, so he takes the blame for the most ridiculed line in the song "And there won't be snow in Africa this Christmastime"; there are, of course, many places on the African continent that get snow. The original line had been ". . . there won't be snow in Ethiopia" – which didn't fit; it was one too many syllables and sat awkwardly in the melody. *Africa*, meanwhile, sat perfectly. It was a hasty nip and tuck, but one that has come in for much criticism over the years – not just for its factual inaccuracy, but because of the implication that the entire African continent was somehow homogenous. It makes the lyric feel overgeneralised and othering.

Does 'Do They Know It's Christmas?' deserve the occasional kicking it gets for its lyrics? Yes and no. It *is* something of a blunt instrument, lyrically. Even its title isn't exactly thought through: Ethiopia's 60% Orthodox Christian population would likely still have marked Christ's birth, even amid their sorrows, though since they celebrated Christmas on 7 January, in line with other Orthodox churches, chances are they wouldn't be doing so just yet. "Where nothing ever grows, no rain or rivers flow" would be fine without the word *ever* … Ethiopia's drought was severe, but not permanent. The country has regions with fertile land, seasonal rains and flowing rivers, though its climate varies widely. Such lyrics added weight to a cynical interpretation that's followed the song through the years: "white saviours" swooping in to rescue a rich and sophisticated culture it perceived as primitive – at best it was cloth-eared and patronising, at worst actually kind of racist. It's a harsh interpretation, and not helped by the fact that only two artists of colour appear on the song; Kool & the Gang's Robert Bell and Shalamar's Jody Watley, neither of whom, despite being among the best singers in the room, has a solo line.[7] The campaign to supply emergency aid to famine-struck Ethiopia was, by necessity, powered by images of suffering. None of that thinking was in the DNA of the project, which was a sincere mission to help desperate people, but that doesn't make the criticisms invalid.

---

[7] Bell's appearance, especially, caused a ruckus among the British stars. No one wanted to embarrass themselves in front of a singer *that* good.

And yet Geldof and Ure's song, on balance, wears its good intentions on its sleeve and wears them well. Geldof's lyrics are piercing and pin-sharp when they need to be. We *do* live in a "world of plenty" and that '80s excess contrasted ever more sharply with the images of Ethiopia's need as Christmas approached. After gently appealing to our sense of seasonal charity in the first verse ("Throw your arms around the world"), the song sticks in the knife in the second. The world beyond our artificially frosted and fairy-lit windows is one of "dread and fear" where the only water to be found, as Geldof says in one of his best lines, sang by Sting, "is the bitter sting of tears".[8] We'd had *Miserable Christmas* songs before, of course, but rarely are their themes this stark, this direct. The kicker comes at the end of the verse with one of the song's most often discussed lines, a line that was given to U2's Bono: "Well, tonight, thank God it's them," sings the devoutly Catholic singer, his voice sounding urgent and desperate, "instead of you." To some it's an astonishingly harsh lyric ("Cruel, imperious, myopic disdain," wrote the journalist Wyndham Wallace in a 2014 essay for *The Quietus*. "Is this really the most we can expect people to do: to pat themselves on the back and praise the Lord for taking care of them?") How could we be grateful this was happening to *anyone*? And yet the line speaks to something fundamental, something everyone feels when seeing images such as those relayed from the camp at Korem: *There but by the grace of God go we*. It's an astonishingly confrontational lyric, one that stops you in your tracks. It shames us. It makes us feel guilty. Perhaps that's one of the reasons people dislike it so much. Bono himself understood that straightaway. When handed the lyrics to the song he pointed straight at that line and said, "I'll sing anything but that." To Geldof, though, it *had* to be Bono. U2 weren't even especially famous at that point, and at the recording some of the bigger acts wondered what such small fry were doing among the great and the good of British pop. The answer was *that* line. And in Bono it found its most perfect expression. "He just has a profound rage," Geldof told *Rolling Stone* in 2014. "If you listen to the way

---

[8] Sting wasn't super keen to sing a line with his own name in it. Yet it gives his delivery an added and effective bitterness.

the emotion of the song scales up, that's the big powerful explosion. That became a phenomenon, which none of us expected."

'Do They Know It's Christmas?' ends on a rousing refrain of "Feed the world", the term that became the song's slogan: its one-line pitch. A phrase that really did cut through the cynicism and politics and boil the cause down to its most basic, vital message: Feeding the hungry. It's that, more than anything, that connects 'Do They Know It's Christmas?' to the season. It goes back to Dickens and *A Christmas Carol*: "it is a time of all others when Want is keenly felt and Abundance rejoices." Geldof's inspiration, as he asserts in his autobiography, was John Lennon, who in 'Give Peace A Chance' and 'Happy Xmas (War Is Over)' created perfect slogan choruses, reducing complicated emotional and political narratives to a catchy soundbite that defined the song: "all we are saying is give peace a chance", "war is over if you want it". "Feed the world" sits among them.

The Band Aid project was announced to the world on page five of the *Daily Mirror* on Saturday 24 November, the day before recording was scheduled, under the headline "The Top 20 On One Record". That week's *Record Mirror* also carried a news splash, stating that "Wham! David Bowie, Paul Young, Duran Duran, Spandau Ballet, Frankie Goes To Hollywood, and Paul McCartney are just some of the stars to be featured on a special single to raise money for the starving in Ethiopia," the latter report either glossing over or unaware that McCartney, Bowie and the Frankie boys were appearing only via telephoned message on the B-side. It was enough publicity to ensure that a smattering of fans and paparazzi alike were gathered outside SARM the following day as recording got underway and artists started to turn up.

Recording commenced early in the morning on Sunday, 25 November, though a lot of the legwork had been done the previous day at Ure's studio, where Sting, Paul Weller and Duran Duran's John Taylor had added bass and guitar and, in Sting's case, backing vocals (he'd later brag that his backing vocals forced everyone else to follow his phrasing). Addressing the cameras the following morning a bleary-eyed Bob Geldof admitted "at the minute there's only me and Midge here … ask me again [how it's gone] at the same time tonight." If Geldof was worried, he needn't have been. In dribs and drabs, the stars began to arrive. Most in low-key ways – Sting strolled casually around the corner with a coffee and that morning's *Observer* looking like he was getting ready to walk the dog, while a brutally hungover Duran Duran and Spandau Ballet both turned up in the limos their labels had put on for them. The two bands had been on the same German TV show the previous evening and had spent the rest of the night trying to outdrink one another before, quite literally, racing each other's private jets back to Heathrow in time to do "Bob Geldof's thing". Once the two bands saw every-one else turning up on foot or in cabs, or in Bananarama's case, tumbling out of a tiny two-door Golf GTI, they began to worry about the optics. "It occurred to me," wrote Spandau's Gary Kemp in his memoir, "that the black Daimler Princess we were riding in did not strike quite the right tone of humility for such an event as the recording of a song highlighting the starvation of a nation." His brother Martin, writing in his own book *Ticket to the World*, agreed: "Here come Spandau Ballet, turning up to help the starving chil-dren of Ethiopia in a luxury car, having just raced Learjets across the Channel, swanning through Heathrow escorted by ten policemen per band member." He had a point.

Still, the Band Aid recording was notable for its camaraderie and good cheer. This was a group of people who were rarely all to-gether in the same room, and most found they got on relatively well, with egos checked at the door and rivalries discarded. "There hasn't been one individual that had an ego problem," SARM's co-owner, Jill Sinclair, says on the song's making-of documentary. "Everybody has completely mucked in, nobody has been difficult in the slight-est." Few harsh words were exchanged, though a characteristically grumpy Paul Weller did pull George Michael aside and castigate him for calling Arthur Scargill a "wanker" at a recent miner's bene-fit.[9] (George's response was to deploy the same insult again: "Don't be a wanker all your life. Have a day off.") The press had constantly pitted Duran and Spandau against each other, yet here they were,

---

[9] "He really did annoy me. He just seemed to be enjoying it all far too much. When I met him I got the impression that the only place he was leading the miners was further and further up their own asses," George told *The Face* the following year.

chummy as anything. Boy George and Simon Le Bon had swiped at each other in the press, but on arrival[10] the former grabbed the latter's hand and pulled him before the crowds saying, "Let's put some rumours to bed." Everyone mucked in, workshopping their parts as Ure doled them out, putting their own spin on their lines, elevating the song – especially in the case of the two Georges (Michael and Boy) who added octave jumps and vocal inflections, creating two of the song's best hooks. Status Quo's Rick Parfitt and Francis Rossi, meanwhile, larked about like rock's Chuckle Brothers, keeping spirits up by supplying the banter[11] and, inevitably, the cocaine. Phil Collins arrived to play some live drums, nailing his parts in two takes. Most turned up without doing their hair or make-up, despite the presence of the cameras filming for a music video and a documentary.[12] It was an uncynical and rather fun day. Everyone was there for the right reasons. The controlled chaos of the recording, including the camera crews, journalists, photographers, wives, girlfriends, children and pet dogs lent proceedings a festival atmosphere, a real sense of joy that's audibly present in the music that was created that day. Some had misgivings about the song itself – George Michael, apparently *hated* it, finding it far too depressing for a Christmas single. "A bit rich," wrote Martin Kemp, "seeing as his Christmas single, released that same year was all about getting your heart broken by a lover on Christmas Day." But no one let misgivings leak into their performance.

Mixing the record took all night, Ure getting increasingly annoyed as his cast leaned into the convivial party atmosphere and

---

[10] Many, *many* hours late – Boy George had begun his day in New York, where Culture Club had just played a huge show at Madison Square Garden. Geldof had called his hotel room and yelled at him through his hangover until, decently chastised, George hopped on Concorde at his own expense and made it to the recording by early evening. Once he realised the rest of the chart had turned up in his absence ("every cunt except you," as Geldof delicately put it) there was no way he was going to be outshone. "He sang his lines perfectly," wrote Ure, "then swanned out into the studio to spread mayhem and gossip."

[11] Constantly calling Ure "Mudge" and, later, "Smudge" is pure Spinal Tap.

[12] The exception being Duran Duran, who had actually arranged for a make-up artist to meet them at Heathrow, which was slightly cheating.

refused to leave, not getting that he had a job of work to get finished. As the biggest names in the country finally headed back to their lives, Ure and Geldof worked diligently into the night, including phoning stars to collect messages to be overlaid across the instrumental for the B-side.[13] There was no time for anything else – the song had to be ready for mastering that day, and would be sent for pressing straight afterwards. It was Geldof, the mastermind behind the whole thing, who took the final word on the recording: "This record was recorded on the twenty-fifth of November 1984. It is now eight a.m. on the twenty-sixth. We've been here twenty-four hours and I think it's time we went home. So from me, Bob Geldof, and Midge we say good morning to you all and a million thanks to everyone on the record. Have a lovely Christmas. Bye."

---

[13] Most notorious, and thankfully absent from the final version was Steve Norman from Spandau Ballet: "I'd like to say hi to all of our friends in Ethiopia. Sorry we can't make it down there this year, but maybe we'll get to tour there next year." "I owe whoever edited that Band Aid music video the coldest, crispest pint of their lives for not stitching us up and including any footage of that," wrote Martin Kemp.

Chapter 11
1984 PART THREE –
WE ALL STAND TOGETHER

Or how Band Aid changed the world

Bob Geldof didn't go home that morning. Instead he bolted across London to Radio 1's West End studios and offered them an exclusive play of the song. When they said they'd listen and consider it, Geldof stopped offering and started demanding. As usual, it worked. 'Do They Know It's Christmas?' made its radio debut on "The Nation's Favourite" just hours after recording had finished, with Geldof introducing the song on Simon Bates' mid-morning show. "Let's make this the biggest selling record of all time," he said. "'Mull of Kintyre' sold about two and a half million …. But there's 56 million people in this country. We can easily beat that. It's only £1.30. That's how cheap it is to give someone the ultimate Christmas gift – their life." He finished with a devastating soundbite: "It's pathetic, but the price of a life this year is a piece of plastic with a hole in the middle."[1] The response was immediate. The station began to play the record on the hour, every hour – unheard of for any song, even on the A-list. Meanwhile, that morning's *Daily Mirror* had hit the streets, the story taking up fully three quarters of the cover under

---

[1] "I thought I was a pious, over the top twat," he later admitted in his autobiography.

177

the headline "BILLION DOLLAR BAND! – Superstars sing for Ethiopia", accompanying a picture of George Michael, Bob Geldof, Sting and Simon Le Bon that went the width of the page. The centre spread of the paper carried the entire "class photo", featuring 36 of the 37 stars who appeared on the record – the picture having been taken while Boy George was still somewhere over the mid-Atlantic. The other tabloids, though lacking the insider access of the *Daily Mirror,* carried the story too. Everyone had photographers outside SARM that Sunday, even if they couldn't get through the door. Band Aid was *news*.

Things ratcheted up that week when the video premiered on BBC One – not, as you'd expect, on *Top of the Pops,* but just *before* it. The show's rules dictated that a song couldn't be featured ahead of its release, and despite pre-orders for the single at this point already passing 100,000, producers simply wouldn't budge. Geldof's solution was both unprecedented and completely audacious – he convinced BBC One controller Michael Grade to shift the entire evening's programming back by five minutes in order to show the video for 'Do They Know It's Christmas?' immediately ahead of that week's show. The screening went ahead almost as a party-political broadcast; essentially the only commercial advertisement that the BBC has ever shown. It was introduced by David Bowie, who listed the grim statistics ahead of the premiere: that, if something were not done, 4,000 children under the age of four would starve to death every day in Ethiopia in 1985. "I hope that you will buy a copy of this record over the Christmas period," said Bowie. "If you can't afford it, club together with someone else to buy a copy. You know that the money will go to the Ethiopians. Thank you." The video may not have featured on the following episode of *Top of the Pops* itself, but Band Aid made sure its presence was felt. Every artist performing in the studio – from presenters Janice Long and Peter Powell to Slade, Nick Kershaw, Kool & the Gang (whose singer, Robert Bell, was the only performer that day who had actually been on the Band Aid record), Alvin Stardust, Black Lace and current No. 1 Jim Diamond – wore a Band Aid "FEED THE WORLD" slogan T-shirt. You couldn't buy better publicity. Indeed, the reverse was true – not only was every star asked to wear a T-shirt, they were also asked to pay for it themselves ("a cool six nicker a go," reported

Melody Maker), with the fee going to the Band Aid Trust. Which, universally, they coughed up.

'Do They Know It's Christmas?' was released on 7 December, inevitably dooming Frankie Goes To Hollywood, who's 'Power of Love' had ousted Jim Diamond, to a single week at the top. The music press all carried adverts for free, though editorially their tone was rather cynical. *Melody Maker*'s gossip column, 'Talk Talk Talk', boasted at how its writer had been "shamed over our champers by Honest Bob Geldof's Career relaunch … *sorry*, heartfelt attempt to prick the consciences of the entire Western world." The paper's actual review of the single was rather more sympathetic, calling out the cynicism that dismissed the song as "a crass exploitation of a terrible natural catastrophe by a fading star desperate for publicity and self-promotion" as "simply cruel". That said, none of the music press reviews were particularly enamoured of the song itself. *Melody Maker* called it "inevitably, something of an anti-climax … which veers occasionally toward an uncomfortably generalised sentimentality." *NME* declared the single "The Turkey" of the week. Its' minimalist review, in full, read: "Millions of Dead Stars write and perform rotten record for the right reasons."[2] "Great cause," said a picture caption under the record's sleeve, "shame about …". *Record Mirror* was equally brutal: "It's pretty awful actually," said the paper's Andy Strike, "cringingly embarrassing lyrics about snow in the desert – that kind of thing, and a 'tune' that is forgettable." Strike went harder than his music press colleagues, however, questioning the deeper motivations of those involved: "It all seems a bit suspect to me. Does this mean the 'cream' of British pop can rest on its laurels for another 25 years and turn a blind eye to hardship? … wouldn't it be nice if all the acts involved had donated the mega bucks they'll make from their own Xmas records this year? The old colonial spirit lives on. Rule Britannia." Perhaps in response to this, but more likely out of characteristic human decency, Wham! announced shortly afterwards that they would indeed be donating royalties from 'Last

---

[2] This was a reference to that week's Single of the Week, 'Chicken Squawk' by Millions of Dead Children, a radical animal rights manifesto offshoot from US hardcore punks Millions of Dead Cops. *NME* in the '80s could be just a trifle self-righteous.

Christmas', released that same day, to Ethiopia. Of all the reviews, *Sounds* probably summed it up best: whatever you thought of the song, "it deserves to sell by the truckload".

Fortunately the wider public really didn't care what the music press had to say. They got their music news from the radio, the TV and the mainstream press – and those institutions were pushing Band Aid like nothing before. By the time the single was released, presales were at 200,000. That figure swelled to a million actual sales within a week of the disc hitting stores – the fastest-selling single in British history. Come the chart rundown it had comfortably dislodged Frankie at No. 1, and, for good measure, kept Wham!'s 'Last Christmas' at No. 2 – something George Michael tried very hard to be gracious about, despite being rather bitter behind the scenes ("it would irk him terribly," wrote Andrew Ridgeley in his memoir. "Not being regarded as the best by his audience, or peers, was one of his greatest sources of irritation.") During the recording of the single George told Paula Yates, filming for *The Tube*, that his ideal scenario would be for 'Do They Know It's Christmas?' to go to No. 1 and then be replaced by 'Last Christmas' in time for the big day itself. It quickly became very clear that this wasn't going to happen. Band Aid would stay at No. 1 well into January and was still in the charts as March rolled around.

To say the public responded is an understatement so great as to render the statement meaningless. It took three weeks for 'Do They Know It's Christmas?' to become the biggest-selling single in British history, surpassing 3 million sales just before the end of the year (a record it would hold for another 13 years, until overtaken by Elton John's 'Candle in the Wind', rewritten to commemorate the death of Diana, Princess of Wales). Eventually it sold four million copies in the UK, and eight million worldwide. It would have been a US No. 1, if not for the strange way the American charts were put together, combining sales, jukebox plays, radio and TV. On pure sales, at least according to Bob Geldof, it was outselling the No. 1 record, Madonna's 'Like A Virgin', by 400%. Eventually it would clear a 1.5 million US sales. Geldof's initial hope for the project was to raise £75,000 that could be donated to Oxfam or a similar charity. Band Aid's opening blast, across Christmas 1984 and into 1985, raised

£8 million. That was quickly turned into 1,000 tons of grain, 150 tons of high energy biscuits, 1,335 tons of milk powder, 560 tons of cooking oil and 470 tons of sugar. Rather than work through an existing charity, the Band Aid Trust was set up to administer the money and to ensure it got to the right places.[3]

This wasn't *just* a pop record, clearly. This was that rarest of things – a cultural phenomenon. Partly it was a way to unlock the helplessness that we inevitably feel in the face of horror on the scale of the Ethiopian famine. This was something people could actually *do*. A tangible action connected to a genuine, physical result. Buy a record. Save a life. It became simple, totemic. It's also no coincidence that this was a Christmas record. Celebrating the season through acts of charity was built into a British Christmas, as Dickens himself had noted. As the UK ramped up for the party season, it was hard to shake off the awful suffering happening on the other side of the television screen. Buying a copy of 'Do They Know It's Christmas?' became a salve for that feeling of guilt.

And yet, there was something about the impact of Band Aid which went beyond compassion for Ethiopia, beyond empathy, beyond even Christmas. The early '80s was a time of real division. Conservative vs Labour, North vs South, working class vs middle class, Unionist vs Republican, intellectual vs everyman, the miners vs the establishment, poverty vs wealth, the *Sun* vs the *Daily Mirror*, the *Sun* plus the *Mirror* vs the *Guardian* plus *The Times* – us vs them. 'Do They Know It's Christmas?' became a leveller and a unifier. Here was something we could all agree on. We were coming together. For Christmas. In many ways, that held an appeal that went *beyond* charity.

The song had sunk into culture, like a moisturiser soaks into skin. It no longer belonged to its creators. Within weeks it belonged to, well, Christmas. Very few songs achieve that. "It's strange to hear it now," wrote Martin Kemp, "Like [Spandau hits] 'Gold' and 'True' it's one of those songs that became so big that ... they've detached

---

[3] In this they were advised by George Harrison, who reached out especially to make sure the Trust got its accounting sorted. A decade earlier he'd organised the Concert for Bangladesh, raising money for another humanitarian disaster, but had been appalled to discover a lot of the funds raised were mismanaged.

themselves from me and exist now in the ether." It achieved penetration almost unheard of for a pop song – that Christmas it was added to carol concerts in schools across the country, included in Nativity plays and sang by door-to-door carol singers who donated the money they collected to famine relief. No one involved in Band Aid benefited financially from it, at least not directly, and thus it belonged to everyone, crossing borders of class and ideology. In a time of division, here was something that brought the country together. A pure, distilled and unspoilt manifestation of Christmas itself, in all of its forms. An editorial in *The Times* highlighted the record's spiritual value, especially noting the line "But say a prayer", and argued that engaging with the song, whether you realised it or not, was in itself an act of prayer: "to feel a deep and indescribable pain at the sight of strangers in distress … is to pray." And yet despite Bono, on the day of recording, teasing the profoundly atheist Geldof that he'd written a hymn, 'Do They Know It's Christmas?' speaks to a version of the season that goes way beyond its Christian roots. British Christmas songs, as we've discussed, are often celebrations of the season itself – a tradition going back centuries. The Band Aid single was Christmas distilled: giving, togetherness, celebration, community and, yes, if you looked for it, spirituality. It had everything. The most Christmas of Christmas songs. Of course people were going to respond.

It's that personal investment which generated fury across the board when the government refused to budge on VAT. No matter how many copies were sold, it seemed, Her Majesty's government would take her cut. The recommended retail price for the record was £1.35 (though to Geldof's fury, some shops did charge more in order to profit a little themselves), but after manufacturing and distribution costs and tax, only 96 pence would make its way to Ethiopia. The biggest bite of the pie was the tax. "Sir, I wonder where indeed our present Government is leading us," a Reverend James M. Cowie wrote in a letter to *The Times*, "when it begins to tax and profit from money given to feed starving children … It is a sad reflection upon our government and way of life that bureaucracy and policy should so conspire to rob starving children of the food from their mouths." The Rev. Cowie was not alone in his disgust. The pressure on the Government came from all sides, with a cross-party delegation of more than 100 MPs writing to Chancellor Nigel Lawson asking the Treasury to make an exception. "The amount may not be large compared to the Government's total revenue," wrote the campaign's spokesman, a young Labour MP by the name of Tony Blair, "but it would make a vital difference to famine relief." Those involved in the record itself remained coldly furious. "I'm disgusted," Bob Geldof told the *Daily Mirror*, "the Government is acting like Scrooge." Phillip Rusted, the accountant handling the money on behalf of the Band Aid Trust, gave the most damning verdict: "The only [people] making money out of this is the Government." Mrs. Thatcher, though, appeared unmoved. "How, in fairness, could we contribute the VAT raised on the Band Aid record to the fund-raising cause, but refuse it in all other cases?" she asked the House of Commons. This, said the *Guardian* in a withering editorial, "betrays an over-riding lack of fairness to the children of Ethiopia for whom the contributions are intended ... The issue has already got to the stage where official stubbornness can only be explained by a reluctance to be seen climbing down rather than a rational decision ... a tax on hunger (Christmas or no Christmas) sticks in the craw." The *Daily Mirror* was blunter still: "Tax scrooges cash in on star charity disc" went its headline. The pressure and outrage led to an uncharacteristic Christmas climbdown for Thatcher – eventually it was agreed that the Treasury would make a donation to the Band Aid Trust matching the figure it had taken in VAT. Perhaps the Prime Minister had been visited by three ghosts?

The legacy of Band Aid is astonishing. Materially, of course that's easy to measure – the Band Aid Trust has raised approximately £140 million across its first 40 years. No small part of that was the gigantic Live Aid concerts staged across the world the following year, the London leg of which culminated in Geldof and Ure leading an all-star cast through a live version of 'Do They Know It's Christmas?'. Band Aid would spawn three direct sequels: Band Aid II, in 1989, in response to another crisis in Ethiopia, Band Aid 20 in 2004, sparked by the dire need of people in war-torn Sudan, and 2014's Band Aid 30, prompted by an unfolding Ebola epidemic in West Africa. The sad reality is that an urgent humanitarian catastrophe could probably be found to justify a Band Aid record in any given year. Each new iteration was a snapshot of the moment, reflecting the sounds and stars of the day. Each was a chart-topper, though Band Aid 30 peaked early and didn't make Christmas No. 1. A fortieth anniversary mix, Band Aid 40, was released in 2024, combining elements of the 1984, 2004 and 2014 records,[4] although partly due to there being no "new" element, and partly from a wave of bad press questioning whether the concept was now rather dated and raising the old spectres of self-serving white saviours, colonialism and clunky lyrics, this latest iteration failed to bother the charts at all.

Outside of Band Aid itself, imitations mushroomed up across the world. Most famous, inevitably, was USA For Africa's 'We Are the World', instigated by Harry Belafonte, who felt Black America needed to step up and to help its African cousins. Written by Lionel Richie and Michael Jackson and produced by Quincy Jones, it was a slicker, starrier and somewhat sicklier operation than its UK progenitor, though its heart was undeniably in the right place. Canada had Northern Lights, Germany had Band für Afrika, Spain had La Hermandad while the Dutch kept things simple with Band-Aid Nederland. Each took the original Band Aid as its template. 'Do They Know It's Christmas?' had created a new visual grammar for pop charity records – stars in big headphones, gathered around studio microphones. Moments of camaraderie captured on camera, interspersed with footage of human suffering to sharpen the impact. Candid aside looks and awkward giggles, arms around each other's shoulders for the finale. You can still see that template in any charity record now, and it's been parodied ruthlessly.[5] Inevitably those

---

[4] Curiously the 1989 version was absent, with the excuse given that the multi-track tapes had been lost over the years. It's also possibly because Band Aid II, produced by hit makers of the moment, Stock, Aitken and Waterman, is also the most disposable of the four generations. With the exception of Kylie Minogue and Cliff Richard, none of the stars featured on it have had any sort of extended legacy and most – Sonia, Big Fun, Bros and D Mob – are unfamiliar to modern audiences. The cast of the other versions, the likes of Robbie Williams, Chris Martin, Ed Sheeran and, inevitably, Bono, have survived longer in the public consciousness.

[5] Most effectively in Pulp's 2002 video for 'Bad Cover Version', which saw the band rerecord their song entirely using a galaxy of tribute artists (including one to Jarvis Cocker himself), in the style of Band Aid.

subsequent videos are all more polished affairs than the original 'Do They Know It's Christmas?', and far more knowing and intentional. There's a naivety to the 1984 Band Aid recording and a genuine sense of freshness and sincerity that could only happen once. No one was turning up to 'We Are the World' without doing their hair and make-up first. No one was strolling in off the street with a coffee at Band Aid 20. There's an innocence to Paul Young's bad skin, Andy Taylor's tangible hangover and the bags under Bob Geldof's eyes that we wouldn't see again. After the success of Band Aid, everyone knew what to expect.

The charity single is now an inevitable part of the Christmas No. 1 season. Ten of the No. 1s in Christmas week between 2000 and 2024 have been charity records, usually by collectives – the Military Wives, the Justice Collective, Lewisham and Greenwich NHS Choir, and various iterations of LadBaby (including the project's creative nadir, a cover of 'Do They Know It's Christmas?' itself called 'Food Aid') – more of which, I'm afraid to say, we'll discuss later. Like Band Aid, the musical quality of these songs was secondary to the causes they were raising money and awareness for – though unlike Band Aid, which is genuinely a great pop song, there was often little substance. Over the years there's been Ferry Aid, Hear 'n Aid, Childliners – and the very unfortunate 'Doctor in Distress' by Who Cares?, a collective of *Doctor Who* fans attempting to save their favourite show as it faced the axe. Between 2008 and 2011 *The X Factor* released charity singles every November featuring that year's finalists. All took their visual cues from the original Band Aid – which had changed the landscape of music. Before 'Do They Know It's Christmas?' pop charity singles were few and far between, and they rarely featured credible artists. After 1984 they were commonplace, and a legitimate response to tragedies of any kind. They helped raise money, of course, but beyond that they were a way for people to react and express emotions that perhaps they couldn't find the words for themselves. A way to feel you could do *something* and feel less helpless, even if it was just buying a song. Pop music is remarkable like that. And not *just* music: Comic Relief, Sport Aid, Sport Relief, Stand Up To Cancer (many of which have tie-in singles recorded in the Band Aid mode), all of them have their roots in Band Aid. "The real legacy ... is that young kids don't think that charity is such a fuddy-duddy thing to do," wrote Midge Ure in his memoir. "My kids and their schools do it all the time, and they don't feel embarrassed or that it is out of place or uncool to care. I believe that Band Aid is directly responsible for that."

Band Aid's other significance is more concerned with its present than its legacy. 'Do They Know It's Christmas?' was the crowning moment for an entire British pop generation – the generation that had its roots in the spontaneity and creativity of punk and the escapism of the Blitz Club and the New Romantics. Theirs was a scene that had always been building to something – and this was it. With some irony, a generation of artists often painted as narcissistic and shallow above all else were defined by a remarkably pure act of altruism. Band Aid was that generation's peak and many of the acts involved slipped into decline, fast or slow, soon afterwards – there are nearly 40 artists on the track, but only George Michael, Sting, U2, Paul Weller and Bananarama would grow their careers in the following years. The very biggest international names on the session – Duran Duran, Spandau Ballet, Boy George, Ultravox, Kool & the Gang, Status Quo – would decline through the rest of the decade, scoring a few more hits before either disbanding or settling into a new career as an oldies act, something that would benefit Duran and Quo in particular, though neither would ever be what you'd call *current* again.[6] (Duran Duran are still headlining festivals in the mid 2020s, Quo toured consistently until Rick Parfitt's death in 2016.)

Meanwhile, the story of Band Aid unfolded as a redemption arc for Bob Geldof. The man who had begun 1984 staring at the commercial abyss, plugging away at a desk at Phonogram, hustling for airplay on a single nobody wanted to hear, ended it on the way to becoming "Sir Bob" – a figure of international repute and moral authority. The knighthood would come later, in 1986, following the massive success of Live Aid, but the trajectory was set. By December 1984, Geldof had metamorphosed from fading pop star to global humanitarian. The Boomtown Rats, the vehicle that had carried

---

[6] I imagine Duran Duran will be horrified to be lumped in with Status Quo, but it's a comparison I'll stand by. Everyone is an oldies act if you wait long enough.

him to fame, would fall apart as his new role took precedence. The band would limp on until 1986, and there would be some respectable solo records, but Geldof's days of being defined by his music were effectively over.

Not everyone was impressed by the Band Aid phenomenon, of course. Morrissey, the famously contrarian frontman of the Smiths, gave voice to a strain of criticism that ran beneath the surface of the praise and plaudits. In an interview with *Melody Maker*, he delivered this withering assessment: "One can have great concern for the people of Ethiopia, but it's another thing to inflict daily torture on the people of England. It was an awful record considering the mass of talent involved." His was a minority view, but not an isolated one. There were many in the music press and beyond who found the song mawkish, simplistic or patronising, even as they acknowledged the good intentions behind it. Some even questioned the intentions – Leeds anarchists Chumbawamba would famously title their 1986 debut album *Pictures of Starving Children Sell Records*, including a thorough evisceration of popstar charity on a song titled 'How To Get Your Band on Television'.

These criticisms hardly dented the project's momentum, however. The transformation of Geldof from rock star to humanitarian figurehead was complete and irreversible. He was now Saint Bob, a man whose moral outrage could be directed like a laser beam at the world's injustices. The curious thing about Geldof's career pivot was how natural it seemed. His charisma, his gift for direct communication, his refusal to be cowed by authority or celebrity – all these qualities that had made him a compelling frontman now served him perfectly in his role as humanitarian spokesperson. In many ways, the transition was smoother and more logical than anyone might have expected. This was a man discovering his true calling. As the years went by, Geldof would build a diverse portfolio of businesses, including television production companies, travel firms and tech investments. He maintained a toe in the water of celebrity, appearing on various TV shows, but his primary public identity remained tied to humanitarian causes.

We can see Band Aid as both a beginning and an end. It was the start of a new era of celebrity philanthropy and a template for how pop stars could leverage their fame for causes beyond themselves. But it was also a last hurrah for a particular moment in British pop – glossy, glamorous, commercially dominant and caught at the peak of its powers. It would be downhill from there for a while ("the last 12 months has been the most boring period for pop music [in years]", Virgin A & R Jeremy Lascelles told *Music Week* in 1986). It's tempting to see the Band Aid recording as a kind of graduation cere-mony – the moment when this generation of pop stars grew up and embraced their responsibilities as global citizens. But that would be too neat, too pat. The reality is more complex and more interesting. Band Aid didn't represent a repudiation of what had come before; rather, it was a natural extension of it. The same creativity, the same ambition, the same willingness to think big that had characterised the best of British pop in the early '80s was now being channelled towards something beyond entertainment. The fact that the record itself divided critical opinion seems, in retrospect, almost irrelevant. What matters is that it happened at all – that for one brief, shining moment, British music harnessed its considerable powers for some-thing beyond itself. If a Christmas No. 1 was the ultimate prize in pop, 'Do They Know It's Christmas?' was one that was shared by everyone. The song endures because it's a cultural touchstone – a reminder of a time when pop music seemed capable of anything. It's a remarkable achievement: a Christmas No. 1 that changed the world. It was a high that British pop would spend the rest of the decade attempting to recapture.

Chapter 12
NOW! THAT'S WHAT I CALL CHRISTMAS!

In which all bets are on and the canon is established

The Christmas No. 1 was already a big deal before 1984: the sought-after crown jewel of pop music, the big prize, but that year had taken it to the next level. 'Do They Know It's Christmas?' had created a cultural moment that was inexorably tied to the Christmas chart, and it did so while heading up a playlist stacked with enduring classics at a peak moment in British pop. The songs of December 1984 would still be soundtracking the season 40 years later. It future-proofed the concept, embedding the goal of having the biggest record at Christmas deeper and more indelibly into popular culture and fixing it there, probably forever. "It's become a tradition," local DJ radio John Simon told *The Northern Echo* the following December, "and you know what we British are like for that." Tellingly, by 1985 there had been an apparently unspoken agreement across the British press to award the concept a definitive article. No longer was it *a* Christmas No. 1, it was now *the* Christmas No. 1, spoken about in the same way people said "Booker Prize" or "Oscar". 1985 also saw the final piece in the puzzle of the now-annual media story fall into place – betting. This was the first year that a bookmaker, William Hill in this case, encouraged its customers to take a gamble on this most hallowed of chart placements, publishing official odds well ahead of the event. The media, of course, loves a properly gamified, quantifiable story, and betting odds officially turned the annual chart jamboree into a legitimate sporting event – and we could all participate.

The first official Christmas No. 1 betting odds were sent out as a press release by William Hill on 22 November, a month ahead of the chart announcement, and were covered in several tabloids and music papers. The bookmaker had the rereleased 'Do They Know It's Christmas?' as a 1/2 favourite, which was hardly worth a flutter. Next most likely was Madonna's 'Dress You Up' at 3/1; Elton John's new single, 'Wrap Her Up', featuring George Michael on backing vocals, was at 4/1; Wham!'s 'I'm Your Man' at 5/1; a reissue of John Lennon's 'Jealous Guy' at 6/1 and, giving George a third entry, the rereleased 'Last Christmas' at 8/1. Several other songs, including offerings from Lionel Richie, Feargal Sharkey, Julian Lennon, Black Lace, Marillion and two from Paul McCartney were somewhere between 10/1 and 14/1.[1] What strikes you, looking back at those odds, is how woefully inaccurate they'd turn out to be. Elton's 'Wrap Her Up' is now rarely mentioned and didn't even break the Top 10. In fact, most of those names were nowhere close to taking the prize. The most glaring error, however, is the absence on that list of the *actual* 1985 Christmas No. 1 – Shakin' Stevens 'Merry Christmas Everyone'. The bookmakers had Shaky at a lowly 25/1 ... so far down the list that most of the papers running the press release didn't even bother to mention it. The single had gone in low at 38 on 3 December, picking up massive radio play and climbing to 10 by the following week. That, of course, meant a *Top of the Pops* slot was inevitable, which worked its usual magic. By the 15th it was at No. 2, at which point the odds had been shortened to 3/1, though 'Do They Know It's Christmas?' remained favourite at 5/4. The lure of sugary Christmas cheer proved too strong, though, and on Christmas Eve Shaky displaced Whitney Houston's 'Saving All My Love for You' at No. 1, costing William Hill £10,000 in payouts in the process.

It was a curious oversight, and an expensive one for the bookmakers, who presumably thought Band Aid's success was

---

[1] "Whatever that means," as *Smash Hits* astutely put it.

unstoppable (in the end it halted at No. 3) and would shield them from rogue options coming up on the outside. What they seemed to have completely missed was that Shakin' Stevens, though never what you'd call cool, was *absolutely massive* in the mid 1980s. The Welsh-born singer had made his name as a rock and roll revivalist, though with none of the genuine excitement or raw sex of the '50s stars he was aping, which other rockabilly throwbacks like the Stray Cats channelled far more successfully. Instead, Shaky was slick and safe, idolising and aping mid-period Elvis with a cheeky hip swivel that had made him something of a housewives' choice. He'd had his first No. 1 in 1980 with a cover of the old '50s hit 'This Ole House', and since then had enjoyed a string of smashes, rarely missing out on the Top 10. His most recent album, *Lipstick Powder and Paint*, however, had rather underperformed, though it had still generated two respectable hit singles. It was likely that the album's performance (it peaked at 37) affected his Christmas odds that year, though the fact he had a seasonal single on the way and an incredibly loyal fanbase should have tipped off observers that he could cause an upset, especially as he had some festive form – his cover of the king's 'Blue Christmas' had gotten to No. 2 just a few years earlier.

'Merry Christmas Everyone' had been in Shaky's gyrating back pocket for over a year by that point – it had been recorded in 1984, and was originally planned for that winter. Stevens has said many times over the years that he decided to kick its release down river to 1985 to avoid clashing with Band Aid, though it's a claim that can be taken with a healthy pinch of salt – 'Do They Know It's Christmas?' was a *very* last-minute project. Had a Shakin' Stevens single been in the works for Christmas 1984, promo would already have been underway, news articles would have announced its coming, records would have been sent out to press and radio, and manufacture would probably have begun… all before the Band Aid crew had assembled on that Sunday in late November. It's far more likely that Shaky and his team were running scared of an extremely strong Christmas chart, even without Bob Geldof sticking his nose in. Band Aid was an unknown quantity, but they'd have been well aware that Wham!, Frankie, Paul McCartney, Queen, Gary Glitter and more all had festive songs coming out. "Not blowing my own trumpet, but 'Merry Christmas Everyone' came across to me as a number one record," he told *Classic Pop* in 2014. "I didn't want it to be stuck at number two". His instincts were good – the song was absolutely Christmas No. 1 material ... but probably not in a year as crowded as 1984. Giving way to Band Aid, of course, sounds far more honourable than "I didn't think I could beat Wham!".

Also lengthening his odds would have been the music press reviews. 'Merry Christmas ...' was *not* well received. The *Evening Standard* called it "wimpy", *Record Mirror* reckoned that "Shaky's on thin ice here ... somebody definitely left the sixpence out of this one." "Soppy, plodding ... bad even by his own standards," said the usually pretty genial *Music Week*. Only the canny *Smash Hits* had it right, glossing over the actual quality of the song to predict that "Shaky and his reindeer are trotting away before starters orders en route to the Christmas No. 1 slot." What was consistently over-looked is how oddly timeless 'Merry Christmas Everyone' sounds. There's very little here that pins it to the mid '80s; it could just as easily have been a hit in 1975 or even 1965. It has a sort of sonic universality. Lyrically, it's a textbook British Christmas hit, essentially just listing things about Christmas people enjoy – falling snow, children playing, parties and celebrations, old songs, presents ... frankly it has all the depth and subtlety of an IKEA teaspoon. The melody, though? Irresistible. The song, by occasional Stevens collaborator Bob Heatlie (who earned the lion's share of the estimated £130,000 of annual royalties it generated right up to his death in 2023) zips along with a breezy jollity that inevitably pulls you along. It is, admittedly, almost astonishingly inoffensive (as, if we're honest, is Shakin' Stevens), but by gum it works. Sometimes a song this milk mild becomes so paper-thin, so nearly invisible that no one pays attention. Sometimes, though – and this was a textbook example – the appeal is so general and so universal that it transcends the normal chart audience, becoming the one single that a lot of people would buy that year. Such records are extremely well suited to the December market and it's still a surprise that the bookmakers didn't see this one coming. And like Band Aid, Wham! and Frankie before it; like Slade, Mud and John and Yoko before *them*, 'Merry Christmas Everyone' would become a true perennial. In Britain in particular, it's embedded so deeply into our Christmas soundscape that its opening bars can bungee the hardest of hearts back to their childhood in seconds. It was also another example of a Christmas No. 1 being a career peak that wouldn't be repeated. As with Slade, Wizzard, Mud and two thirds of the stars on the Band Aid record, that much sought-after Christmas hit would also be Shaky's last major single. He never had another No. 1, broke the Top 10 only once more and slid slowly into nostalgic obscurity.[2]

The mid '80s is also the point when the soundtrack to British Christmas, as it would stand for at least the next 40 years with very few changes, would be locked into place. Those same songs – 'Happy Xmas (War Is Over)', 'Merry Xmas Everybody', 'I Wish It Could Be Christmas Everyday', 'Lonely This Christmas', 'I Believe In Father Christmas', 'When A Child Is Born', 'Mary's Boy Child', 'Wonderful Christmastime', 'Stop The Cavalry', '2,000 Miles', 'Last Christmas', 'The Power of Love', 'Do They Know It's Christmas?', 'Merry Christmas Everyone' – would return year after year, played on local radio stations and in supermarkets, appearing in television commercials either in their original forms or as anodyne covers, woven into the season itself with a life distinct from the artists that created them. More songs would join that list over the next four decades ('Fairytale of New York', 'Driving Home for Christmas', 'Mistletoe and Wine', 'Stay Another Day', 'All I Want for Christmas Is You'), but not as many as you'd think and at a decreasing rate as time goes on. What we start to see is a canonisation process, a list of the officially sanctioned Approved Christmas Songs. That process begins in 1985 with the release of *Now – The Christmas Album*.[3]

The *Now!* series, a collaboration between Virgin Records and EMI, had been introduced in time for Christmas 1983 with the aim of updating the rather neglected compilation market, which up to that point had been dominated by budget titles packed with filler or, in the case of the notorious *Top of the Pops* albums of the 1970s, featuring hits rerecorded entirely by session musicians. Realising how often they were licensing their own records to inferior

---

[2] Shaky still tours every once in a while and is always well received – he's got a loyal fanbase. He's still making music, too. In 2023 he released *Re-Set*, an album of surprisingly authentic, rootsy country songs. It's a genuinely great record.

[3] Also known as *The Christmas Tape*, *The Christmas Compact Disc* and, later, *The Christmas Video*, depending on the format you bought.

compilations produced by rival labels, Virgin execs Jon Webster and Steven Navin hit upon the idea of cutting out the middleman and creating a compilation of their own, using the artists they could already access. Virgin, the label of Culture Club, Heaven 17, Human League and Phil Collins, was enjoying a run of astonishing success at the time, and Webster and Navin came to the quick conclusion that by approaching just one other label, EMI – who had, among others, Duran Duran, Rod Stewart and Tina Turner – they'd have access to most of the year's biggest hits. The resulting album was titled *Now That's What I Call Music*, inspired by a poster hanging in Virgin boss Simon Draper's office. The concept was a huge and immediate success, hitting over a million sales in December alone and becoming a comfortable Christmas No. 1 album.[4] Once established, the series would become a mainstay of the British musical landscape, and from 1984 onwards there would be two and later three entries per year, with occasional genre-specific spin-offs. *Now II* followed quickly in Summer 1984 and by Christmas of 2025 the main series will have reached *122*. At their peak the compilations were selling in excess of two million copies for each new entry.

The Christmas Album, released in November 1985, was the first spin-off from the main series, and collected the various festive pop hits of the previous decade or so, plus a few older tracks, including an obligatory outing for Bing's 'White Christmas'. Christmas compilations, of course, were nothing new – carol collections had been around since before the launch of the LP itself, but outside of Phil Spector's classic *A Christmas Gift For You,* pop-focused albums were rare, and a record comprised mostly of *British* Christmas pop songs was basically unknown. *The Christmas Album* succinctly recognised and catalogued the emergence of festive pop hits as a uniquely British phenomenon, cannily noting John and Yoko's 'Happy Xmas (War is Over)' as a year zero and going on from there, with an honorary bonus appearance for the Beach Boys' 1963 'Little Saint Nick' – the only non-Spector seasonal pop moment of the '60s worthy of note. Collected here was almost every festive-themed

---

[4] The album chart, of course, has its own Christmas No. 1 every year, though aside from a sheer sales achievement the position has never held any particular cultural cachet in the way that topping the singles chart has and does.

UK Christmas No. 1 from Slade in 1973 through to Band Aid in 1984,[5] plus a few other big hits that had missed out on the top spot: Wizzard's 'I Wish It Could Be Christmas Everyday', McCartney's 'Wonderful Christmastime', Wham!'s 'Last Christmas', Mike Oldfield's 'In Dulci Jubilo', Jonah Lewie's 'Stop the Cavalry' and Greg Lake's 'I Believe in Father Christmas'. Keeping things current were the also-rans of 1984: Queen's 'Thank God It's Christmas' and Glitter's 'Another Rock and Roll Christmas'. We also get Shakin' Stevens' 1982 cover of 'Blue Christmas', pulling double duty by both taking Shaky far more seriously than William Hill had and saving Virgin from having to fork out for the Elvis original. Given Stevens' ownership of Christmas 1985, it proved to be a sound financial decision. Of the 18 tracks here, only Bing Crosby and the Beach Boys predate 1972 – Virgin/EMI had been able to pull the compilation together almost entirely from near-contemporary hits. Forty years on and the tracklisting, with only a few exceptions, reads as wall-to-wall classics.

Younger readers may struggle to appreciate the cultural importance of compilation albums in the pre-streaming era. A household's copy of *The Christmas Album* would become the musical backbone of countless family celebrations, pulled out every year, and its arrival on the turntable, or in the CD player or tape deck, would mark the official commencement of the celebrations. These collections represented the only practical way families could access all these seasonal hits affordably; acquiring music in the 1980s demanded both effort and cash. Singles cost around £1.30 (roughly £5 in today's money), while albums, priced at around £8.99, offered remarkable value by comparison – essentially bulk-buying your festive soundtrack. The compilation's physical presence in homes, stacked beside the turntable awaiting its annual spin, gave it an authority that today's ephemeral playlists simply cannot match. Its tracklisting became the definitive statement on which songs mattered at Christmas, a musical advent calendar with lasting cultural impact.

As a result, *The Christmas Album* was a huge success, selling 750,000 copies by the end of the year and outselling even *Now 6*,

---

[5] With the exception of Boney M.'s 'Mary's Boy Child', probably for rights reasons.

the latest entry in its parent series. It's not a huge surprise, given that it was, as *Record Mirror* said, "a simple but brilliant variation on the *Now* theme … it's the definitive Christmas party album". By the end of the year it had become the first Christmas album to hit the No. 1 spot. It would go on to be a consistent seller, updated many times, eventually being rebranded as *Now That's What I Call Christmas*. What's remarkable is that, however much the tracklisting has expanded (the 2024 triple LP version runs to 54 songs, for example), almost every song on that first release has remained on the tracklisting. Only Gary Glitter, for obvious reasons, has fallen off permanently, though 'Blue Christmas' tends to be upgraded to the Elvis original – but that's okay since Shaky's 'Merry Christmas Everyone' joined the ranks fairly swiftly. Many more Christmas pop compilations would come and go, and almost all of them, in the UK at least, contained almost all of the songs that the *Now* team had selected.

What was happening here was the establishment of the Christmas canon – the approved list of hits that would permanently soundtrack Christmas in the UK. *The Christmas Album* played a major part in this, something that's proven by the inclusion of two specific tracks which we now accept as perennial visitors. Firstly there was Elton John's 'Step Into Christmas', a song that had peaked at No. 23 back in 1973, had never been included on any greatest hits and hadn't been performed live since 1974. Elton's name, of course, was valuable to the compilation, but it's unlikely many people would have singled out the LP because they wanted to own *that* particular song. It's one of the few tracks on here where the artist was more important than the title. It added some star quality, and as an unintentional consequence completely refreshed a largely forgotten single, adding it to the permanent list of canon Christmas songs. Secondly there was Chris de Burgh's 1975 song 'A Spaceman Came Travelling'. This was comfortably one of the oddest Christmas records ever made, in which the Biblical Star of Bethlehem is revealed to be an alien spacecraft. You have to give de Burgh marks for originality – very few festive songs have the bottle to include lines like "Then the stranger spoke, he said do not fear / I come from a planet a long way from here". The song, which is certainly epic, audacious, almost hymnal and ludicrously catchy but also deeply weird and faintly naff, had failed to make the chart on its initial release. De Burgh himself remained a cult act for the rest of the '70s, and a mid-selling album artist in the early '80s. 1986 would give him a global mega-hit in the shape of 'The Lady in Red', but prior to that he'd never had a UK hit single. His 1984 album, *Man on the Line,* had reached No. 11 but had hardly set the world alight. The inclusion of 'A Spaceman Came Travelling' wasn't going to shift many copies of a Christmas compilation in of itself. This was purely a filler track – decent enough, by a respectable-ish name, and presumably affordable. It added value to the album only by expanding it. And yet its inclusion effectively canonised the song. As *The Christmas Album* became the soundtrack to present wrapping, tree decorating and (via supermarket plays) Christmas shopping, 'A Spaceman Came Travelling' was embedded into the annual playlist along with Slade, Wizzard and the rest. De Burgh would rerecord it for release over Christmas 1986. It peaked at No. 40, but that was enough to confirm its place in the festive perennials. It's since sold 400,000 copies.

Almost as interesting are the songs that *aren't* here. Had the compilers opted to include Showaddywaddy's 'Hey Mister Christmas' or Gilbert O'Sullivan's 'Christmas Song', would we have been hearing those every year as well? Are they any better or worse than 'A Spaceman Came Travelling'? What about the Snowmen's 'The Hokey Cokey'? Or Kate Bush's 'December Song'? If they'd opted for Elton's 'Cold as Christmas (In the Middle of the Year)' instead of 'Step Into Christmas', would the latter have remained a footnote in his career? Curation decisions based on availability, price and, presumably, not a small amount of personal preference ended up defining our annual celebrations. It is, when you think about it, *fascinating.* For the artists involved, inclusion on Christmas compilations could have a huge impact – but for the grace of God, Showaddywaddy's Dave Bartram might now own a substantially bigger house than he currently does.

What's curious is that as the canon was established, it also started to become ring-fenced. 1984 had been the peak for new Christmas songs we would return to year upon year. There would be more to come, of course, but never at the rate they appeared between 1973 and 1984. The Christmas No. 1 spot itself continued to be a goal, but the sheer Christmassiness of the songs vying for it declined substantially, and while some apparently evergreen hits would latch themselves onto the season, like 'The Power of Love', others simply came and went, grabbing the title and then passing into history like a football team having a fluke season. 1986's winner, for example, was a quickly forgotten rerelease of Jackie Wilson's 1957 R & B classic 'Reet Petite (The Sweetest Girl in Town)'. Earlier that year an animation studio called Giblets had produced a stop-motion video of the song on spec, as a showcase for their abilities. The clip had been featured during a six-hour edition of BBC 2's *Omnibus* dedicated to the history of the music video, hosted by John Peel and John Waters, and had made quite the splash ("anyone who saw [it] ... couldn't fail to be impressed," said *Music Week* that June). The clip was so effective that it inspired a mini renaissance for the song on pop radio, which in turn prompted record label SMP to reissue the original disc. A spike in sales meant the Giblets video was shown on *Top of the Pops* (Wilson wasn't available to perform, having died the previous year) and the song's innate, punchy zest did the rest. Some 700,000 copies later, it was the Christmas No. 1, and would stay atop the hit parade until 17 January and hang around on the chart for another month. Giblets would go on to create several music videos, most notably for the Housemartins' indie pop hit 'Happy Hour', another stop-motion clip delivered long before 'Reet Petite' was reissued. With some irony, the Jackie Wilson song that Giblets helped to reawaken would beat the Housemartins' a capella cover of the Isley Brothers' 'Caravan of Love' to Christmas No. 1. Neither song would make it into the Christmas canon.

The tail end of the decade generated precious few new songs to add to the annual list. The Pet Shop Boys, then in their imperial phase, snagged the 1987 win with a brilliant synth-pop cover of Elvis' 'Always on My Mind' – a classic, yes, but despite its timing one that wouldn't be attached to future Christmases at all. According to the bookies, its' stiffest competition was to be Rick Astley, who'd covered Nat King Coles' chocolate-smooth 'When I Fall In Love'[6]

---

[6] Mindful of the success of 'Reet Petite' the previous year, Cole's record label decided to rerelease his original version of 'When I Fall in Love' and put it in direct competition with Astley's. It got to No. 7, while Rick peaked at 2 but

(William Hill reckoned over half of the £20,000 in bets they'd taken on that year's Christmas No. 1 had been for Rick Astley), and a forgettably silly cover of 'Rockin' Around The Christmas Tree' by Mel & Kim (comedian Mel Smith and singer Kim Wilde), released to raise money for Comic Relief.[7] As per usual, the bookmakers initially overlooked the real contender – a bittersweet duet by the Pogues featuring Kirsty MacColl called 'Fairytale of New York'. It was probably the last true Christmas masterpiece to emerge from British pop.[8]

Formed in 1982 as Pogue Mahone (Gaelic for "kiss my arse"), the Pogues crawled out from London's punk scene, drawing some of its spittle-flecked urban aggression and blending it with traditional Irish folk. Their frontman, Shane MacGowan, was a walking contradiction – a once-pretty London-Irish boy with an encyclopaedic knowledge of traditional music and a profound self-destructive streak. By 1987, his rotting teeth were becoming a music press punchline, and his on-stage performances could veer from transcendent to incoherent, often in the same song. The band's first three albums – *Red Roses for Me* (1984), *Rum Sodomy & the Lash* (1985) and their then-forthcoming *If I Should Fall from Grace with God* – established them as critical favourites with a ferocious live reputation, though they remained ever outside of the mainstream. They were the last act you'd expect to challenge for a Christmas No. 1.

And yet 'Fairytale of New York' is a little miracle – a booze-soaked Christmas hymn, intimate yet universal, bitterly realistic yet hopelessly romantic. The song had taken two years to complete, beginning life in 1985 as a bet between MacGowan and Elvis Costello, who was then producing the group and now challenged him to write a proper Christmas duet. The initial version was shelved, but the idea lingered. MacGowan eventually reworked it with his bandmate

---

had fallen two places to No. 4 by Christmas week. Buying a classic original as a protest vote against a new cover version wasn't just a phenomenon of the download and streaming era.

[7] The whole project was conceived entirely off the back of a pun: there was a successful pop duo at the time called Mel and Kim.

[8] I am aware this is comfortably the most controversial statement in this whole book, but damn it, I will fight this corner and die on this hill.

Jem Finer into a story of Irish immigrants in New York – a drunk, reminiscing about a tumultuous relationship that began full of dreams on a Christmas Eve but deteriorated into recriminations and regret.

Recording the female part proved challenging (originally it was a duet with Pogues bass player Cait O'Riordan, who quit the band late in 1986) until producer Steve Lillywhite suggested his wife, the acerbic and criminally underrated singer-songwriter Kirsty MacColl. Her clear, unsentimental voice, loaded with character and class, provided the perfect foil to MacGowan's slurred, wounded delivery. The result was magical, enduring, heartbreaking – a song that's neither a straightforward celebration nor a rejection of Christmas sentiment, but something more complex. It's a Christmas song for adults – people for whom the shine has been knocked off the season by the realities of life and love. People who've been around a bit. What 'Fairytale of New York' understands better than almost any other seasonal song (save perhaps Joni Mitchell's gorgeous 'River') is that the season is as much about what *might have been* as what *is*. It's a new take on *Miserable Christmas*, a yearning not just for something lost, but something that never will be. The emotional heft of Christmas, once again, amplifies not just joy but loneliness, not just togetherness but separation. The Pogues captured that tension perfectly, grand strings and Spider Stacy's penny whistle clashing with gutter poetry and kitchen-sink spite.

Upon its release in November 1987, the song was met with widespread acclaim from the UK music press. It was a comfortable 'Single of the Week' in *Sounds*, as it was in *Record Mirror* which dubbed it, with some justification, "the most wonderful Christmas record ever" and "staggeringly and drunkenly inspirational". Future *Loaded* founder James Brown, writing in the *NME*, acknowledged the Pogues had "claimed the art of the ballad to be their own – on the strength of 'New York' they deserve it." Even publications as far afield as the *Vancouver Sun* were calling it "the best Christmas song since John Lennon's", despite the single not even being released in Canada.

Though it went in low, as independent records tend to, debuting at No. 40 in the week of release, a record *this* good, at Christmas of all times, couldn't go unnoticed and it picked up speed quickly.

This was never a single that was going to be stuck in the *NME*/John Peel indie ghetto. "As our technical staff just pointed out, [it's] a bit Radio 2 really," Peel himself said after premiering the song on his show that November, "but then again some of my best friends listen to Radio 2." It took just a few weeks and an absolute peach of a *Top of the Pops* performance for 'Fairytale of New York' to become a genuine Christmas No. 1 contender, which given that it began life with odds of 50-1 is pretty remarkable. Ultimately, though, it didn't have enough in the tank to take it all the way. The Pet Shop Boys were at the peak of their powers, on a bigger label, and had a song that was not only an Elvis cover but handily free of the relatively fruity language to be found in the Pogues' hit. It was a close-run thing, though, and of all of the post-Band Aid British Christmas hits, it's 'Fairytale of New York' that has the most enduring legacy. It sold respectably in its first year, a UK No. 2 and an Irish No. 1, but grew in stature with each passing December. It would re-enter the charts continuously, particularly after the advent of downloads and streaming. Its tale of love, loss and rancorous nostalgia grows more potent as the years pass. The song represented Christmas as many actually experienced it: messy, complicated, tinged with both sweetness and bitterness, a time for memories good and bad. In a season increasingly dominated by mechanical cheer, 'Fairytale' had an authenticity that made it stand out both as a seasonal song, and also in the turgid chart landscape of the era. "The temptation was to walk away from this thing called pop altogether and start listening to anything and everything else," as the *Guardian*'s Adam Sweeting wrote in despair that Christmas, "a sentiment that may account for The Pogues selling so many copies of their excellent Christmas drinking song."

By the mid '90s, it had already ascended to classic status, joining the emerging Christmas canon that had been codified by the *Now* compilations. It had become as much a part of the British Christmas soundscape as Slade or Wham! – piped into pubs, supermarkets and Christmas parties, despite containing language that would have been bleeped from daytime radio any other time of year. Its inclusion on numerous compilations (including the expanded *Now* Christmas volumes) cemented its status. At the time of writing its official sales, incorporating streaming figures, stand at 3.5 million.

The song has so far outlived two of its creators – Kirsty MacColl died tragically in a boating accident in Mexico, just before Christmas 2000, adding another layer of bittersweet nostalgia to the song's annual appearances. MacGowan himself, defying all medical probability, would continue to perform it each December, his health deteriorating but his legend growing. For a song about damaged dreamers, there was something oddly appropriate about its most enduring interpreter being so visibly ravaged by time and excess, yet still somehow so very present. He died in 2023, again just before Christmas. At his funeral in Nenagh, Tipperary, the surviving Pogues were joined by Irish singers Glen Hansard and Lisa O'Neill for a suitably raw performance of 'Fairytale of New York' which raised both goosebumps and glasses.

As popular tastes changed and reality shows began to dominate the Christmas chart, 'Fairytale of New York' came to represent something more authentic – annual and increasingly tedious culture war arguments about the use of the word *"faggot"* aside.[9] Here was a Christmas song with dirt under its fingernails, whisky on its breath and romance in its heart, a song that defied easy categorisation and commercial calculation yet spoke to the complex emotions of the season better than almost anything before or since. As far as Christmas pop songs go, it has yet to be bettered.

---

[9] It's a hateful term, of course, but in the context of a song sung by homeless junkies in the docklands of New York in the mid '80s, it scrapes a pass. Neither Kirsty MacColl nor Shane McGowan were precious about omitting the word, which both accepted as problematic. MacColl often used "you're cheap and you're haggard" when performing, and McGowan had no time for the commentators banging on year after year about political correctness. In 2020, when right-wing agitator Lawrence Fox told his followers on Twitter to buy the uncensored version of the song in defiance of the BBC's use of a tamer edit, the official Pogues account replied: "Fuck off you little herrenvolk shite."

Chapter 13
DO THEY KNOW IT'S CLIFFMAS?

The dawn of the '90s sees the chart stuck in the past,
but there is a monster on the horizon . . .

The turning of a decade always leaves fallow ground at the top of charts, and so it proved once again as the '80s ticked into the '90s. Despite the thrills of acid house, hip-hop, Hi-NRG and the social revolution that dance music was ushering in, things had rather sputtered to a halt as far as the Christmas hit parade was concerned, where across 1988, 1989 and 1990 a new version of 'Do They Know It's Christmas?' provided the filling in a Cliff Richard sandwich. Band Aid II was an attempt to repeat the magic of the original, five years on, though the biggest takeaway from this version was that pop was once again in the doldrums. This time Geldof had handed the job off to the Hit Factory of Stock Aitken Waterman, aka SAW, the unholy alliance of producers and songwriters Mike Stock, Matt Aitken and Pete Waterman. The trio had dominated British pop in the latter half of the decade, attempting to replicate the Motown/Brill Building trick of knocking out catchy songs to order and finding pretty faces to sing them. They'd had massive hits with Bananarama, Dead or Alive and Rick Astley and struck commercial gold when they'd taken on *Neighbours* star Kylie Minogue at the height of the show's British popularity, inevitably signing her real-life and on-screen boyfriend Jason Donovan, and making the

203

duo into something of a pop culture sensation. Their saccharine but oddly likeable duet 'Especially for You' had been Christmas No. 2 in 1988. Every so often SAW would birth a dancefloor masterpiece: Dead or Alive's 'You Spin Me Round (Like A Record)', Mel and Kim's 'Respectable', Bananarama's 'Venus', Kylie's 'Better the Devil You Know', but they were just as likely to churn out box ticking dross for the long-forgotten likes of Sonia, Big Fun, Sinitta and the Reynolds Girls. At their best they were Hi-NRG fun with a knowing sense of camp. At their worst they were, well, Jason Donovan's 'Too Many Broken Hearts'.

One of the underlying themes of this book, the Christmas stuff aside, is to track the evolving nature of Britain's music and pop culture by revisiting the chart in the same week every year. The Band Aid records do this perfectly. The 1984 version sparkled with pop stars. It had *everyone* – including, thanks to Sting, Wham!, Duran Duran and Culture Club, some of British pop's biggest global names. Band Aid II was a much smaller affair. For a start, either through a lack of personal charm, a lack of adequate time (which hadn't been a problem for Geldof) or maybe through a lack of interest from the pop community in general, SAW's Pete Waterman was able to pull together just 16 stars – less than half of the original record's 37-strong cast. And though Kylie, Jason and twin heartthrobs Bros were legitimately big league international artists and Lisa Stansfield, for example, had one of the biggest hits of the year, there was a *lot* of padding here from the SAW stable and elsewhere: Big Fun, Sonia, Chris Rea, Wet Wet Wet, Technotronic, Cathy Dennis, the Pasadenas, long-forgotten singer Glen Goldsmith and, oddly, former 10CC frontman Kevin Godley, probably better known at that point as a music video director.[1] There was also the aforementioned Cliff Richard, whose pop legacy is unarguable but who was hardly the coolest of the cool.

If Band Aid '84 was a snapshot of British pop in a peak moment, then Band Aid '89 was Kylie and Jason, plus whoever was available. It was a weaker version of the song, too. "We found a way to make it more dance orientated," wrote mix engineer Phil Harding in his

---

[1] As part of Godley & Creme he'd done Frankie's 'The Power of Love' back in 1984.

book *PWL: From the Factory Floor.* "Most people would rightly say that it's an inferior version but at the time it seemed totally the right thing to do." "True to the original, but ... updated," Kylie told ITN at the time. What it actually was, despite the megawatt charm of Kylie herself, who opens the record, is *charmless.* The original was rough around the edges, giving it far more of an identity. Those edges have been sanded down here, taking much of the song's character with them. Band Aid II sounds dated and formulaic, nailed sonically to the year it was made in a way that the original record doesn't. SAW had produced almost 30% of that year's hit records, including five No. 1s and fifteen Top 5s, and they were the sound of 1989: very catchy, bright, slightly tinny and woefully lacking in depth. Their trademarks were well in evidence here. It's something Geldof himself had anticipated. "It'll be the sound of 1989," he told ITN on the night of recording, adding, rather knowingly, "For good or ill."

The song was a comfortable No. 1, selling around half a million copies, which is mid-range for a typical Christmas hit of the time but peanuts compared to the original. Band Aid II was the ninth biggest selling song of the year – the first version had been the biggest selling single *ever.* Some might blame charity fatigue for that – appeals to donate to overseas causes, especially in Africa, had been pretty constant across the last five years, but no small amount of the blame must be given to a very, very ordinary-sounding 1989 pop record severely lacking in iconic stars.

One name that stands out on the Band Aid II cast list is that of pop elder Cliff Richard, who despite his longevity and his importance as a foundation stone of British pop, seems woefully out of place among SAW's bright young things, at least from the vantage point of the twenty-first century. While Cliff's very early career had seen him launched, with reasonable justification, as the British response to Elvis, his rock credibility hadn't survived Beatlemania, and he'd evolved quite happily into a family-friendly variety act. His conversion to evangelical Christianity in the early '60s had come to define his image – which, since his faith was incredibly important to him, isn't something he minded much. It did, however, place him in the very safe, very middle of the road aisle of popular culture. He never stopped having hits, but it had been many years since the kids had listened to Cliff. For a long time his audience had been the less groovy Christians, young-at-heart grans and your mum's slightly weird friend. You'd be amazed, however, how big that demographic is – his fan base might not have been a very cool one, but it was *massive*. Cliff fans were dedicated, often obsessively, and much ridiculed, but there were plenty. In fact, since 1958 Cliff had managed a Top 10 hit in very nearly every year in which he'd released music.[2] His 1989 song 'The Best of Me' had been his 100th single, and nearly all of them had been hits in some form.

Still, given that the Band Aid brief had always been "current pop smashes", the appearance in the video of a 49-year-old man of God wearing groovy shades and looking down the barrel of the camera as he sang (the only person in any Band Aid video to do so) does rather jar alongside the extremely youthful *Smash Hits* crop surrounding him. His appearance can be partly chalked up to his recent work with SAW on the generic dance-pop of 'Just Don't Have the Heart', a Top 3 earlier that year. Mostly, though, he was there because it was Christmas. And Cliff Richard had some serious Christmas form.

It was Cliff who claimed the first Christmas No. 1 of the '60s with a fairly harmless, twangy little ditty called 'I Love You', recorded with his backing band, the Shadows. It was neither festive nor, if we're honest, memorable. However, it did establish a pattern, and although it would take almost 30 years for Cliff to snag the Christmas No. 1 again, he would usually have a song out for the lucrative December market, and that record would usually be a respectable hit. By the late '80s he'd become something of a national institution, and in 1988, his 30th year in showbiz, he'd sold out a 50-date UK tour – 200,000 tickets – in 72 hours. He capitalised on its success with the mother of all slightly naff Christmas singles, a cheerful waltz called 'Mistletoe and Wine'. The song had been written for a Victorian-themed musical, *Scraps*, an adaption of

---

[2] It's remarkable. Every time his popularity seemed to be on the slide, this would turn out to be a temporary affliction. It did seem like his number was finally up in the late '70s, when 1979's 'Green Light' peaked at 57. Then, just a few months later, he had a No. 1 smash with 'We Just Don't Talk Anymore' and he was back in the game.

Hans Christian Anderson's *The Little Match Girl*, which had aired on television the previous Christmas. In that version it had been a bierkeller-style drinking song, reeking of spilled ale, and performed by Twiggy.[3] Cliff sweetened the whole thing and insisted on adding some Christian messaging. The end product was, of course, *incredibly* naff, but it was also ludicrously catchy and extremely accessible. Cringey it may be, but there's something wholesome and decidedly uncynical about 'Mistletoe and Wine', which Cliff sings with gusto in the video, a scarf slung around his shoulders, arms swinging from side to side as the snow falls. His fanbase ate it up, of course, but this was a song that was always going to travel further – it was probably the most straightforwardly *Christmassy* Christmas No. 1 for a decade. It's a brandy-blazing plum pudding of a song, un-subtle but jolly. It sounded like a carol, like a song you'd known forever. Not necessarily one you particularly liked, admittedly, but one you couldn't get out of your head. It was a radio smash hit (even pop-focused Radio 1 played it). Children sang it in carol concerts. Builders hummed it while they worked. The postman whistled it on his rounds. You couldn't help yourself. It gave Cliff the biggest selling record of 1988, and provided a hell of a springboard into the following year – a year in which he celebrated his hundredth single with a sold out, two-night stand at the 72,000-seater Wembley Stadium followed by another four Top 20 singles, including a No. 2 and a No. 3. Given all of that, his appearance on the Band Aid II record wasn't that surprising at all: 1989 had been as much Cliff's year as anyone else's … though that doesn't say much about the freshness of the music scene of the time. Cliff would follow his 1988 Christmas No. 1 and appearance on the *1989* Christmas No. 1 by snagging the first Christmas No. 1 of the new decade, just as he had 30 years before. The song was 'Saviour's Day', a retread of the same musical ground as 'Mistletoe and Wine' but, if anything, even more overtly religious – though a little less charming, and it was notably less successful. It did, however, give Cliff Richard the honour of a

---

[3] Who you'll remember had some form playing penniless Victorians at Christmas in cheap-looking TV shows – it had been a decade since *Bing Crosby's Merrie Olde Christmas*, but she hadn't lost her touch.

fairly remarkable statistic – the only artist to have a No. 1 hit in the '50s, '60s, '70s, '80s and '90s.

The two singles tied Cliff even tighter to Christmas, and he'd be chasing that high again for the rest of his career. From 1988 there was a Cliff Richard single in the Christmas Top 40 for seven years in a row, and he would go on to release occasional festive albums, making one last serious play for Christmas No. 1 with 'The Millenium Prayer' in 1999.

'Mistletoe and Wine' and 'Saviour's Day' had been Christian-leaning pop, but 'The Millenium Prayer' was something else – an unabashed hymn, putting the words of 'The Lord's Prayer' to the tune of 'Auld Lang Syne', taking advantage of the end-of-a-century mania that was unavoidable at the time – a surprisingly calculated move for such an overtly religious man. Sir Cliff, as he was now known following a knighthood in 1995, first offered the song to EMI, the label he'd recently parted company with after a 40-year relationship. The response, as Cliff reports in his memoir *The Dreamer*, was "we don't think this is a hit". The label offered to release it all the same, despite no contractual obligation to do so, but feeling that EMI had drastically underpromoted his recent releases, Cliff opted to take it elsewhere. Eventually it was offered to Papillon Records, an offshoot of Chrysalis designed to deal with "heritage" artists. The label took it on hungrily ("This is Cliff Richard's Christmas single? And *we* can release it? *Now*?" is how Cliff describes their response), the singer declaring he would donate his portion of the royalties to children's charities.

When the single was released late in November, it proved surprisingly controversial. BBC Radio 2, the natural home for such artists, declined to add it to their playlist, prompting predictable if ludicrous "Cliff Banned By The BBC!" headlines and fury among the pop legend's devoted fanbase. "It's totally unfair!" Carol Hall, the 33-year-old president of the London and Surrey Cliff Richard Fanclub ranted to the *Independent*. "Why should they dictate what we hear? What right do they have to write Cliff off?" Ms Hall even organised a protest outside the station, though only a dozen people turned up. There was a call from Christians to boycott Radio 2 – "I find it quite unbelievable that BBC Radio 2 has unilaterally decided to totally reject a record, which, based on advanced sales alone, could make it to the No. 1 spot in the charts at Christmas," said Peter Kerridge of London radio station Premier Christian Radio. "The ban is even more incredible when one considers that Cliff will be donating the proceeds to children's charities." The furore was such that the BBC was forced to put out a statement pointing out that, though the song hadn't been added to playlists, its DJs were all free to give it a spin should they want to and, as such, the single quite emphatically "has not been banned". The corporation's argument was that while they were "supportive of him as an artist ... his new single was considered not to be of broad enough appeal to be on the playlist", adding that "all singles on the playlist must be suitable for mainstream programmes." You can certainly see their point. There's a market for this stuff in America, where Christianity is tied to big bucks. In the UK, though, where church attendance had been falling for half a century, a 60-year-old star bellowing the actual Lord's Prayer didn't seem to have a place in a chart dominated by boy bands and two-step garage. Even fellow Granny-botherer Tom Jones, no stranger to a bit of gospel, had reinvented himself with an album of duets with current pop stars like Robbie Williams, the Stereophonics and dance producer Mousse T.[4] The main contender for Christmas No. 1 that year was Irish boyband Westlife, whose double A-side covers of ABBA's 'I Had a Dream' and Terry Jacks' 'Seasons in the Sun' featured music just as earnest, just as middle of the road and with equal granny appeal to Cliff's, but with the bonus of a built-in teenybopper fanbase. In comparison, 'The Millenium Prayer' felt like a step too far. The idea, too cringey. Cliff himself, too past it. *Of course* EMI weren't keen. *Of course* the BBC weren't interested. The whole thing was a folly.

And they were all, sort of, right. 'The Millenium Prayer' wasn't Christmas No. 1. The Westlife army and an old classic with true crossover appeal proved too strong. Released the week before Christmas, the insipid 'I Had a Dream'/'Seasons in the Sun' swept straight to the top, giving the Irish heartthrobs their fourth consecutive No. 1. And yet, in another sense the naysayers and the snarks were also completely wrong about Cliff – 'The Millenium Prayer'

---

[4] The duo's floor filler 'Sex Bomb' is probably the most enduring hit from that album, still played in clubs today. Strange but true.

was a *massive* hit. The single had come out mid-November, follow-ing ITV's airing of *An Audience With Cliff Richard* on prime-time Sunday night television. The TV show concentrated Cliff fans and the Cliff-curious into one place, and culminated with 'The Millenium Prayer'. It was, for the audience concerned, better than a *Top of the Pops* appearance. What also helped (and this is among the most controversial opinions in this book) is that 'The Millenium Prayer' is a genuinely stirring record. It's built around a compulsive, rat-a-tat drum beat that offers real momentum as an entire orchestra swells around it, soon joined, inevitably, by a gospel choir. Cliff sings with more conviction than he'd delivered in decades, breaking out of his usual bland croon to rip little ad libs over choral parts. At one point he hits a falsetto a man two third's his age would envy. Cliff had begun his career in 1958 as the British Elvis, and with 'The Millenium Prayer' that had come full circle – you could easily imagine the King releasing this exact record in his '70s gospel pomp. The Cliff fans came out of the woodwork in droves – he was still a massive name. That December he played a ten-night run at Birmingham's National Indoor Arena, climaxing with a double whammy of 'Saviour's Day' and 'The Millenium Prayer', Cliff soar-ing on wires over the audience. A huge chunk of the country's active Christians, of whom it turned out there were still plenty, bought the song on principle. Buoyed by all of this and the wave of *Banned by the Beeb* publicity, the single swept straight to No. 2 at the end of November, rising to top the charts the following week, where it stayed for three weeks before being ousted by Westlife at the very last minute. In the end it spent 16 weeks on the chart and sold a million copies – the third biggest selling single of 1999, giving Cliff his 14th (and final) No. 1 single. In a 60-year career in music it was his bestselling record. Its success, however, was tinged with just a shade of disappointment for the man himself – he ultimately missed out on a fourth Christmas No. 1, which would have equalled the Beatles record. Worse, had he clung on to the top spot into the new year, he'd have managed an even more remarkable feat: a No. 1 in six consecutive decades. Cliff remains convinced to this day that, had he put the single out a couple of weeks later, both prizes would have been his.

Meanwhile, back in the early '90s, Cliff's domination was rather telling of a fairly drab chapter in the Christmas charts, and by extension in British pop itself, which lingered for the first few years of the new decade. In 1991, following Freddie Mercury's death from AIDS, a rereleased 'Bohemian Rhapsody' became the first recording ever to return to the Christmas No. 1 spot. It's a brilliant record, of course, and its second wave of a success was a fitting tribute to one of the all-time greats, gone too soon, but it's hardly a festive treat. It's been Christmas No. 1 twice now, and we still don't consider it a Christmas record, and besides, when the crown jewel of the pop year is awarded to a song from 16 years ago, it's not necessarily indicative of a healthy musical market. There was no real battle for the Christmas No. 1 that year. No stakes and little fun. The only actual Christmas song in the charts was a rerelease of 'Fairytale of New York', lurking in the lower regions. The 1992 Christmas chart, meanwhile, had some signs of life dotted through it that suggested British pop was beginning an upswing – the Stereo MC's 'Step On', the Prodigy's 'Out of Space', and in Take That's 'Could It Be Magic', the first real stirrings of one of the acts that would dominate the decade. Still, the top of the charts was nothing to write home about. That year's Christmas No. 1 was Whitney Huston's world-conquering mega-hit 'I Will Always Love You', which had been in the top spot since the start of December and would occupy it throughout January. At No. 2 was Michael Jackson's all-time worst single, 'Heal the World', an overly worthy, saccharine dirge about global togetherness. There's rarely any fun to be found when the Christmas charts are dominated by gigantic US artists. Christmas No. 1 has never held cultural weight for American acts, and for these two superstars especially, this was just another territory in a global campaign. Christmas was never really built into the plan. It had been a good few years since anyone had really given battle for the festive top spot, and longer since anything surprising or even particularly interesting had happened. Thank goodness, then, for 1993.

The 1993 Christmas No. 1 was about as far from an American superstar as it is possible to be. It wasn't Michael Jackson, it wasn't Whitney Houston and, despite a superficial resemblance, it wasn't Meat Loaf, whose power ballad 'I'd Do Anything For Love (But I

Won't Do That)' had sat at No. 1 for most of October and the whole of November. No ... the 1993 Christmas No. 1 was 'Mr Blobby' by Mr Blobby. And it's unlikely that could have happened in any other country on Earth.

Let's make no bones about this. The whole Mr Blobby phenomenon is entirely strange, and it peaking with a Christmas No. 1 is both the weirdest twist of the whole saga while also being, somehow, the most appropriate possible outcome. Mr. Blobby was, and indeed is, an anarchic monstrosity originally conceived as a parody of a children's TV character. He's more than 2 metres (7 feet) tall, shaped something like an aubergine with legs, made of lurid pink foam with splodged yellow polka dots, wears nothing but a bow tie and has googly green eyes with huge lashes, a flat, piggy nose and a massive, slightly crazed and unmoving clown's smile. He can say only three words: *blobby, blibby* and *blob*, and he falls over a lot, generally taking whatever and whoever is around crashing to the floor with him. The character had originated on a Saturday teatime variety show called *Noel's House Party*, broadcast on BBC One and hosted by the then ubiquitous broadcaster, Noel Edmonds. Blobby was conceived by *House Party* producer Michael Leggo and writer Charlie Adams as a just-believable-enough children's TV character that could be used to prank minor celebrities on the show's popular 'Gotcha!' segment. Obviously Blobby would have to be retired after a single series, since by then the secret would be out and the character would be useless for pranks. What happened next, however, took the show's producers entirely by surprise: *audiences loved Mr Blobby*. According to Edmonds over half of the show's fan mail was Blobby based. Children took him at face value and enjoyed his pratfalling antics, while adults responded to a character that both sat in and satirised the slapstick tradition.

Blobby became a mainstay of *Noel's House Party*, coming on every week to stagger about and knock things over. At an outdoor live show in the summer of 1993, filmed in front of a couple of thousand people, Blobby was greeted like a rock star. Merchandise started to appear – bedspreads, lemonade, bubble bath, dolls, stationery, socks. By the autumn, just over a year since his first appearance, Mr Blobby was *everywhere*. That November, readers of Newcastle's *Evening Chronicle* newspaper voted Mr Blobby the

nation's favourite choice to replace Graham Taylor as the manager
of the England football team. The story was picked up widely to the
point that bookmaker William Hill assigned him odds (100,000/1:
tempting enough for one anonymous punter from Reading to place
a £5 bet).[5] When prime minister John Major opened up suggestions
for future knighthoods to the public, his office was flooded with
calls for Sir Blobby.

Earlier that year, the show's producers had received a phone
call from the Destiny Music record label, a fairly minor imprint of
Warner Chappell, proposing a Mr Blobby single. Michael Leggo
agreed on one condition. "I rather grandly said: 'We'd only consider doing a single with Mr. Blobby if it's going to be Christmas
No. 1,'" he told *Vice* in 2021. "He said: 'You're on'." The single,
simply titled 'Mr Blobby', was released on 22 November. Radio 1,
recently rebranded as "One FM", focused on new music and now
uber-credible, immediately declared they wouldn't be playlisting it.
William Hill gave it 50/1 odds of bagging the festive top spot. No
one was taking it seriously. And then things went *crazy*.

The song itself is awful, obviously, but it's awful in a way that's
practically avant-garde; a post-modern, surrealist joke. It opens by
nodding to Richard Strauss's *Also sprach Zarathustra*, and thus the
opening to Stanley Kubrik's *2001: A Space Odyssey*; moves into the
jaunty, squelchy farts of the fictional *Mr Blobby Show* theme used
on the *Noel's House Party* segments; breaks with a drum roll into
a Hi-NRG dance tune sang by not one but *two* children's choirs
(both prestigious, too – the choirs of King's College and Brentwood
Cathedral Music); veers from *Goon Show*-style talky verses into that
raspberry-blowing TV theme and back into a dance record; and
then, somehow, for the finale, combines all of that at once. The
video parodies Shakespears Sister's recent hit 'Stay' in which a looka-
like of the band's Marcella Detroit (intercut with shots from the

---

[5] The world of betting odds is very weird indeed. Other figures given odds by
the bookies to manage the England team that year included Michael Jackson
(500,000/1). This effectively means that someone at William Hill had sat down
and calculated that Mr Blobby, an entirely fictional character, was *five times
more likely* to be England manager than Michael Jackson, who was (apparently)
an actual human man. The world is a strange place.

actual 'Stay' video) gives Blobby a moonlit sponge bath while he convulses manically, and Robert Palmer's 'Addicted to Love', complete with stony-faced, sexy lady backing band. It also features *Top Gear*'s Jeremy Clarkson cameoing as Blobby's driver, *Countdown*'s Carol Vorderman teaching him maths and lines of school children following the pink monster around like he's the Messiah. It's *insane*. "You will stare at your radio in disbelief," said the *Northern Echo*. "A record which science will one day be able to prove could have been written by an amoeba with a casiotone keyboard."

For some it was a baffling nightmare, for others an absurdist laugh. But for younger children, especially, it was catchy and funny and had a video with an oddly loveable pink giant knocking everything over. To the disgust of many but the surprise of few, and with very little radio support, it sold 200,000 copies in its first week and went in at No. 3 behind Elton John and Meat Loaf. The following week it leapfrogged them both and hit the top spot with two chart weeks left before Christmas. It had already sold 450,000 records. William Hill's odds on a Blobby Christmas dropped from 50/1 to 33/1 to 7/1, at which point Noel Edmonds himself declared that he'd put £1,000 bet on a Blobby win. The character was also media gold: the BBC's three Blobby suits were dispatched across the country to do in-store appearances, delighting children with pratfalls and cuddles. For the important appearances he was always played by the "official" Blobby actor, Barry Killerby, previously known more for his Shakespearean stage work ("I was doing *Measure for Measure* when I got the gig," he told the *Evening Standard*), who inhabited the suit for TV appearances in which he crashed haplessly through the *GM:TV* and *Top of the Pops* studios.

Newspapers would do anything they could to add a Blobby angle. When it transpired that Prince Edward's new girlfriend, Sophie Rhys-Jones, worked for the PR company promoting the single, she was quickly dubbed Blobby's Girl and Buckingham Palace was asked for the Queen's opinion (she declined to give one). A photoshoot in *Smash Hits* saw him tangled in Christmas decorations and covered in flour. On 10 December, Mr Blobby was the guest editor of the *Sun* ("there we were thinking he'd been in charge all along," sniped the *Evening Standard*). The *Daily Mirror*, meanwhile, did a rather pointless expose of Blobby actor Barry Killerby and his wife,

Felicity, in which it revealed juicy details like "the Blobbys live in a three-bedroom semi-detached home in suburban south London" and that the "Blobby Mobile" was an "L-Registered Peugeot 306 XR in a shade of John Major-grey". Perhaps the most tantalising morsel in this vigorous piece of investigative journalism comes when the reporter asked Mrs Killerby if she would care to "describe her life as Blobby's girl", in which we learn that "she replied 'no' and slammed her front door." The piece carries three separate bylines.

Away from the gutter press, sociologists, psychologists and broadsheet writers were attempting to decode and explain Blobby-mania. "Mr Blobby is *Monty Python* without the politics," Leicester University's Stephen Wagg told the *Independent*. "A lot of television worships itself. Mr Blobby appears to undermine that. He is a maverick, anarchic element." Meanwhile, Dr Mike Money[6] of Liverpool John Moores saw Blobby in terms of the theory of "collective unconscious" proposed by philosopher Carl Jung in the early twentieth century. "Mr Blobby is a clear manifestation of the trickster character that appears in many societies," Dr Money told Merseyside's *Daily Post*, referring to a "benign anarchist" such as a jester. "He's a clear indication that people think things should be different – that it's time for a change," he continued. "Perhaps it's because we've had the same political party in power for so long." Noted psychologist Dr Stephen F. Blinkhorn[7] told the *Independent* that Blobby was likely a symptom of "anteretrograde Korsokovian psychosis" in which a rare collective hallucination of a pink and yellow monster was shared by the whole country in anticipation of their Christmas boozing. Another psychologist interviewed in the same paper had a less intellectual perspective: "It's simply that people are being subjected to such marketing and hype that some of the mud sticks," said Martin Lloyd-Elliot. "This is not reflecting our culture or some mysterious section of the British psyche ... it's a transparent con." It's clear that none of these experts had studied the history of Christmas in Britain, else they'd surely have speculated that, what Blobby *actually* was, was a return to the days of Lords of Misrule and Bean Kings, when festive celebrations were entrusted to the hands of an assigned agent of chaos.

---

[6] Stephen Wagg and Mike Money are, honestly, really their names.

[7] Also his real name.

"Proper" music types were appalled. *Top of the Pops* presenter Tony Dortie publicly called the song "dross" and doubled down when Blobby's record company demanded a retraction. "If they want an apology they are just whistling in the wind," he told the *Hull Daily Mail*. "It was fair comment and they know it." The *Guardian*'s Caroline Sullivan called the song "rancid". Meanwhile, a Chrysalis Records exec told the *Mirror* that Blobby was symptomatic of a decline in British pop as the industry focused on cash-grab, one-hit wonders over developing long-term careers ("HAS BLOBBY RUINED POP?" was the paper's summary). "At Christmas time," an HMV spokesman told the *Independent*, "everyone's taste disappears." One of the few positive responses came from a young music exec who wrote into industry bible *Music Week*. "Am I the only person in the record business not connected with Mr Blobby's single who was pleased to see it go to No. 1?" pondered one Simon Cowell, A & R consultant to Arista Records and future creator of *The X Factor*. "We have done nothing but pour scorn on this single … if we as an industry continue to ignore the under elevens here, perhaps they will never get into the habit of buying records. What may seem 'crap' to your average record company executive, is obviously bringing pleasure to hundreds of thousands of youngsters and that is what counts."

The song was dethroned after just a week at the top by the latest release from boy band Take That. 'Babe', comfortably the group's weakest single, had been the bookies' favourite for Christmas No. 1 that year; and it did seem that, for once, they'd gotten it right. Despite an astounding 80% leap in Blobby's sales week on week, "the That" (as *Smash Hits* endearingly referred to them) were in their imperial phase, and 'Babe' became their third consecutive No. 1. Groups in that position always try for the Christmas prize. It's part of the playbook; a way to cement their ascendency. Blobby had sold half a million singles, but the Christmas No. 1 dream seemed to be over. Take That had bided their time and owned their moment. "All but the most charitable have ruled out his chances of regaining [No. 1]," said the *Daily Express*'s Andrew Preston, sagely. "Fate can be cruel." Blobby's Christmas No. 1 odds rose to 20/1, since artists rarely bounce back to the top of the charts after losing the position, while Take That's fell to 1/8: a virtual certainty.

And then something remarkable happened. Take That ran out of fans. Despite having thrown everything at the campaign, including discounted sales, special edition CDs with free calendars and framed pictures of Mark Owen, and despite absolutely dominating the pop press, sales started to slip. 'Babe' was the third single taken from the band's hugely successful *Everything Changes* album, and compared to their previous two, the robust and danceable 'Pray' and 'Relight My Fire', this ballad sung by Mark Owen felt weedy and thin, holding little appeal outside the (admittedly large) Take That faithful. The band's army of fans had turned up in the first week to buy the single, sure, but sales momentum was slowing. Blobby, meanwhile, was gaining ground, sailing past 600,000 copies.

The bookies noticed first. A surge of bets started coming mid-week, leading some at William Hill to speculate that sales data had somehow been leaked. "All of a sudden at lunchtime we were inundated with punters wanting to place bets of up to £1,100 on Mr Blobby," a spokesman for the bookies told the *Daily Mirror*, "when according to all the pop experts Take That should already be past the post." Blobby's odd's were shortened to 3/1 and betting was promptly suspended. Come Sunday, it was 'Mr Blobby' by Mr Blobby that was announced as the Christmas No. 1 – the first record in 25 years, at any time of the year, to be knocked off the top spot and then return. William Hill was forced to pay out £100,000 in Blobby bets, including a not inconsiderable £8,000 to Noel Edmonds, who presumably wished he'd had his flutter a little earlier when the odds were still at 50/1.

Awful novelty records hitting the top of the chart for Christmas is, of course, by no means unusual – we've seen it plenty of times before, from 'Ernie (The Fastest Milkman in the West)' to 'There's No One Quite Like Grandma' to 'Long Haired Lover From Liverpool'. 'Mr Blobby', though, does rather stand out. It was awful in an entirely new way. This was a very '90s version of a novelty hit … more knowingly grotesque, more media saturated, and more catastrophically unmusical. For much of the adult population its success was baffling, and though plenty of people had tried to explain Blobby's appeal – by referring to a British anarchic comedy tradition, tying it to *The Goon Show* or *The Young Ones*, for example – no one had quite been able to nail it. "[Blobby] is not some aberration of taste but an intrinsic part of British culture," wrote the *Sunday Times*. "But it's not the part we like to boast about, especially around the Americans." The Americans were indeed baffled: "watching Mr. Blobby at work, his green plastic eyes spinning maniacally, one has to wonder whether his appeal to this nation of Shakespeare, Milton and Philip Larkin isn't a bit more complex," speculated the *New York Times* from across the pond. "His frozen smile has a malevolent curve. Blobby is Barney without his medication." People talked about this cheeky spirit of maniacal chaos cheering up a disaffected Britain mired in recession and struggling with an identity crisis in the post-Thatcher age. "Some commentators," summarised the *New York Times*, "have called him a metaphor for a nation gone soft in the head." Ultimately it was Simon Cowell who got it right in his letter to *Music Week* – this was a children's song, and young children genuinely loved it, just as in the past they'd loved Pinky and Perky or the Chipmunks, and in the future they'd love 'Baby Shark' and *Teletubbies*. It was really no more complicated than that.

Like most novelty hits, Blobby's moment in the sun was brief – despite big talk by the record label ("we've learned a lot – wait till the album next year," a Destiny representative told *Music Week*) the resulting LP, *Mr Blobby – The Album*, sold poorly and an attempt at another festive hit, 1995's 'Christmas in Blobbyland', peaked at 36 before vanishing. Even *Noel's House Party* ultimately phased Blobby out. The Blobby moment had passed. Recently, however, he's seen something of a revival, with millennials who loved him the first time around, as very young children, getting a kick out of seeing him appear on panel shows to destroy sets and create chaos. On a 2022 episode of the reality TV competition *RuPaul's Drag Race UK*, two of the contestants, independently of one another and much to the bafflement of American host RuPaul Charles, interpreted a "100 years of the BBC" theme with drag queen looks inspired by Mr. Blobby … it's clear we've grown quite fond of the strange pink monster. There's a feeling that Mr Blobby, like the Christmas No. 1 phenomenon itself, is something uniquely and weirdly British. Something no one else has. And while the song rarely gets played (because it's awful), and even Blobby's progenitor, Noel Edmonds, has long since lost the affection of the public, somehow the United Kingdom still keeps a little Blobby in its heart.

Chapter 14
ALL I WANT FOR CHRISTMAS IS YOU

In which British pop gets its act together

While no one can claim that the 1993 Christmas No. 1 was a creative peak, it did, at the very least, remind people that the December charts could be exciting, unpredictable and have high stakes. Depending on your perspective, either the biggest boy band in the country had been denied their rightful crown – having been "stuffed by a piece of pink and yellow plastic", as a William Hill spokesman put it to *Music Week* the following year – *or* a ridiculous underdog had put a monkey wrench into the spokes of the conventional music industry … and Britain *loves* an underdog. Either way, after a fallow period where the most important chart of the year had felt rather predictable (global stars, charity records, Cliff Richard), the Blobby phenomenon had been *news*. The Christmas No. 1 was once again providing watercooler moments. When the bookies are paying out £100,000, you have to wonder *just how much more they must have taken*. More than that, Christmas 1993 showcased a UK music industry starting to get its mojo back. The two major contenders after all, had been *British* records, none more so, and while Take That had stumbled at the finish line, it hadn't taken the shine off an extraordinary year of massive hits. The era of the British boy band was now in full swing, and Take That were merely the forerunners – also in the chart that week were Bad Boys Inc, and though they don't have much of a cultural footprint 30 years down the line, they got the full *screaming fans* treatment at the time. More significantly, and nipping closest at the leader's heels, were London four-piece East 17, in the Top 10 with the brilliant 'It's Alright', their biggest hit so far. 1994 would be their peak, and by the end of that year, with the arrival, among others, of PJ & Duncan, 2wo Third3, Worlds Apart, Ultimate Kaos and, most significantly, Ireland's Boyzone, boy band dominance would be complete.

East 17 had been formed in 1991 as a vehicle for 21-year-old East London dancer, rapper and songwriter Tony Mortimer, discovered in a gay club[1] by a friend of former Bros/Pet Shop Boys manager Tom Watkins, who, once made aware, was impressed enough to offer a management deal – but only if Mortimer found himself a band. He quickly rounded up local teenager Brian Harvey, who combined the voice of an angel with the grubby vibe of Dickens' Artful Dodger, to handle the vocals and two beefcake friends, John Hendy and Terry Coldwell, to dance and basically make up the numbers. The quartet were named after their Walthamstow postcode: E17. Much as the Rolling Stones were marketed as a sketchy, rebellious antidote to the charming and squeaky clean Beatles, East 17 quickly became the anti-Take That. The Manchester band had settled into a non-threatening image of boys you'd happily take to your nan's for tea, but East 17 came off as thugs who'd probably rob your grandad's false teeth. The difference was emphasised by the music the two produced. Take That made pure teenybop pop, flecked with disco and Hi-NRG: danceable but also cute and occasionally a little soppy. East 17, meanwhile, had elements of house music and hip-hop: edgier, cooler, a little more grown-up. The kind of group that could also appeal to older, more musically savvy teens and, crucially, straight men – two demographics that had no time for Take That. Between them, the two acts came to define the boy band era in the UK and were head and shoulders above the competition, thanks mostly to the elements they had in common: genuinely gifted songwriters in Tony Mortimer and Gary Barlow, and charisma machines with distinctive singing voices in Brian Harvey and Robbie Williams. By Christmas 1994, East 17 were almost as

---

[1] Which Mortimer claims he'd stumbled into by mistake because he liked the music.

big as their rivals. Their debut album, *Walthamstow*, had been a No. 1 and five of their first eight singles had been Top 10s. A second album, *Steam,* had gone top three that October,[2] and as is traditional for massive pop bands, they'd been careful to keep a ballad back for the Christmas market.

'Stay Another Day' had come out of an intense, six-week writing session the previous summer in which Tony Mortimer was basically asked to vomit out his band's entire second album, sharpish. Their debut had been, for the most part, a harder, dance-focused record and Mortimer was keen to expand his musical palette with a couple of out-and-out ballads, inspired partly by American hard rock band Extreme, who'd broken out of their lane with the massive, lighters-aloft weepie 'More Than Words' and gotten away with it. Plus, as a lifelong Prince fan, he knew the value of having a heart-wrenching torch song to break up a funky album. The phrase *stay another day* had popped into his head when a friend's terminally ill father had clung on for another 24 hours after his family had been told to prepare for the worst. In Mortimer's head this became connected to his older brother Ollie's suicide, four years previously, and the words he wished he could have said to him. Some ambivalent lines and the smart insertion of the word *baby* meant the song could also be interpreted as the end of a romantic relationship, taking the edge, just slightly, off the bleak theme. When producers Phil Harding and Ian Curnow asked Mortimer how he envisioned it sounding, he told them to throw the orchestral kitchen sink at it: "Go for it, guys," Harding remembers being told, writing in his book *Pop Music Production: Manufactured Pop and Boybands of the 1990s*, "take it all the way – timpani's, brass and strings, make it really over the top!"

The band's management and label were overjoyed, rightly sensing a massive hit. However, there were two problems to overcome. Mortimer was initially resistant to releasing 'Stay Another Day' as

___

[2] The success wasn't reflected in that December's annual *Smash Hits* poll winners awards, where the only gongs they took home were for "worst group" and, for Brian Harvey specifically, "least fanciable male" and "worst haircut". It's worth bearing in mind that these awards were voted for by readers, and *Smash Hits* was very much Take That territory.

a single. The song was too personal, and too close, and he couldn't stand the idea of answering the inane questions that would surely come from the teen mags and pop shows: "So what's your new single about?" It took label boss Colin Bell telling him that the song was a classic in waiting to nudge him over the edge. The second problem was that Brian Harvey absolutely *hated* it. East 17 had been built around Mortimer's songs, but it was very much Harvey's soulful voice that had sold them. By their second album he was leaning into cooler, American R & B styles. To him, 'Stay Another Day' was too saccharine and required too basic a performance. "We were trying to get him to sing like The Beatles," session singer Tee Green, who helped arrange the vocals on the album, told Phil Harding for his book, "and he was trying to do R. Kelly." At one point Harvey was so dismissive of the song that Mortimer had to be held back from punching his lights out. Eventually he was coaxed through it, line by line, resisting all the way. It took two whole days. Once finished, though, even Brian Harvey had to admit that the song was an obvious hit. Manager Tom Watkins was instantly convinced it was a Christmas No. 1.

The Christmassy vibe had been arrived at by serendipity – producers Curnow and Harding hadn't had time to mix the bass and drums before a planned summer break, so had sent the label a *work in progress* version featuring the vocals and orchestral backing only. The song ended with the peeling of tubular bells, part of the *throw the kitchen sink at it* brief Mortimer had given his producers. That simple addition, added as a way to resolve the drama of the swelling swings, timpani's and brass at the song's climax, brought it firmly into Christmas territory, with the notes falling like snow into the same descending scale commonly used by church bells. It conjured images of bright, frosty Christmas mornings. You half expected Ebenezer Scrooge to pop his head out of a nearby window to yell, "You boy! What day is this?" at Brian Harvey.[3] The producers had intended to add the bass, drums and other, poppier elements into the song on their return. As it turns out, everyone loved it as it was and the pair were instructed, in no uncertain terms, to leave it

[3] To which Harvey would presumably have replied: "Shove off, mister" and flicked the V-sign.

untouched. To Tom Watkins, as he says in his memoir, those chiming bells "sounded like the ker-ching of cash registers ringing out."

Like Frankie Goes To Hollywood's 'The Power of Love' before it, 'Stay Another Day' had become a Christmas song by default. It certainly hadn't been written as one, but once the seasonal vibe was identified leaning in was the obvious thing to do. An initial video was shot featuring the band singing around a piano, but was rejected in favour of a second attempt, which had the boys in immaculate, fur-trimmed white parkas, singing in the snow, a pair of ski goggles dangling around Tony Mortimer's neck. It became their defining image. The song was well received, too. The *Guardian* called it a "beautiful thing", while noting the cynical festive positioning and pointing out that the bells at the end had more than a hint of "Buy! Buy! Buy!" about them. "A tinkling piano, a gorgeous melody, a sweet and soulful lead vocal," noted the *Sunday Mirror*, "those little devils from East 17 have gone all angelic for Christmas … [it] leaves Take That's recent efforts looking very sad indeed".[4] William Hill quickly set odds at 8/1, making the single joint-third most likely to be Christmas No. 1 … though the betting odds were getting increasingly hard to take seriously, since the list the bookmaker published included Mr Blobby, the Beatles and Take That, none of whom were releasing a single, and had Captain Sensible's cover of the 'Hokey Cokey' as more likely to get that all-important chart crown than East 17, Wet Wet Wet or Cliff Richard.[5] 'Stay Another Day' entered the chart at No. 7 on 26 November, jumped to No. 1 the following week, displacing Baby D's dancefloor classic 'Let Me Be Your Fantasy', and stayed there until 7 January, fending off novelties from TV puppets Zig and Zag, a new version of the theme

---

[4] The only bad review came, surprisingly, from *Smash Hits*, who had the stars of the TV hit *Gladiators* reviewing the singles that week. "Like a Big Mac advert," said Saracen. "I don't like it very much," said Trojan. "I haven't got any East 17 and I won't be getting this," finished Scorpio. They collectively rated it at two stars. Which is one star more than they gave Boyzone's 'Love Me for a Reason', so Tony and the boys can at least feel smug about that.

[5] Yes, *another* attempt to get the 'Hokey Cokey' to Christmas No. 1. I genuinely can't work out what it is about that song that keeps people trying it. This version peaked at 71.

to Saturday morning kids show *Mighty Morphin Power Rangers*[6] and a clear play for Christmas No. 1 by the ascendent Oasis with their eight-minute Beatles impression, 'Whatever'. Throw into that two US megastars with rare, bona fide Christmas songs in Bon Jovi's cover of 'Please Come Home for Christmas' and Mariah Carey's 'All I Want for Christmas Is You', and you had one of the healthiest December charts in a decade.

It's worth pausing here to discuss 'All I Want for Christmas Is You', because though it wasn't Christmas No. 1 (and still hasn't been, at least at the time of writing), though it wasn't British, and though it wasn't taken especially seriously at the time, it's arguably the last true, gold-plated, iconic Christmas pop song to be added to the canon. Indeed, it will probably outlive all but a handful of the songs mentioned in this book. When 'Stay Another Day' has been forgotten, and 'Driving Home for Christmas' is a pop footnote – when even 'Merry Xmas Everybody' is remembered fondly only in Wolverhampton care homes – Mariah's holiday classic will endure. Of the modern pop era's Christmas standards, only 'Last Christmas' can really match it for staying power.

'All I Want for Christmas Is You' is one of those rare songs that transcended mere pop and ascended into a wider role in culture. It's been turned into a book, a film and a meme. It's a plot point in *Love Actually*. It's the one you will hear in the pub, the taxi, the dentist, the school disco and the Nativity play with your nephew. For many, its first play of the year marks the beginning of Christmas (Radio 1/Radio 2 DJ Scott Mills has a tradition of playing it in September for that very reason). Mariah and co-writer Walter Afanasieff built the song as a deliberate homage to Phil Spector's *A Christmas Gift For You* – all maximalist production, sleigh bells and Wall of Sound rhythm section, and it helps that it's incredibly well written. The lyrics hit a precise emotional tone – romantic, yearning, warm without being cloying. The performance is outrageous: Mariah at the height

---

[6] Both of these had been willed into existence by Simon Cowell, who was making good on his letter to *Music Week* of the previous year in which he'd lambasted the wider industry for neglecting the children's market. He wasn't finished yet.

of her vocal powers, but playful rather than obnoxiously showy. And it moves more than most Christmas songs dare. It skips, struts, dances, *gallops*. It's also oddly timeless. 'All I Want For Christmas Is You' doesn't really sound like 1994 and Mariah holds back on the vocal acrobatics that would have tethered it to the pop-R & B of the time. It also doesn't sound like the '80s or the '70s. If anything, it's closest to the sound of the mid '60s – though it has a contemporary brightness that stops it feeling like pastiche. It's a record that exists out of time. Like the best Christmas songs, it doesn't belong to a year or a decade or an era. It belongs to *Christmas*.

It didn't reach No. 1 in the UK on release. It didn't need to. Like 'Last Christmas', it slowly took up permanent residence. Streaming, downloads and chart rule changes eventually nudged it to the top spot in 2020 – though not Christmas No. 1. It was dethroned in Christmas week, as we'll see – 26 years after its release, and after a combined 105 weeks on the chart. The longest gap ever for a chart-topper. A good pub quiz fact, yes, but one that illustrates the point: this was a permanent migration. A song that just kept returning until we admitted it had always lived here. It's tempting to call it the last great Christmas pop anthem, and perhaps it is. If nothing has quite matched it in the decades since, and that's not from lack of trying (the likes of Leona Lewis and Kelly Clarkson have attempted to beat Mariah at her own game) – but because 'All I Want For Christmas Is You', with all its exuberance and its channelling of a half century of the Christmas pop that came before, firmly closed the door behind it. After that, what was left to say?

Meanwhile, like so many Christmas No. 1s, East 17's proved to be their career peak. They never had another chart-topper, and while rivals Take That managed to go out on their own terms and at the top of their game, announcing their split in early 1996 (Robbie Williams flying the nest early, on his way to becoming Britain's biggest solo pop star), East 17 fell apart like a clown car. Brian Harvey got the sack after making some extremely ill-judged comments about ecstasy in an interview and Tony Mortimer walked out a few months later, not really seeing the point anymore.[7] But while it may

---

[7] The band revolved through various reunions in various combinations over the next 30 years. In 2023 they made a play for the Christmas No. 1, donning the

The Story of the Christmas No. 1

have been the beginning of the end for East 17, 1994's Christmas chart heralded a blossoming for British pop, which was entering a period of energy, creativity and confidence it hadn't known since before Band Aid – though it took a little while for things to really settle.

The following year's Christmas chart reads like a tug of war between decades. The 1995 Christmas No. 1: 'Earth Song', Michael Jackson at his most insufferably messianic. Like most US megahits that top the Christmas chart, the song felt incidental rather than festive. It could have been a hit in June. Below Jackson, improbably, 'Wonderwall' – not by Oasis, but by the Mike Flowers Pops, a lounge music cover delivered with an impeccably arched eyebrow and full 1960s pastiche. It's a far more representative snapshot of Britain in 1995 than Jackson's performative histrionics – fun, self-referential but never self-*reverential*. The real Oasis were there too, just a few places down, with the original 'Wonderwall', still hanging around three months after its release. This was smack in the middle of Britpop, the catch-all phrase for the jangling, '60s and '70s indebted indie rock that had defined the year, marking a confidence in British guitar music that celebrated its own past and present. All of Britpop's Big Three were in that Christmas chart – Oasis with 'Wonderwall', Blur with 'The Universal', Pulp with 'Disco 2000'.

And then it gets odder. At No. 5: 'Free as a Bird' by the Beatles – a brand-new single, stitched together from a John Lennon demo and issued with the full weight of *Anthology*-era reverence. Just below that, Queen's 'Heaven for Everyone', drawn from unfinished Freddie Mercury material. It's a Christmas chart that feels crowded with endings. Posthumous singles. Covers of recent hits. Throwbacks and farewells. Even the new songs sound borrowed from somewhere else – retro pastiches, reworked album tracks, year-end mop-ups. In Britain itself, something similar was happening. John Major's government was on its last legs, trying to maintain the momentum of the Thatcher years while simultaneously distancing itself from them.

---

white parkas once more for a song called 'Merry Quitmas', an anti-smoking anthem with a video where, and I'm not making this up, Santa dies of lung cancer. It didn't chart.

226

After so long in government, the Tories had burned through their best and brightest, and those left seemed to be constantly mired in accusations of corruption or vice. The public was losing patience, the tabloids were feeding off scandal, and Tony Blair's New Labour was starting to smell like inevitability. Change was in the air, both politically and culturally. Britain was feeling its oats – you could see it in the Britpop groups, of course, but that was nothing compared to the bomb that would explode across pop culture in 1996 in the form of five young women and a "zig-a-zig-ah".

From 1996 to 1998, the Christmas No. 1 wasn't really up for grabs. It belonged to the Spice Girls. Three years in a row, the best-selling single in the most-watched chart week of the year came from the same act – a feat not seen since the Beatles, and repeated only once afterwards. These were pop smashes by the biggest chart act in the world, and yet, somehow, they were also Christmas songs – not in subject, necessarily, but in atmosphere, intent, and timing. In 1996, it was '2 Become 1' – soft-focus, and romantic,. In 1997, 'Too Much' – velvet strings, Bond chords, Hollywood pastiches in the video. These were both the traditional "album ballads held back for Christmas". In 1998, 'Goodbye' a sleek, mournful glide into the girl's new era – their first single without Geri 'Ginger Spice' Halliwell, who'd departed the group, cracking under the strain of being in the most famous pop band in the world. By this point there wasn't an album to take a single from; 'Goodbye' existed because by this third year their simply *had* to be a Spice Girls Christmas single. Each song was different. Each one everywhere. Like Cliff Richard or Paul McCartney before them, they owned the season for a spell. The Beatles had Beatlemania, Cliff had the church.

The Spice Girls' Christmas hat-trick coincided with a moment of national self-belief – not always justified, not always attractive, but definitely present. The mid to late '90s saw a burst of energy in British life. Cool Britannia, New Labour, Britpop, the Lottery, Euro 96, the Millennium Dome. Britain, or at least the idea of it, was getting a rebrand – younger, slicker, brasher. The Spice Girls, like Oasis, arrived at exactly the right time to soundtrack that moment. They were flashy, confident, aggressively British – and, crucially, everywhere. The group had been put together in 1994 after answering a trade magazine ad looking for girls who could sing and dance – they were technically a manufactured group, originally called Touch, who found their final form when they ditched their original management, renamed themselves and leaned into their differences. There was no lead singer and no matching outfits. Instead there were five personalities, quickly given nicknames by the pop press: Scary (Melanie Brown), Sporty (Melanie Chisholm), Baby (Emma Bunton), Posh (Victoria Adams) and Ginger (Geri Halliwell). Between them, they offered a cartoonish but effective version of modern femininity – laddish but glamorous, assertive but marketable. Their debut single, 'Wannabe', went to No. 1 in summer 1996 and stayed there for weeks. It was followed by a run of five consecutive No. 1s, a feature film, a world tour, and the most astonishingly comprehensive merchandising and endorsement campaign of any pop act in living memory.

In a sense, they represented the logical endpoint of everything the 1995 chart had been building towards. The Beatles' return, Blur and Oasis mining the past for the present, Mr Blobby still haunting the Top 40 like a bright pink spectre of festive pop gone wrong. The Spice Girls took all of the retro styling, the media saturation and the nods to national identity and made it streamlined, international and choreographed. Where Britpop had always carried a slight sense of irony, the Spice Girls were completely sincere. They wanted to be massive. They were. They also understood Christmas pop. Not just the release date, but the mood. '2 Become 1' landed in December 1996, just after the girls turned on the Oxford Street Christmas lights in London, with the full power of a major label push behind it – CD singles, picture discs, magazine covers, and a New York-set video that, while not *specifically* Christmassy, certainly had a twinkly, winter vibe. The single was about romance,[8] technically, but the packaging was pure Christmas: fairy lights, blurred backgrounds, city skylines after dark, and a Christmas classic, 'Sleigh Ride', on the B-side. It's emotional and pretty and slow enough to feel seasonal. A song for the end of a party, not the middle of one. Of all the three Spice Christmas singles, this is the only one that tends to crop up on seasonal compilations. It just about makes the canon.

---

[8] And, genuinely, safe sex.

'Too Much' in 1997 was a different proposition – more musically ambitious, more grown-up, more self-aware. This was the second single from *Spiceworld*, the girls' second album, which had a film to go with it and a promotional campaign that ran on caffeine and international licensing deals. '2 Become 1' was a handy ballad that could be packaged up for the December market , but 'Too Much' was far more cynical. With one Christmas No. 1 behind them, this was precision tooled for that specific goal. It's a Christmas No. 1 as brand extension – a seasonal flagship for a pop movement. By 1998, though, that movement was softening. Geri had left, the film was out, the world tour had happened. 'Goodbye' – the final Spice Girls Christmas No. 1 – was specifically a closing of a chapter, though in truth it may have been the closing of the book. It was slick and low-key, and there was a real sadness in it. It worked as a tribute to Halliwell, which was absolutely the intention (though behind the scenes the remaining girls were furious with her for bailing at the top of their game), but it was also a sign that things were changing, and there were cracks in the girl's previously bulletproof confidence. This was fragility. It was difficult to shake the feeling that the song existed only because there *had* to be a Spice Girls Christmas single, especially with the world questioning whether they could survive the departure of, arguably, their driving force. They didn't bother to do another Christmas single. Having proven their point, with the remaining four buckling under the pressure in their own way, the group went into a two-year hiatus to focus on solo projects. Though a third album would emerge in 2000, it badly undersold, and they consciously skipped the Christmas element. They never quite got their mojo back.

Between them, the three singles sketch a neat arc: from intimacy to scale to transition. A band arriving, a band at the top, a band shifting into something else. It's easy to be cynical about the whole thing – they were a product, after all – but they were a product people actually wanted. Not just bought, but played. The Spice Girls were the last act to truly *own* Christmas.[9] Their three-year run coincided with a moment when Britain believed, briefly and loudly,

[9] On statistics alone, there is one more artist to come who could argue that they "owned" Christmas. I strongly disagree. We'll get to that soon enough.

in itself. Pop mattered again. The charts still felt like they mattered, too. The country had a story it wanted to tell, and the Spice Girls were more than happy to narrate. After that, things got messier. The millennium arrived. The bloom came off New Labour's rose. Reality TV changed how stars were made. The internet changed how hits were measured. But for three years an uncynical connection between pop and the season still held. It felt obvious. It felt easy. It couldn't last.

Chapter 15
HOW THE GRINCH STOLE CHRISTMAS

In which reality TV dominates the season and the bottom falls out of the pop market

By the turn of the millennium, the rules of the Christmas No. 1 had been long established. No one was surprised, for example, when a garage-flavoured version of the theme to the likeable and wildly popular CBBC show *Bob the Builder* bagged the spot in the year 2000 – young children absolutely adored that show, and the song was irresistibly catchy. It sold 600,000 copies and its closest competition, extremely dull Irish boy band Westlife, couldn't compete. Essentially the continuity Boyzone, Westlife were another Simon Cowell project which, by that point, automatically indicated a kind of empty pop, spread thinly as possible to go as far as possible, appealing to the widest possible demographic and thus, by extension, no one in particular. A few years earlier, Cowell had huge success by giving TV actors Robson Green and Jerome Flynn a run of early '60s hits like 'Up on the Roof' and 'Unchained Melody', squeezing all the fun and sex out of the songs and flogging them to old ladies. Westlife got similar treatment. They were the first boy band aimed as much at housewives and grannies as at teenage girls. Few acts get both the grey *and* pink pound. Westlife, somehow, managed it – an act designed to offend so few people that they end up being offensive through sheer blandness, at least to those of us who like our pop

231

with some life shaken into it. Still, the five lads (shortly to become a quartet after the departure of Bryan McFadden) were monstrously successful. Their 2000 Christmas release, 'What Makes a Man', was their seventh single and the previous six had all topped the UK chart. In any other country they'd have had a second consecutive Christmas No. 1 in the bag. Fortunately, the topsy-turvy logic of the December charts had robbed them of that. 'Can We Fix It' is hardly a masterpiece, but it's *so* much more fun than the alternative.

Still, Westlife are as good an indication as any that the spark in British/Irish pop was spluttering since the days of Take That, East 17, Britpop and the Spice Girls. The record biz, in the very last throes of its boom years, was starting to play things very safe. The industry was now thoroughly spooked by the rise of file sharing and MP3s, a threat that made the home taping of the '80s and '90s seem positively harmless. The CD era had given record execs the world over a decade of being able to swim like Scrooge McDuck in vast pools of money – but it had also given every customer a fully digital catalogue of music that was *incredibly* easy to rip to a computer and share on the burgeoning internet with barely any loss of quality. The year 2000 saw a series of court cases against Napster, the most commonly used file sharing app, which forced the service to restrict its flow of copyright material, but it was too late. Genies were out of bottles, cats were out of bags. Replacement software – LimeWire, KaZaA, eDonkey, Soulseek – mushroomed, the demand encouraged by the growth of digital MP3 players and supercharged by the launch of Apple's iconic iPod. Digital music, with no physical product attached, was here to stay and the record industry had completely failed to prepare. The business would never have it so good again, and the decline would only get steeper. The Christmas season had always underpinned the rest of the year, delivering 40% of annual sales. Risky swings at the December charts were to become increasingly rare.

The 2001 Christmas winner was no less predictable. Robbie Williams, comfortably the country's biggest star, had bagged a duet with Hollywood goddess Nicole Kidman, having a moment of her own thanks to her star turn in Baz Luhrman's huge film *Moulin Rouge*. The pair had covered Sinatra's classic duet 'Somethin' Stupid', a smart choice for the inexperienced Kidman, as it needed very little in the way of vocal range but required a performance with bags of character. You didn't have to be a fortune teller or a William Hill bookmaker to predict its success. The rest of the chart was largely business as usual, though it still held a little unexpected Christmas magic: No. 2 was Gordon Haskell's 'How Wonderful You Are', a gentle jazzy number by a 55-year-old session musician who'd spent the previous decade or so slogging on the pub circuit. The song, released on the tiny Flying Sparks label, had been championed by Radio 2 DJ Johnnie Walker and become a hit via word of mouth, eventually selling 400,000 copies, bagging Haskell a record deal with East West worth a reported £2.4 million. Alas, it would be his only hit.

Looking at the 2000/2001 Christmas chart in general, the usual turn-of-the-decade stagnation was pretty clear. There were no real standouts, few classics and a sense of treading water. If the British music industry was going to continue to sell festive product in significant amounts – something it needed more than ever – it was going to have to find a new Christmas No. 1 playbook and a new mechanism for star-marking. And in 2002, amid alarmingly declining sales of singles across the board, it found one. On television.

TV singing competitions were nothing new. British telly had been pitting hopefuls against audience applause from the 1950s right into the 89s, with *Opportunity Knocks* and *New Faces* offering a leg-up to the likes of Les Dawson, Lenny Henry and Marti Caine. These were often rough-edged affairs, cheap sets, wobbly vocals, light entertainment masquerading as talent scouting, but they hung around for decades and for a while they worked. They even created a few chart stars – Renato Pagliari, of 1982 Christmas No. 1 fame, had been on *New Faces* in the '70s, and Sheena Easton had found early success on a BBC documentary series called *The Big Time*. In 1990, ITV's *Stars In Their Eyes* refreshed the format as something softer and sillier: not a launchpad for pop careers, but a place for supermarket managers to be Marti Pellow or Chris de Burgh for the night, before removing the fake ponytail or bushy eyebrows and vanishing back into obscurity.

The real shift came in early 2001, when ITV launched *Popstars*; a documentary format ported over from New Zealand, which followed the assembly of a manufactured pop group from open auditions to release day. It was the first time the public were invited behind the scenes – to see the decisions, the rejections, the infighting. It felt like access, even if it was clearly shaped for drama. The show was huge – 12 million people tuned in to watch the final line-up of the band be revealed, and the resulting group, Hear'Say, were an instant, if short-lived hit. They were given a decently uplifting debut single titled 'Pure and Simple',[1] which went straight to No. 1, selling 550,000 copies in its first week and becoming, briefly, the fastest-selling debut in UK chart history. The band were given their own Saturday night variety show, and even made the cover of *NME*. It wasn't built to last, however. Within 18 months, they'd been dropped, and a group formed of the show's runners-up – Liberty X – was outperforming them both commercially and critically.

But *Popstars* had opened the door. That autumn, ITV returned with a new format: *Pop Idol*, technically unconnected to *Popstars,* though very clearly inspired by it (the creators of the former attempted to sue), this time presented as a gamified reality TV talent competition rather than a fly-on-the-wall documentary. Created by Simon Fuller, who'd previously managed the Spice Girls and S Club 7, it focused on solo singers, the voting was public, the final rounds took place in front of a live audience and the tone was more polished – equal parts talent contest, panto and soap opera. The judging panel included radio DJ Neil 'Dr' Fox, publicist Nicki Chapman, record producer Pete Waterman and, stepping in front of the camera properly for the first time,[2] A & R man Simon Cowell, who quickly became the breakout star thanks to his knack for vicious but extremely pithy put-downs. It was a huge hit. The final, in February 2002, drew 13 million viewers. Winner Will Young

---

[1] Originally meant for a band called Girl Thing, a recent Simon Cowell signing that had failed to make any impact, the song was a transparent retread of Oasis' 'All Around the World'. Oasis themselves made no comment on the release, presumably because no one could listen to the famously light-fingered Noel Gallagher complaining about his songs being ripped off and keep a straight face.

[2] If you discount the odd interview and a trial run auditioning popstars for a short-lived feature on *This Morning with Richard and Judy*.

released a double A-side – 'Evergreen' and 'Anything Is Possible' – which sold 1.1 million copies in its first week, breaking Hear'Say's short-lived record for fastest-selling debut, and would go on to be the biggest selling single of the entire decade. Runner-up Gareth Gates followed with a cover of 'Unchained Melody' that enjoyed first week sales of nearly 900,000. These were numbers the industry hadn't seen in years, almost unheard of outside of Christmas. What *Pop Idol* proved, more than anything, was that a Saturday night TV show could deliver a guaranteed No. 1 and sell CDs by the truck-load. The interactivity, by public phone call/text vote, was the final piece of the puzzle; it gave the audience a sense of ownership of the artists and an investment in their careers. *Of course* people would rush out and buy the songs and support their favourites – they'd been with them all along. ITV, and the record labels it partnered with, had found their model.[3]

Not to be outdone, the *Popstars* team stole the format right back (taking judge Pete Waterman with them) for *Popstars: The Rivals*, broadcast in the run-up to Christmas 2002. This time the concept was competitive: build a girl group and a boy band in parallel and have the public vote on the members. The panel now featured Waterman, Boyzone/Westlife manager Louis Walsh and former Spice Girl Geri Halliwell, between them responsible for four Christmas No.1's. At the end of the process we would be left with one boy band, to be managed by Waterman, and one girl band to be managed by Walsh, who would then battle out in the charts. The prize? Well, that was obvious. *Everyone* knows what the ultimate prize in pop is.

What's telling here is that the question immediately became "Which of these songs will be the No. 1?", not "Can either get a Christmas No. 1?". Massive success was a given. And that was in spite of a strong chart that year in terms of superstars. Robbie Williams' single

---

[3] The BBC tried to respond with *Fame Academy* – a kind of televised songwriting boot camp where contestants lived together in a boarding school and learned how to channel their feelings into an acoustic guitar. It was well meaning and less brutal, but lacked the drama. It produced one No. 1 – David Sneddon's 'Stop Living the Lie' in early 2003 – and then faded out, quietly.

'Feel', in retrospect one of his best, was released toward the end of November, and Blue, the country's biggest boy band at the time, had covered Elton John's 'Sorry Seems to Be the Hardest Word', dragging Sir Elton himself along to feature on the record. Both would have had Christmas No. 1 in their sights. There was the usual massive American names as well – Eminem ('Lose Yourself'), Christina Aguilera ('Dirrty'), Pink ('Family Portrait'), Jennifer Lopez ('Jenny from the Block') and Avril Lavigne ('Sk8er Boi'). All artists at the peak of their popularity, all releasing songs that are considered among their best. Despite this, the coverage at the time was around the *Popstars* winners "battling it out for the Christmas No. 1". Nothing was expected to upset the apple cart; though Louis Walsh quietly agreed to move Westlife's next single back into January. Just to be sure.

This was the first example of a pattern that would dominate the decade's December charts – that the Christmas No. 1 was the rightful, God-given prize for winning a TV singing competition. It made sense. These competitions were about making superstars, and the crowning achievement of a superstar in British music is to top the charts at Christmas.

Except, of course, that it wasn't.

What everyone was ignoring, what the record industry *must* have known, was that, by now, the idea that the Christmas No. 1 was some sort of beautification or confirmation of pop greatness was entirely an industry myth and a media construct. It wasn't actually true. The Spice Girls had been the exceptions, not the rule. Slade, Boney M., Human League, Shakin' Stevens, East 17 – these were all acts that were huge at the point they had a Christmas hit, but none of them ever had a No. 1 again. Having a Christmas No. 1 didn't guarantee any form of longevity or legacy, unless as part of the mythology of the Christmas No. 1 itself. It simply meant you, or maybe just your song, were popular *now*. With the exception of the Spice Girls, who cleverly built it into their brand, none of the global megastars who achieved the feat – the Jacksons, Houstons, Queens, McCartneys, Pink Floyds (and later, the Ed Sheerans and Clean Bandits) – did so by actively trying to get a Christmas No. 1. Those who came to be defined by their festive hits rarely had a legacy outside it. And the makers of *Popstars*, *Pop Idol* and, later, *The*

X Factor knew this. And that betrayed their true intentions. These competitions were about creating immediate product. They were about success *now*, not forever.

The team behind *Popstars* was right about one of their singles being a dead cert for Christmas No. 1, though they were wrong about just about everything else. The two freshly minted groups were chosen in separate finals, the boys on 23 November and the girls the following week, and the two singles were formally launched with performances on 7 December. No episode got above nine million viewers, falling short of the peaks of *Pop Idol* and the original *Popstars*. The new boy band, signed to Jive records, was christened One True Voice and from the start, even before the line-up was finalised, they were the favourites to bag the big prize, with William Hill offering odds of 4/6 – some of the shortest ever given for a Christmas No. 1 in early December – making them as close to a sure thing as you'll find in betting. Their single was a double A-side, with 'Sacred Trust' as the focus track – a mid-pacer written by the Bee Gees and originally intended for Backstreet Boys, who'd rejected it. In the end the Gibb brothers had used it as filler on their latest album. The flipside, 'After You're Gone (I'll Still Be Loving You)', was a textbook slushy boy band ballad co-written by Waterman and the band's Daniel Pearce. The boys were handsome and tastefully styled and had more than a hint about them of Blue, the UK's current biggest boy band. The fact they'd been paired with the bigger name, Pete Waterman (an "industry legend" as the show went out of its way to remind us), and that the boy's final was scheduled first, made it very clear which group the producers considered the priority. When *Smash Hits* agreed to a *Popstars* feature, it was One True Voice that got the cover. There was a problem, though – both sides of the single were *terrible*. The Bee Gees had been responsible for some gold in their time, but 'Sacred Trust' is no 'Jive Talkin''. It's not even a 'You Win Again'. Compared to the other song on the disc, however, it was a masterpiece. Waterman and Pearce's track was utterly limp; a musical wet lettuce, devoid of soul, romance or a hook you could whistle ("It's nothing like what you'd expect from me or the group," Waterman proudly told *Music Week*, inadvertently putting his finger on the problem). The single got its premiere on Terry Wogan's Radio 2 show, which is rather telling. The man who'd championed 'There's No one Quite Like Grandma' and 'The Floral Dance' wasn't exactly a cutting-edge tastemaker. This was meant to be a contemporary pop product, not a cute novelty. What became very quickly apparent, what was utterly unavoidable in fact, is that One True Voice, in terms of music, presentation and personality, were deeply *boring*.

Meanwhile, Polydor records, who had signed the girl group, working with minimal input from manager Louis Walsh, had decided that, since everyone assumed they'd be the also-rans anyway, they may as well take a big swing with their artist. The five-piece band, comprising Sarah Harding, Cheryl Tweedy, Kimberly Walsh, Nicola Roberts and Nadine Coyle, was named Girls Aloud, given a neon-and-chrome, futuristic punk style and handed an absolute *banger* of a single in 'Sound of the Underground' written by the cutting-edge Xenomania production team.[4] The song, a mash-up of drum and bass beats and surf guitar, was exciting and sexy and didn't really sound like anything else happening in the pop mainstream; certainly not in the girl band sphere, where Sugababes had established a sort of arm's-length cool and an impression of sophistication. Girls Aloud were, by design, far messier and more fun. The whole campaign, from the girls' image down, was vibrating with attitude and energy – ads for the song carried the perfect tagline: "Buy girls … bye boys!" It worked, too. The tide turned in the girl's favour extremely quickly – pretty much as soon as anyone heard both songs. Journalist Peter Robinson, for example, who wrote the official companion book to *Popstars: The Rivals*, was played the two singles early – before the band's line-ups had been finalised. That afternoon he went straight to the bookies and put £50 on the girls to win.[5] Hearing the two songs side by side, there was no contest at all, it was a no-brainer. The public almost unanimously agreed with him. 'Sound of the Underground' went straight in at No. 1 for Christmas week with 213,000 sales, compared to 'Sacred Trust''s

---

[4] This had originally been recorded by another Polydor girlband, Orchid, whose deal had fallen through. The Girls Aloud version still has the original backing vocals on the chorus.

[5] "The odds were ridiculous at that point. It paid for my Christmas," as he told Michael Cragg for his book *Reach for the Stars*.

148,000. Girls Aloud went on to become one of the biggest pop acts in the country. By August of the following year, One True Voice had split up.

Girls Aloud won the battle, and *Popstars: The Rivals* certainly won the chart, so in a sense it was mission accomplished. The celebrations, however, were masking a bigger problem. Sales of 213,000 is a very strong hit at any other time of the year, but for Christmas week it's on the average side (the Spice Girls' '2 Become 1' had managed 450,000 for example), and it was a notable drop-off from the sales Hear'Say, Will Young and Gareth Gates had achieved with their debut singles, despite 'Sound of the Underground' being a substantially stronger song. Partly this could be chalked up to the chart battle gimmick itself – by definition, fans of the *Popstars* show were being asked to buy one or the other single, not both, splitting the vote. However, even combined with the No. 3 record – 'Cheeky Song (Touch My Bum)' by fellow *Popstars* alumnae Cheeky Girls[6] – the three singles took a week to equal what Will Young's 'Evergreen' had sold on its first day. CD singles were simply not selling in the numbers they had previously. December's combined music sales had dropped 44% in two years, and 2002's Christmas week sales were 33% below what they had been in 2000. However, there was *some* good news. Those final week figures may have been poor compared to 2000, but they were slightly higher than they had been in 2001. The injection of reality TV into the marketplace had caused a small bounce back. The industry took the lesson.

It took a few years for the pattern to settle, however – 2003's Christmas chart was a straight fight between a haunting if miserable cover of Tears for Fears' 'Mad World' by obscure American singer

---

[6] *Popstars: The Rivals* actually generated the whole top three that year. The Cheeky Girls were two twins from Transylvania, who'd auditioned on the show and been booted out early. They then signed a hasty deal with Telstar records and put out the Europop novelty 'Cheeky Song' while the series was still airing. It was dreadful, obviously, but such is the power of (a) reality TV and (b) weird novelty singles at Christmas, it ended up selling 88,000 records. They managed another three Top 10 hits, including the following year's 'Have A Cheeky Christmas'. Later, one of the twins dated Liberal Democrat MP Lembit Öpik. Strange but true.

Gary Jules, and a jaunty attempt to revive the Christmas No. 1's glam rock prime by tongue-in-cheek hard rock band the Darkness, titled 'Christmas Time (Don't Let The Bells End)'. The latter was a fine single, and one that's had some staying power in the canon – though it feels like it's fading a little, 20 years on. Theirs was one of the first conscious efforts to "save" the Christmas No. 1, restoring it to it former greatness. That year's was one of the most heated Christmas battles in some time, and one that did its job. The UK's combined music sales had dropped by another 30% that year, but the healthy competition in Christmas week inspired a huge spike, with sales jumping a remarkable 93% week on week and once again proving that the festive period was utterly vital if the singles market were to survive. It didn't escape anyone's notice that reality TV was still playing a role – another contender was Ozzy and Kelly Osbourne's duet on the old Black Sabbath ballad 'Changes', which had hit No. 1 a week previously, its popularity based on the success of their fly-on-the-wall docusoap *The Osbournes*. Also in the mix was the cast of the second season of *Pop Idol*, covering John Lennon's 'Happy Xmas (War Is Over)' for charity. The two records ended up at 3 and 5 respectively. In the end, Gary Jules pipped the Darkness at the post, once again proving Britain's collective desire to wallow in misery at the alleged "most wonderful time of the year", but the real winner was the music industry. A million and a half singles had been sold that week, and though Nos. 1 and 2 had gone to some encouragingly rogue choices, the two reality TV options had certainly played their role.

2004, meanwhile, saw everyone clearing the decks to make way for a twentieth anniversary Band Aid single; a new 'Do They Know It's Christmas?' raising money for an ongoing humanitarian catastrophe in the Darfur region of Sudan. Produced by Nigel Godrich, who'd made his name working with Travis and Radiohead, it was a far better version of the song than 1989's, and represented a far healthier British pop scene – among the stars present were Robbie Williams, Sugababes, Dizzee Rascal, Will Young, Chris Martin, the Darkness and a returning Bono, who once again took on his much-loathed and still-powerful line, here giving it a more compassionate reading that sands its edges down, just a little.[7] For good measure, the backing band for the song was built around Paul McCartney on bass, Travis' Fran Healy on guitar, Radiohead's Thom Yorke and Johnny Greenwood (piano and guitar respectively) and Supergrass drummer Danny Goffey. Not too shabby, and a large part of the reason that Band Aid 20's take on 'Do They Know It's Christmas?' sounds far, far less dated 20 years on than the 1989 version did within just a few years. The song was a predictable smash, selling 200,000 copies a week for most of December and staying at the top for a month, becoming comfortably the biggest selling single of the year and selling as much as the rest of the Top 20 combined.[8] It would be another 18 years before an actual Christmas song would be No. 1 at Christmas again.[9]

This was a good record for a good cause, which briefly revived the flagging singles market. It was also an ending. Almost 50 years since Bill Hayley's 'Rock Around the Clock'[10] became the UK's first million seller, the 2004 version of 'Do They Know It's Christmas?' would be the last song ever to sell a million physical copies in Britain (or the US for that matter). A digital chart, tracking legal downloads from services like Apple's iTunes Music Store had been launched that year, although they weren't yet counted in the official Top 40, and by the end of December downloads were outselling CDs for the first time. The singles chart was mattering less and less – the BBC had even relegated the flagging *Top of the Pops* to BBC 2, after 40 years on BBC 1. The times, they were a-changin'.

---

[7] The Darkness' Justin Hawkins apparently pushed *hard* for that line, correctly identifying it as the most important in the song. The press made quite a fuss over the "feud" between Bono and Hawkins at the time. I've always suspected this was fabricated, or at least inflated, for the extra column inches it would provide. That line works because it is deadly serious. Justin Hawkins' appeal is rooted entirely in the fact that he *isn't*.

[8] If you're keeping count, by the way, this was Paul McCartney's seventh contribution to a Christmas No. 1, and eighth if you count his message on the b-side to the original Band Aid, though that's pushing it.

[9] And when it came it turned out to be *the same song*. And really not worth the wait.

[10] Unofficially a Christmas No. 1; see Chapter two.

It was into this market of evolving formats and sinking sales that Simon Cowell launched *The X Factor*. Much as *Pop Idol* had built on the format of *Popstars*, *X Factor* was a straight lift of *Pop Idol*.[11] Cowell's twist was to expand the format, creating different categories – solo singers aged 16–25, solo singers aged *over* 25 and groups, who could be any age but were inevitably young boy/girl bands. It was the first time this later generation of TV talent shows had cast the net wider, particularly opening the door to older people, and it instantly made the shows more relatable, while inevitably adding more grotesques to be mocked in the early audition rounds. Cowell resumed his position on the judging panel, as he had with *Pop Idol*, this time joined by Louis Walsh and Sharon Osbourne – both legitimate music managers with TV experience. Each judge would then mentor one of the categories, meaning that once the show entered its live, audience-voted stage they were in competition with one another, something they took quite seriously. The first season of the show began in September 2004 and was a modest hit, not reaching the heights of the first *Pop Idol* series and not competing with BBC One's *Strictly Come Dancing*, but coasting along at a reasonable eight million viewers. Though the series climaxed in mid-December, winner Steve Brookstein, a 35-year-old soul singer from London, was never lined up as a Christmas No. 1 contender. 'Do They Know It's Christmas?' was squatting like a toad at the top of the charts, and it was generally assumed that attempting to unseat a charity record at Christmas wouldn't be great optics, and would certainly be unsuccessful anyway. Cowell cannily launched the first *X Factor* winner's single, a thin, karaoke cover of Phil Collins' 'Against All Odds', in the week following the Christmas chart – in time to still be a stocking filler, but not in visible competition with Band Aid. It went in at No. 2 in the week between Christmas and New Year, and unseated 'Do They Know It's Christmas?' the following week to become the first No. 1 of 2005.

There's a neat symbolism in the first *X Factor* winner knocking a Christmas song off No. 1 – it foreshadowed the next decade or so

---

[11] And just as the producers of *Popstars* had taken legal action against *Idol*, *Pop Idol* creator Simon Fuller later attempted to sue Simon Cowell over *X Factor*. As the saying goes, there is no honour amongst thieves.

of the December charts. From the 2005 series onwards, the winners' single would be timed specifically to go straight in at No. 1 for Christmas week. As Brookstein himself told the *Guardian* a few years later, Cowell had effectively "bought the rights to Christmas", adding dryly that "from now on it's called *X-mas*". On the surface this was, again, the old chestnut of crowning a new pop superstar with the most "coveted prize" in the industry. Ultimately, though, it was more about selling as many records as possible, as quickly as possible, by releasing a song in the biggest sales week of the year, given there was no guarantee that an *X Factor* winner would still be a name that would shift product further down the line. The reality TV track record was patchy – Will Young and Girls Aloud had managed sustained careers, while One True Voice, Hear'Say, Gareth Gates, Steve Brookstein, Michelle McManus (winner of *Pop Idol*, series 2) and the winners of the BBC's *Fame Academy* had all dropped off the face of the Earth within six months. The real goal, one that Cowell wouldn't admit to out loud, was legitimising the *X Factor* brand and his own reputation as a king maker. Forty years of British culture had given the Christmas No. 1 a weight and currency. By owning the Christmas chart, year upon year, Cowell was able to leach that cultural magic for himself. Who but the most powerful man in pop could literally dictate the Christmas No. 1? The biggest chart of the year was to become an extension of *his* show.

The system worked. Series two of *The X Factor* was won by genial 21-year-old Shayne Ward, whose debut single, 'That's My Goal', was a comfortable Christmas No. 1, with first week sales of 600,000. Thanks to a new rule that counted downloads in the main chart so long as they also had a physical release, the song was available for purchase the moment the show ended.[12] It set the precedent – seven of the next ten Christmas No. 1s would be *X Factor* winners. Almost all of them, the first four certainly, followed a standard formula – a mid-paced, vaguely inspirational ballad, sometimes written especially, sometimes recycled, with a big chorus and key change near the end, allowing for some vocal acrobatics

---

[12] Physical product was still considered the more important medium – the show featured TV presenter Andi Peters dispatched to the pressing plant and hitting "go" on the machines that manufactured the discs.

and, occasionally, a gospel choir. The video would feature a montage of clips from the show, highlighting the winner's "journey". Leona Lewis, an obvious star with a remarkable voice, took first place in 2006 and was given 'A Moment Like This', originally released as Kelly Clarkson's *American Idol* winners single. It sold almost a million copies between physical sales and downloads, denying poor Take That a Christmas No. 1 for a second time with their reunion hit, 'Patience' … though they probably felt better about it than they did being beaten by Blobby. In 2007, Leon Jackson took the crown. A likeable, if not especially memorable figure, he shifted 400,000 copies of his cover of Mariah Carey's 'When You Believe' and outsold the rest of the Top 10 combined. *X Factor* seemed untouchable. The Christmas No. 1 had become, in the words of the *Guardian*'s Helen Pidd, "as predictable as elections in North Korea".

By 2007, William Hill and Ladbrokes were, for the first time, refusing to take bets on the Christmas No. 1, giving the *X Factor* single completely unassailable odds of 100/1 and paying out early on existing bets. At one point William Hill turned down a punter who tried to put a £1 million bet on anyway – a canny attempt to earn themselves a cool ten grand. Instead, bookmakers started taking bets on the Christmas No. 2 ("The best of the rest," as Ladbrokes called it). "The annual *X Factor* single has wiped out a national institution," a William Hill spokesman told the *Irish Examiner* that year. "There's little real competition for the top single on Christmas Day, so we've opened a book to open the race up again." Alas, voting on the Christmas No. 2 didn't fire the imagination and there was very little take-up. There was, however, one quirk of the 2007 chart that did make it interesting – the records found at numbers 4, 6, 16, 18, 20, 22 and 24: the Pogues' 'Fairytale of New York', Mariah Carey's 'All I Want For Christmas Is You', Wham!'s 'Last Christmas', Wizzard's 'I Wish It Could Be Christmas Everyday', Slade's 'Merry Xmas Everybody', Andy Williams' 'It's The Most Wonderful Time of the Year', Shaky's 'Merry Christmas Everyone' and the 1984 version of 'Do They Know It's Christmas'.

Earlier that year, bowing to increasing pressure from the labels (and to the vocal dismay of retailers), the Official Charts Company had finally changed the rules around eligibility and started to count legally downloaded songs in the main chart without an accompanying physical release. By now, downloads made up 80% of the UK singles market and CDs were becoming less important – it was only the *X Factor* Christmas releases that sold actual discs in any significant numbers. The CD era, and thus the era of physical music formats that had begun with wax cylinders in the nineteenth century, was coming to a close. Downloads were cheaper – the UK wasn't immune to the global recession and what was becoming known as the *credit crunch* was biting hard. They were also more convenient. Why bother to go to a shop and fork out £2.99 for a disc that you would use just once – to rip the songs to your computer and transfer them to your iPod – when you could pay 79p for the lead track, get it instantly and not have yet another bit of plastic taking up space? The new rules meant that any song, be it a single on a major label, a self-released demo or a long-forgotten album track by artists big or small, could enter the UK charts with no need for manufacture or inventory. It was the biggest change in 54 years. And when, late in 2008, it was announced that the *X Factor*'s winner's single was to be a cover of Leanord Cohen's 'Hallelujah', several people considered the new rules and all had the same idea at once. It was time to fight back.

Chapter 16
I'M STREAMING OF A WHITE CHRISTMAS

In which the magic fades and the world moves on

And that, more of less, is where we came in, way back at the start of this book. By now there was plenty of very vocal opposition to Cowell's monopolising of the Christmas chart, but 2008 wasn't the year to unseat him. There were some solid attempts, of course – various campaigns were launched to get this or that classic song to the top, not least the Jeff Buckley version of 'Hallelujah', but in order for that to happen the weight of feeling against Cowell and the show had to be stronger than the product on offer. Alexandra Burke, that year's winner, was one of the better *X Factor* champs, a compelling performer and a great vocalist with plenty of star quality, and since she'd been handed, in 'Hallelujah', one of the greatest songs ever written, Christmas No. 1 victory was assured.[1] Burke's debut single

---

[1] Not that the *X Factor* version is a particularly good take. It really doesn't need the gospel choir. Or the key change, and it doesn't particularly suit Burke's soul diva style – she'd just duetted with Beyoncé, for heaven's sake. It would be far better suited to fellow contestant Diana Vickers, who used it as her audition piece that year. A lot of people at the time speculated that the choice of single meant that Cowell and his team were expecting and hoping for Vickers to take the title.

became, by quite some margin, the year's biggest seller, eventually topping out at 1.3 million sales – it made her the first solo female act to sell a million singles in the UK.[2]

2009, however, was a horse of a different colour. Cowell and his team had gotten complacent, and though the show itself was becoming bigger year on year, the end product was easier for the public to resist. Joe McElderry, bless him, was a talented singer and a likeable kid, but he wasn't a star anyone was getting especially excited about, and the single he was given, 'The Climb', was insipid – practically a parody of an *X Factor*'s "winner's song". It didn't feel like anyone on the show's team or at Cowell's Syco label had given it more than a moment's thought. Meanwhile, what the public had found in Jon Morter and Tracy Hayden's Rage Against the Machine campaign was a *focus*. 'Killing in the Name' became a rallying point, uniting disparate groups of fans – those who hated *X Factor* for what it represented joining with fans who hated it for taking the fun out of the Christmas chart and fans who hated manufactured pop music and wanted to get a "real" alternative anthem to No. 1. A lot of people bought it simply to bloody Cowell's nose. The British public rarely approves when someone is perceived to be getting ideas above their station. "Me having a No. 1 record at Christmas is not going to change my life," Cowell told a press conference that year as he begged the public not to take their annoyance with him out on his artists. He was entirely wrong. His reputation had become tied to *his* act from *his* show getting that absolutely key chart position. The public took great joy in reminding him that they could take that away if he didn't fulfil his end of the bargain – making really good pop records.

Rage Against the Machine's 2009 victory came at a pivotal point for the mythology of the Christmas No. 1 itself, and in the changing nature of the music industry and the Top 40 in general. It put some excitement back into the December charts, reminding us that this time of year could always be unpredictable, which was part of the fun of Christmas itself, but this would also be the last time there were any stakes or tension in the race. When the following

---

[2] To date, Adele's 'Someone Like You' is the only single by a British woman to have outsold Burke's debut at home with 1.6m.

year's *X Factor* rolled around, a year in which the show reached its all-time ratings peak, Cowell and his team course corrected to avoid a repeat of 2009's disaster. Rather than one generic ballad, producers selected a different song for each of the finalists, with the artists' input. It meant a far closer synergy between singer and song and thus a far stronger product. That year's winner was Matt Cardle, a slightly older, slightly more serious act with a background in rock bands. His winner's single was as far away from 'The Climb' or 'That's My Goal' as it could possibly be: a cover of 'Many of Horror', a recent ballad by Scottish punks Biffy Clyro. It was given some *X Factor* gloss, obviously, as well as a new title – 'When We Collide' – but fundamentally this was an indie-ish alternative rock song, performed with some sincerity. That made it much, much harder for the naysayers to campaign, and though there was an effort to put Biffy Clyro's original in the charts (it re-entered at No. 8) as well as a Facebook campaign to get the old '60s novelty hit 'Surfin' Bird' to the top (it made No. 3), Cardle's debut was untouchable, giving *X Factor* its fourth and final million-selling winner's single.

Cardle's win that year, both in the show and in the charts, heralded a sea change as Britain entered the new decade. In a move that seems unbelievable now, he'd knocked boy band One Direction, who had been put together from rejected solo performers, into third place. The pendulum of public taste was again swinging away from boy bands, and 2011 would be the year of the "serious" singer-songwriter. Of Adele and Ed Sheeran. The Best British Male and Female awards at that year's Brits went to Plan B and Laura Marling – artists who'd come from the underground in one way or another. The industry was honouring what it saw as "real" artists. That's an oversimplification, of course – One Direction would soon dash from under the shadow of the *X Factor* to become the biggest boy band in the world, and there are other pure pop examples from that year. Still, the shadow of perceived "authenticity" seemed to hover over the charts; a sort of anti-genre that pop critic Peter Robinson, writing in the *Guardian*, described at the time as "The New Boring", a trend he defined as "a ballad-friendly tidal wave destroying everything in its path".

Also joining Matt Cardle in the Christmas charts, and absolutely an example of Robinson's "New Boring", was singer-songwriter Ellie

Goulding, whose stripped back cover of Elton John's 'Your Song', sat at No. 5, having featured in that year's John Lewis Christmas advert. The department store had begun a tradition a few years earlier of classy, expensive and tear-jerking seasonal ads, always accompanied by a stripped down and deeply earnest cover of a classic song. The anticipation and celebration of these ads had become an annual tradition that was starting to match the Christmas No. 1 in terms of column inches. Over the next few years these plaintive readings of old classics would all enter the Christmas charts – Slow Moving Millie's cover of The Smiths' 'Please, Please, Please Let Me Get What I Want', Gabrielle Alpins' take on 'The Power of Love',[3] Lily Allen doing Keane's 'Somewhere Only We Know'. These songs became temporary additions to our annual Christmas soundtracks. Bloody miserable ones, admittedly, but then that's always been a part of the British festive experience.

The musical landscape of the 2010s was now completely removed from that of the '70s, '80s and '90s, and many of the old landmarks had fallen by the wayside. *Top of the Pops* had finally been discontinued in 2006 after years of sliding ratings. The growth of digital TV had given many more people access to 24-hour music video stations, and an increase in broadband internet meant streaming music videos online was becoming commonplace – YouTube had launched in 2005, and within a few years would become the first port of call for young people wanting to watch music content, seemingly having as much an appetite for low-quality footage shot on a phone as they did for professionally produced music videos. The "online premiere" became one of the key pieces of marketing in any new single's campaign. *TOTP*'s unique selling point, of being the only way fans could regularly see their favourite acts perform, no longer existed. The show wasn't entirely dead – it would keep its Christmas Day lunchtime slot right up to 2023, but never again would there be new weekly episodes celebrating the latest chart. Nothing came up to replace it, either. The biggest chart music slots on TV were the guest performances on *The X Factor* and *Strictly Come Dancing*. Music magazines had also fallen by the wayside – *Record Mirror* and *Sounds* hadn't survived the '90s, *Melody Maker*

---

[3] Frankie Goes To Hollywood, rather than Jennifer Rush or Huey Lewis.

had halted publication in 2001, *Smash Hits* had been retired in 2006. *NME* would struggle on to 2015, before relaunching as a general pop culture mag to be picked up for free in train stations and in Topshop – and went online only in 2018. The internet and social media had become a far faster and more effective way for artists and labels to communicate with fans. Those things the music press was uniquely good at – curation, context, long-form and entertaining writing, acting as a tastemaker – were outweighed by the instant gratification of internet culture. Only the weightier monthly mags remained, and they weren't aimed at a teenage audience in love with the thrill of the pop single. All of this contributed to leaching the life out of the phenomenon of the Christmas No. 1. It was becoming increasingly hard to make a younger audience, the heart of the record buying public, care.

That said, there were still some wins to be found: physical media may have been declining, but sales of singles spiked in the early 2010s – downloads from stores like Apple's iTunes, Amazon, 7digital and the in-house platforms owned by HMV and Tesco among others were incredibly popular. Buying a single had never been cheaper or more convenient, though it was far less profitable for the industry. The spend per purchase dropped from £1.99–4.99 for a CD single to just £0.79–99 for a download. Still digital single sales were breaking records – 2012 was the peak, with nearly 190 million downloads sold in the UK. When combined with a release aimed at an older market that still bought physical discs, those numbers meant that Christmas sales could be *huge*. As was well in evidence at Christmas 2011, when a charity record by a collective called the Military Wives, a choir of women with husbands serving in the armed forces overseas and championed by BBC Radio 2 and media figures like Piers Morgan, claimed Christmas No. 1 with half a million sales. The song knocked that year's *X Factor* winners from the top spot on Christmas Day itself. Girl group Little Mix, had sold 200,000 copies of their cover of Damien Rice's slightly damp ballad 'Cannonball' – less than half of what the Military Wives managed.[4]

---

[4] Very much suggesting that producers hadn't expected (or perhaps hadn't wanted) the feisty teen foursome to win. They'd won the public's affection on

After almost a decade of dominating the season, Simon Cowell's TV pop machine was finally in decline, with ratings shrinking for the first time – a trend that would continue year on year. The show squeezed out two more Christmas No. 1s – Sam Bailey's 'Skyscraper' in 2013 and Ben Haenow's 'Something I Need' in 2014 – but both had disappointing for Christmas, first-week sales of less than 250,000. The following year, Louise Young's cover of Dylan's 'Forever Young', became the first *X Factor* winner's single to miss No. 1 altogether, peaking at 9. It never passed 100,000 units. No *X Factor* winner's single ever topped the charts again, at Christmas or any time. In 2016 the show made one, final attempt to recapture what it felt was its traditional crown. That year's winner, Matt Terry, was given, for the first time in the show's decade-plus history of December releases, an actual Christmas song – 'When Christmas Comes Around'. Cowell even drafted in Ed Sheeran, arguably the defining male artist of the 2010s, and his regular co-writer Amy Wadge, who wrote a pleasant but rather forgettable and slight acoustic ballad. The kind of thing Sheeran can write in his sleep. It managed No. 3 but had nowhere near the momentum to dethrone beige, coffee table pop act Clean Bandit, whose by the numbers EDM hit 'Rockabye' had been sitting at No. 1 since mid-November and would stay there into the new year. By the time Christmas did indeed come around, Terry's single had dropped to No. 8. It did 200,000 in the end, respectable enough by that point, but barely anyone remembers it. The following year's *X Factor* single was moved to an early December release, as was the one after that. It was an acknowledgement that Christmas No. 1 was now off the table and there was no point in pretending otherwise … and that's despite the show's 2018 winner, the genuinely great Dalton Harris, covering Frankie's 'The Power of Love'.

The 2018 season would be the *X Factor*'s final run and Harris its final winner, ending what was probably the last era of the Christmas No. 1 that could be considered any sort of unique, shared cultural moment – even if that moment itself had little musical value. By the end, the show's ratings had declined by 50%; partly a result of

---

the show by covering En Vogue, Destiny's Child and Lady Gaga. Suddenly they're launched on the chart with a singer-songwriter ballad?

a public that had grown bored with the format, partly reflecting a decline in TV ratings across the board. Those moments when 15 million and more people all watched the same thing at the same time were now vanishingly rare. They certainly weren't happening every Saturday night. The way pop culture was consumed had changed dramatically.

By the time *X Factor* breathed its last, the Christmas No. 1 itself had felt irrelevant for some years. Though the press still framed it annually as a race and the bookmakers still gave odds and encouraged betting, there hadn't been any real investment from the public since Rage Against the Machine's 2009 win. Across the decade, the title had bounced between *X Factor* winners and charity collectives; Military Wives in 2011, the Justice Collective in 2012,[5] the Lewisham & Greenwich NHS Choir in 2015. People had gotten behind those songs, absolutely, but they were more about supporting a cause than they were about pinning down a moment in pop culture. There was certainly no sense of a chart battle. When Clean Bandit and Ed Sheeran took the respective 2016 and 2017 prizes, it was by default: massive pop artists releasing big singles that hung around at the top as Christmas came and went. It didn't feel exciting anymore. It certainly didn't feel particularly fun.

The biggest contributor to the phenomenon's decline had come from a fundamental, and probably irreversible change in the way people consumed music. In 2006, a Swedish website was launched that would allow users to stream a library of content directly to their computers was launched. Spotify gave music fans access to millions of songs in exchange for a subscription fee – or free, if they were prepared to listen to ads every few plays. It launched in the UK in 2009 with a huge catalogue, and was immediately wildly popular. The model Spotify pioneered would eventually make the idea of

---

[5] This raised awareness and funds for the Hillsborough Justice Campaign, a group formed to support the victims and families of the awful 1989 disaster, in which 96 Liverpool fans were killed in a crowd crush at Sheffield's Hillsborough stadium. The single, a cover of the Hollies' 'He Ain't Heavy, He's My Brother', featured pretty much every Scouse superstar still working. On top of the valuable cause it supported, the single gave the Spice Girls' Mel C her fourth Christmas No. 1, and raised Paul McCartney's tally to eight.

owning a single or an album the exception rather than the rule, certainly in the realm of mainstream pop. You can see why it took off. Streaming services are a true jukebox – the embodiment of an almost science fiction idea that any song, from any era could be played at any time. Other streamers soon joined the party – Apple Music, TIDAL, YouTube, Amazon and more – though Spotify was, and is still at the time of writing, by some distance, the market leader. Tied to the growth in smartphones, tablets and cellular data, meaning unlimited music on the go, there was little need to own physical media at all. A monthly subscription got you access to all the music you'd ever want.

If it was just a change in listening methods, however, then the paradigm shift wouldn't be as total as it has been. After all, music formats have been changing every generation or so for a century. Streaming may be the biggest change in consumption since prerecorded songs replaced sheet music and lyric books, but if it was just a matter of format then the same measures of success would apply – the most popular song wins. That's a semblance of democracy, at least. Streaming, however, also brought about a fundamental shift in discovery and curation. Roles traditionally delegated to radio stations were now built into the music store itself, and algorithms and playlists have changed the game dramatically. In the streaming era, a song's performance is often dictated less by conscious choice and more by passive consumption. The dominance of platform-curated playlists means that exposure often depends on fitting a particular mood or formula, rather than any traditional sense of fandom or cultural moment. Songs designed to slot easily into playlists – mid-tempo, melodic, non-disruptive – are more likely to thrive. It's not so much about buying into an artist's narrative, as it once was with *X Factor* winners, or about a communal moment, as it had been with charity singles or mass-purchased novelties. Now, it's about being present in the background noise of daily life. That's reflected in the charts, where long-running hits float along for months, buoyed less by active excitement than by sheer, algorithmically fed ubiquity. In that sense, the Christmas No. 1 has become less a badge of cultural feeling and more an incidental result of playlist mechanics.

The shift from downloads to streaming didn't happen all at once, but the effect was seismic. By the middle of the decade, streaming had started to take over. The Official Charts Company began counting audio streams towards the Singles Chart in July 2014, assigning a conversion rate to equate plays with sales (initially a rate of 100 plays equalled one sale, though that has changed over the years). By 2017, streaming made up the majority of single "sales", and by 2019 it accounted for virtually all of them. This fundamentally changed the nature of chart success. The old system rewarded spikes – release-day purchases, media-driven campaigns, physical sales in huge volume. Christmas, as a high-consumption period, was perfect for that model. But streaming is cumulative and ambient: songs rise slowly, hang around, and only sometimes surge. A huge new hit can sit at No. 1 for weeks without shifting especially high volumes in any given week. The thrill of the Christmas chart – the idea of one song triumphing in a sales battle, with a tangible number attached – no longer applies in the same way.

It means the system is now substantially easier to game. The stakes are so low and the opt-in for the audience is so easy, that anyone with a following can throw themselves into a Christmas No. 1 "race" and stand a pretty good chance of pulling it off, especially if they can convince that audience to download or buy a CD rather than stream. Couple that to the rise of online influencers on YouTube, Instagram and TikTok and you have what is probably the final form and, it has to be said, comfortably the most unlistenable manifestation of the festive pop phenomenon. What you have, bluntly, is LadBaby.

The previous record for consecutive No. 1s at Christmas was three, and it was jointly held by the Beatles and the Spice Girls, both pop culture phenomena and among the biggest artists in the world at the time of their hits. The record for most total Christmas No. 1s by a single artist was four – the Beatles again. LadBaby sailed past both of those milestones. Five Christmas No. 1s. In a row. But this wasn't a band. This was a husband and wife with a YouTube following.

Mark and Roxanne Hoyle had built their online presence as LadBaby through videos about Mark (the "lad") journeying into parenthood (the "baby"), with content that centred on budget-friendly family life, dad jokes and practical parenting hacks. Their transition to Christmas chart contenders began in 2018 with 'We Built This

City on Sausage Rolls', a novelty reworking of Starship's 1985 hit, based on an in-joke from their videos about Mark's fondness for the beloved pastry snack. The formula was simple: take a well-known song, rewrite it with lyrics about sausage rolls, perform it with limited musical polish, and direct all proceeds to food bank charity The Trussell Trust. Their following singles maintained the pastry theme: 'I Love Sausage Rolls' (2019), 'Don't Stop Me Eatin'' (2020, a duet with Ronan Keating), 'Sausage Rolls for Everyone' (2021, featuring, unbelievably, Ed Sheeran and Elton John[6]), and 'Food Aid' (2022), the latter an authorised reworking of 'Do They Know It's Christmas?' featuring tribute artists alongside money saving expert Martin Lewis.

LadBaby's rise coincided with – and cannot be separated from – a staggering increase in food banks across Britain. In 2010–11, the Trussell Trust network distributed 61,000 emergency food parcels. By 2018, when the Hoyles released their first single, that number had risen to 1.33 million. By 2022, their final year at the Christmas top spot, it had reached an unprecedented 2.99 million parcels. More than a third of these went to families with children. Throughout the 2010s, government austerity measures, welfare reforms, rising housing costs and low wages had created a perfect storm of food insecurity – one that the COVID-19 pandemic would only intensify. The reality of this crisis was something Mark Hoyle himself had experienced. As he told *The Big Issue* in 2020: "There was a time, four or so years ago, when we'd just had our first child. We were struggling, you know? We went down to single parent income, we were struggling to put food on the table. At one point, once our bills have been paid we had about £20 a week for food. We know that worry, when you're in a supermarket and you've not got all the money you would like to feed the family." In their book, *Our LadBaby Journey: Success, Sacrifice and Sausage Rolls*, Roxanne tells the story of having a breakdown in a supermarket after going over the food budget by 70 pence and being unable to pay for shopping.

The LadBaby phenomenon embodied a peculiar duality in British society. On one hand, it represented the rise of influencer culture – a world where online personalities with no traditional

---

[6] Giving Elton, tragically, his first and only Christmas No. 1.

showbusiness credentials could leverage their platforms for remarkably outsized cultural impact. Their success bypassed traditional gatekeepers entirely; radio barely played the songs, music critics universally panned them, and television coverage was minimal compared to previous Christmas campaigns. Yet through direct appeals on social media, they mobilised their followers in ways that would have been impossible in previous decades. On the other hand, their success spoke to a growing public awareness of societal failure. The very existence of food banks in one of the world's wealthiest nations represented a profound breakdown of the social safety net.

The music industry establishment mostly regarded LadBaby with thinly veiled contempt. Critics derided the songs as musically crude, technically limited and conceptually one note – which, obviously, they were. The critical reception, though, seemed almost irrelevant to their success. The songs weren't meant to be good in any traditional sense; they were meme-friendly fundraising vehicles wrapped in a dad-joke novelty.

The LadBaby phenomenon highlighted how fundamentally the notion of a hit single had changed in the streaming era. In the days when a Christmas No. 1 required hundreds of thousands of physical purchases, novelty acts needed broad appeal that transcended their core audience. In the digital landscape, where a comparatively modest number of dedicated fans making targeted purchases could tip the scales, the Christmas crown was suddenly accessible to niche creators with dedicated followings. Yet to dismiss LadBaby simply as algorithmic anomalies or chart-gaming opportunists would be to miss the bigger picture. Their five-year run at the top of the Christmas chart represented something far more uncomfortable: charitable giving to prevent hunger was now needed far closer to home than Ethiopia or Sudan.

Christmas has always had a charity element, going back centuries. It's in the almsgiving of the Middle Ages, it's in the collection for the needy at the start of *A Christmas Carol*, it's in the tradition of charity collectives recording Christmas singles. That it should be so necessary in our "world of plenty", on our doorstep, as advanced as we believe our society to have become, is shocking. As Hoyle himself put it, "You know what, I don't think food banks should exist. We're trying to get to the point where people don't need them, because people shouldn't need them. It shouldn't be a problem that anyone faces."

The Hoyles decided to move on from Christmas singles after their 2022 success, burnt out by the trolling they'd received over several years.[7] By that point they'd raised £1.3 million for the Trussell Trust through direct sales and brand partnerships. Unfortunately, with three million emergency food parcels still being distributed annually, it's likely that however much the music industry might wish to move on from sausage roll songs, the social conditions that made them resonate remained stubbornly in place.

What LadBaby had proved, though, is that the Christmas No. 1 was now a long way from being the "biggest prize in pop". Simon Cowell had once said of the position that "there's a tradition of quite horrible songs. I think I've done everyone a favour."[8] And he's right, there have been some stinkers – 'Mr Blobby', 'There's No One quite like Grandma', 'Long Haired Lover From Liverpool' – but those are outweighed by the genuine classics: 'Merry Xmas Everybody', 'Bohemian Rhapsody', 'Don't You Want Me', 'Sound of the Underground'. Mostly the songs that have won the year have been, at the very least tolerable, and often far more than that. The real plunge in quality happens *after* Cowell starts to take an interest. Before him the Christmas No. 1 was patchy, but rarely boring. Of the seven *X Factor* Christmas No. 1s only two, 'When We Collide' and 'Hallelujah', really stand up as records, and even then only as pale imitations of better versions.[9] You'd be hard-pushed to whistle

---

[7] An online rumour that the pair were Conservative supporters who were creaming off the top of their charity work spread like wildfire and the responses made the couples' life a misery. They maintain, pretty reasonably, that all of the profits for their singles went directly to the Trussell Trust (who have confirmed this), and what's more, that they're both lifelong Labour voters. It's pretty clear that their only crimes are to music and comedy. Though those in themselves are probably bad enough.

[8] He has the cheek to specify 'Mr Blobby', apparently forgetting that he'd been so impressed with that record at the time that he'd written a gleeful letter to *Music Week* in celebration.

[9] Leona Lewis's 'A Moment Like This' gets a pass for an extraordinary vocal performance, but the actual song is dull as anything.

many of the songs that earned the spot after 2004, covers aside. The Christmas No. 1, whenever it's mattered at all, has become a sales tool, a marketing gimmick or a rallying cry for good causes. The musical worth has been negligible in the extreme for some time. The LadBaby records are the nadir. They're the first Christmas No. 1 singles in history that no one *actually wants to listen to*. Children loved 'Blobby'. Terry Wogan fans loved St Winifred's School Choir. Most of the Western world seemed to love the Spice Girls. But those sausage roll singles were empty calories – one shot jokes. And not very funny ones. They did good in the world, and we can't begrudge that, but musically they're actively hateful. It's possible they put the last nail in the coffin of the Christmas No. 1. It remains an annual media story, because the media lives or dies on quick clickbait, but as far as watercooler moments, discussed in classrooms and offices and the tearoom of the House of Commons and the newsroom at the *Guardian* go … those days are far, far gone.

But Christmas endures. It comes back every year. And in some ways it's a very different experience to the Christmases of our child-hoods, however old you happen to be. But in other ways – not so much. We still gather, in the dark and the cold. We still eat and drink and give presents. There are still trees and baubles and *The Muppet Christmas Carol*. Christmas Day still remains, for those who celebrate it, a unique point of the year. Its own little pocket reality, unlike any other day we experience. Where the world stops and we turn inwards, to each other. And there's still music. Often, in all honesty, the *same* music. The same couple of dozen songs – songs that we know in our bones. The present, and maybe the future of the Christmas No. 1, is to be found in the past.

Epilogue
MAY YOUR DAYS BE MERRY AND BRIGHT

George Michael didn't live to see his dearest Christmas wish come true. That's one of the great tragedies of British Christmas music. But come true it did. In 2023, 39 years after its original release, Wham!'s 'Last Christmas' finally became the Christmas No. 1, helped along by LadBaby bowing out of the race that year. Its biggest competition came from Sam Ryder, riding high after his Eurovision success the previous summer. His song, 'You're Christmas to Me' – a kind of greatest hits of British Christmas pop – spent so long borrowing the vibe of the classics that it never quite found its own. In the face of our enduring affection for Wham!, it didn't stand a chance. Ryder's track was nowhere to be seen the following December, and that's telling. 'Last Christmas', meanwhile, celebrating its fortieth anniversary, became the first song since records began to hold the Christmas No. 1 for two years running.[1] New Christmas songs, though they crop up from time to time, struggle to find a toehold. The canon is easy to recognise now, because streaming rules mean it dominates the whole chart – take a look at the UK Top 40 for 17 December, 2024:

---

[1] Though it's unlikely to match the *unofficial* holder of the consecutive Christmas award. According to the data in *The Missing Charts*, Bing's 'White Christmas' was No. 1 at the end of December for seven years in a row, from 1945 to 1951.

1. 'Last Christmas' – Wham!
2. 'All I Want for Christmas Is You' – Mariah Carey
3. 'It Can't Be Christmas' – Tom Grennan.
4. 'Rockin' Around the Christmas Tree' – Brenda Lee
5. 'Jingle Bell Rock' – Bobby Helms
6. 'Fairytale of New York' – The Pogues ft. Kirsty MacColl
7. 'Underneath the Tree' – Kelly Clarkson
8. 'Santa Tell Me' – Ariana Grande
9. 'Do They Know It's Christmas?' – Band Aid
10. 'Step Into Christmas' – Elton John
11. 'It's the Most Wonderful Time of the Year' – Andy Williams
12. 'Merry Christmas Everyone' – Shakin' Stevens
13. 'Christmas Magic' – Laufey
14. 'It's Beginning to Look a Lot Like Christmas' – Michael Bublé
15. 'Sleigh Ride' – the Ronettes
16. 'Wonderful Christmastime' – Paul McCartney
17. 'Feliz Navidad' – José Feliciano
18. 'A Nonsense Christmas' – Sabrina Carpenter
19. 'Driving Home for Christmas' – Chris Rea
20. 'Let It Snow! Let It Snow! Let It Snow!' – Dean Martin
21. 'That's So True' – Gracie Abrams
22. 'I Wish It Could Be Christmas Everyday' – Wizzard
23. 'Holly Jolly Christmas' – Michael Bublé
24. 'Happy Xmas (War Is Over)' – John & Yoko/Plastic Ono Band
25. 'Snowman' – Sia
26. 'Merry Xmas Everybody' – Slade
27. 'Winter Wonderland' – Laufey
28. 'Apt.' – Rosé & Bruno Mars.
29. 'Merry Christmas' – Ed Sheeran & Elton John.
30. 'Christmas (Baby Please Come Home)' – Darlene Love
31. 'Run Rudolph Run' – Mark Ambor
32. 'The Christmas Song' – Nat King Cole
33. 'Messy' – Lola Young
34. 'One More Sleep' – Leona Lewis
35. 'Santa Baby' – Laufey
36. 'Mistletoe' – Justin Bieber
37. 'Carol of the Bells' – John Williams
38. 'Holiday Road' – Kesha

39. 'DJ Play a Christmas Song' – Cher
40. 'It's Beginning to Look a Lot Like Christmas' – Perry Como

Thirty-five of the top forty are Christmas songs, most of them decades old. Almost every modern pop single had been pushed out. There's been a lot of talk about how technology ended the idea of monoculture in pop music – that we no longer experience the same moments together. Christmas is the exception. That's nothing new – it's just more visible now. Twenty years ago we were spinning compilation albums in the privacy of our CD players and the chart was reserved for new music. Now, with streaming, we can see a nation's actual listening habits in real time. And it turns out, most of us are still listening to the same old songs after all. Partly, of course, because they're the ones the algorithm serves us.

The numbers are respectable. When 'Last Christmas' finally hit No. 1 in 2023, it did so with around 13 million streams – roughly 133,000 chart units. A strong total by modern standards. But it's no 'Mull of Kintyre' with two *million* sales, or 'Do They Know It's Christmas?' with *four* million. It's not 'Killing in the Name' with half a million downloads in a week. In the streaming era, the Christmas No. 1 no longer guarantees the biggest weekly audience of the year. It might not even make the Top 5.

So what's left? Is there still a reason to care? Maybe – but more for tradition than impact. The crown still carries symbolic weight. It's a marker, especially for charity singles or novelty efforts, and it makes a neat news story. But in a world where music is mostly passive – one track among millions on playlists and feeds – the Christmas No. 1 is no longer the season's centrepiece. The chart hasn't died. But it *has* stopped being a battlefield.

What does that say about us? About Britain? About music? About *Christmas*? Where are we now? Maybe it's simpler than we think. The music of Christmas is part of the box of tinsel and lights we pull down from the attic every year, stitched into school plays, department store speakers, late-night taxis home. The songs that lasted – Slade's wallop and yell, George Michael's broken heart, Shane and Kirsty's lost, lovelorn row – they're traditions, passed down like recipes or decorations, returning each year without anyone needing to ask. And they matter.

Last summer I was performing stand-up at the Latitude Festival, and wandered into one of the late-night tents, for an event hosted by Club de Fromage, a night of cheesy pop usually held in London. It was July. A warm, Saturday night. The tent was full of kids – the average age maybe 20. Some younger, a few older. At around two in the morning, the dancers on stage pulled on Santa hats and fake beards, and the DJ dropped the first few bars of a song everybody knew somewhere deep in their bones. Two thousand kids promptly lost their minds to Shakin' Stevens' 'Merry Christmas Everyone'.[2] A song from 1985, from 20 years before most of them were born. A song that sounds as naff and chirpy now as it did then. A song owned, metaphorically if not literally, by everyone in that tent. It's not even *that* great a song. But every single person knew it. Every bar. Every beat.

Streaming hasn't broken that connection. If anything, it's made it *unbreakable*. We keep playing these songs because they belong to us. They're stitched into our lives, pinned to a particular point in the year. Music as time travel. Songs as a moment in the calendar. The old battles for Christmas No. 1 – the headlines, the chart races, the campaigns – were never really about the records. They were about celebrating something together, gathering in the dark when the year was running out. That's how it started, with Slade, back in 1973. The glow of coloured lights in the gloom. For a time, the Christmas chart gave us that. A rare thing in pop culture that crossed generations. Something you could argue about at the dinner table, somewhere between the turkey and the pudding. Between *Top of the Pops* and *Doctor Who*. Between the dark and the dawn.

And what have we learned? That a Christmas No. 1 is never just a No. 1. Not here. Not in Britain. It's a joke. It's a story. It's a bit of theatre, a marketing stunt, a memory from childhood, a flash of something daft or moving that briefly cuts through the noise. It's a place where taste, sentiment and public mood all crash into each other, then rearrange themselves into something that sounds like Christmas. Nobody else does it like this. Not with this much fuss, or this much feeling. No other country cares who's No. 1 on 25 December. We do. We built it into the calendar. We wrapped it

---

[2] Absolutely *baffling* any visiting Americans.

in snow and sentiment, pinned it to novelty singles, talent shows, charity records, protest campaigns. We turned it into *our thing.* That's the point. Not the chart itself, but the fact that we insist on giving it meaning. It's part of a much older story. Midwinter music, wassailing songs, noisy crowds, sad old ballads, Victorian sentiment, music halls, panto, punk – all still echoing in Slade and Cliff and Rage Against the Machine and Blobby. It's even in LadBaby, a five-year triumph of well-meaning musical crimes that wouldn't be allowed to happen *anywhere* else. The British Christmas is rowdy and reflective, a bit pissed and a bit wistful, driven by cheap jokes and deep feelings. There's always been a melancholy in it. And a bit of rebellion. And a stubborn streak that says, no, this matters, even if we're not sure why.

Maybe that's what makes it British. Not the songs, not the snow, not the bells and choirs, but the way we gather around something that doesn't really matter and decide, together, that it *does*. We make it matter. Just for a week. Just for Christmas.

We still glance at the Christmas chart. Not out of nostalgia exactly, but out of habit. A ritual. Like untangling the fairy lights or posting a card to a cousin you haven't seen for 20 years. Christmas music was always bigger than the Christmas chart anyway. It started as folk songs shouted into the cold, passed through Victorian sentiment, American schmaltz, glam rock bombast, charity records, boy band ballads, and reality TV anthems. It ended up here: a loose collection of songs we dust off every December and sing along to, whether there's a new contender or not. The Christmas No. 1 might not dominate the headlines now. It might never again. But the songs are still here – in the pubs, in the shops, in the taxis home. Still filling the rooms. Still catching us off guard. Still making us cry into our second glass of Baileys. Still connecting us, quietly, stubbornly.

Not sales. Not records. Just the sound of Christmas.

All is calm. All is bright. And every year, without fail, once again we press play.

BIBLIOGRAPHY

Memoirs and Autobiography

Barrett, Marcia. *Forward: My Life With and Without Boney M.* Constable, 2018.

Batt, Mike. *The Closest Thing to Crazy: My Life of Musical Adventures.* Nine Eight Books, 2024.

Bono. *Surrender: 40 Songs, One Story.* Hutchinson Heinemann, 2022.

Chisholm, Melanie. *Who I Am: My Story.* Welbeck Publishing, 2022.

DeMacque-Crockett, Pepsi & Kemp, Shirlie. *Pepsi & Shirlie – It's All in Black and White.* Welbeck Publishing, 2021.

Geldof, Bob. *Is That It?* Weidenfeld & Nicolson, 1986.

Geldof, Bob. *Tales of Boomtown Glory.* Faber & Faber, 2019.

Grima, Charlie. *Aren't You Glad That It's Not Christmas Everyday? Memoirs of a Wizzard Drummer, ex drummer of Roy Woods Wizzard.* Mirag Publications, 2015.

Halliwell, Geri. *If Only.* Bantam Press, 1999.

Harding, Phil. *PWL: From the Factory Floor.* Cherry Red Books, 2011.

Harrison, George. *I Me Mine.* Genesis Publications, 1980.

Hill, Dave. *So Here It Is: The Autobiography.* Unbound, 2017.

Holder, Noddy. *Who's Crazee Now?: My Autobiography.* Ebury Press, 1999.

Holder, Noddy. *The World According To Noddy.* Constable, 2014.

Horn, Trevor. *Adventures in Modern Recording.* Nine Eight Books, 2022.

Hoyle, Mark & Hoyle, Roxanne. *Our LadBaby Journey.* Little, Brown, 2024.

Kemp, Gary. *I Know This Much: From Soho to Spandau.* Fourth Estate, 2009.

Kemp, Martin. *Ticket to the World.* Pan Macmillan, 2013.

Mintz, Elliot. *We All Shine On.* Post Hill Press, 2024.

Morello, Tom. *Whatever It Takes.* Genesis Publications, 2020.

Powell, Don & Falkenberg, Lise Lyse. *Look Wot I Dun: Don Powell: My Life in Slade.* Omnibus Press, 2013.

Richard, Cliff. *The Dreamer: An Autobiography.* Ebury Press, 2020.

Ridgeley, Andrew. *Wham! George & Me.* Michael Joseph, 2019.

Stock, Mike. *The Hit Factory: The Stock, Aitken and Waterman Story.* New Holland, 2004.

Taylor, Andy. *Wild Boy: My Life with Duran Duran.* Little, Brown, 2008.

Taylor, John. *In The Pleasure Groove: Love, Death and Duran Duran.* Sphere, 2012.

Ure, Midge. *If I Was: Midge Ure, An Autobiography.* Virgin Books, 2004.

Waterman, Pete. *I Wish I Was Me: The Autobiography.* Virgin Books, 2000.

Watkins, Tom. *Let's Make Lots of Money: Confessions of a Fat, Rich, Gay Lucky Bastard.* Virgin Books, 2017.

Music Biography

Doyle, Tom. *Man on the Run: Paul McCartney in the 1970s.* Ballantine Books, 2014.

Easlea, Daryl. *Whatever Happened to Slade?* Omnibus Press, 2023.

Fearon, Gary. *After Abbey Road: The Solo Hits of The Beatles.* Robinsong, 2020.

Giuliano, Geoffrey. *Lennon in America.* Cooper Square Press, 2000.

Halstead, Craig. *Boney M. All the Top Forty Hits.* Independently published, 2019.

Hoskyns, Barney. *Glam! Bowie, Bolan and the Glitter Rock Revolution.* Pocket Books, 1998.

Jackson, Joe. *Bob Geldof: The Joe Jackson Interviews Plus.* Self-published, 2012.

Jones, Dylan. *David Bowie: A Life.* Crown Archetype, 2017.

Kozinn, Allan & Sinclair, Adrian. *The McCartney Legacy: Volume 2: 1974–80.* Dey Street Books, 2023.

Norman, Philip. *George Harrison: The Reluctant Beatle*. Scribner, 2023.

Norman, Philip. *John Lennon: The Life*. HarperCollins, 2008.

Norman, Philip. *Paul McCartney: The Biography*. Little, Brown, 2016.

Norman, Philip. *Shout!: The True Story of the Beatles*. Pan Books, 2004.

Paytress, Mark. *Glam!: When Superstars Rocked the World, 1970–74*. Omnibus Press, 2022.

Pegg, Nicholas. *The Complete David Bowie*. Titan Books, 2016.

Read, Mike. *Cliff – The Great 80*. G2 Entertainment, 2020.

Stanley, John. *Cliff Richard: Essential Music*. Independently published, 2022.

Tremlett, George. *The Slade Story*. Futura Publications, 1975.

Turner, James R. *Roy Wood: The Move, ELO and Wizzard (On Track)*. Sonicbond Publishing, 2020.

Van Der Kiste, John. *Roy Wood*. Fonthill Media, 2015.

Williams, Richard. *Phil Spector: Out Of His Head*. Omnibus Press, 2003.

General Music and Pop Culture

Baker, Richard Anthony. *British Music Hall: An Illustrated History*. Sutton Publishing, 2005.

Burford, Andrew. *70 Years of Christmas No. 1s*. Self-published, 2024.

Burger, Jeff. *Lennon on Lennon: Conversations with John Lennon*. Chicago Review Press, 2016.

Checksfield, Peter. *Top of the Pops: The Lost Years Rediscovered 1964–1975*. Independently published, 2021.

Checksfield, Peter. *Top of the Pops: The Punk and New Romantic Years 1976–1986*. Independently published, 2022.

Cragg, Michael. *Reach for the Stars: 1996–2006*. Nine Eight Books, 2023.

Forde, Eamonn. *1999: The Year the Record Industry Lost Control*. Omnibus Press, 2024.

Harding, Phil. *Pop Music Production: Manufactured Pop and Boybands of the 1990s*. Routledge, 2019.

Jones, Dylan. *Faster Than a Cannonball: 1995 and All That*. White Rabbit, 2023.

Jones, Dylan. *The Eighties: One Day, One Decade.* Preface Publishing, 2014.

Lewis, Justin. *Don't Stop the Music: A Year of Pop History, One Day at a Time.* Elliott & Thompson, 2024.

Long, Pat. *The History of the NME.* Portico Books, 2012.

Readiof, Lonnie. *1952-2024 –UK Top 40 Singles Charts.* Self-published, 2024

Rees, Dafydd/ Lazell Barry/ Osbourne, Roger. *Forty Years of the NME Charts.* Boxtree, 1992.

Rosen, Jody. *White Christmas: The Story of a Song.* Scribner, 2002.

Spaeth, Sigmund. *A History of Popular Music in America.* Random House, 1948.

Stanley, Bob. *Let's Do It: The Birth of Pop.* Faber & Faber, 2022.

Stanley, Bob. *Yeah Yeah Yeah: The Story of Modern Pop.* Faber & Faber, 2013.

Gorman, Paul. *Totally Wired: The Rise and Fall of the Music Press.* Thames & Hudson, 2022.

Wade, Ian. *1984: The Year Pop Went Queer.* Nine Eight Books, 2024.

Waters, Steve. *The British Hit Singles January 1940–October 1952: The Missing Charts.* RockHistory Ltd., 2013.

Warwick, Neil; Kutner, Jon; Brown, Tony. *The Complete Book of the British Charts.* Omnibus Press, 2004.

History of Christmas

Flanders, Judith. *Christmas: A Biography.* Thomas Dunne Books, 2017.

Hill, Christopher. *The World Turned Upside Down.* Viking Press, 1972.

Lawson-Jones, Revd Mark. *Why Was the Partridge in the Pear Tree?* The History Press, 2011.

Mengah, Felix. *UK Christmas No. 1s – 1952–2022.* Victor Publishing, 2023.

Miles, Clement A. *Christmas in Ritual & Tradition: Christian and Pagan.* Jazzybee Verlag, originally 1912.

Nissenbaum, Stephen. *The Battle for Christmas.* Vintage, 1997.

General History

Sandbrook, Dominic. *Never Had It So Good: A History of Britain from Suez to the Beatles.* Little, Brown, 2005.

Stewart, Graham. *Bang!: A History of Britain in the 1980s.* Atlantic Books, 2013.

Turner, Alwyn W. *A Classless Society: Britain in the 1990s.* Aurum Press, 2014.

Turner, Alwyn W. *Crisis? What Crisis?: Britain in the 1970s.* Aurum Press, 2009.

Turner, Alwyn W. *Rejoice! Rejoice!: Britain in the 1980s.* Aurum Press, 2013.

Turner, Alwyn W. *Things Can Only Get Bitter.* Aurum Press, 2012.

TV Shows and documentaries

Bing Crosby's Merrie Olde Christmas – CBS (US), ITV (UK), 1977
Last Christmas: Unwrapped – BBC Two, 2024
The Making of 'Do They Know It's Christmas' – BBC Two, 2024
Omnibus: The Story of the Music Video – BBC Two, 1986
TV Hell – BBC Two, 1992
The Wright Stuff – Channel 5, 2000–2018

ACKNOWLEDGMENTS

Ghosts of Christmas past:

I'd like to thank my parents, Julie Williams and Russ Burrows, for decades of wonderful Christmas memories. The older I get, the more I appreciate the effort they put into making Christmas a magical time for us. For many people, Christmas is a time of conflicting emotions and rancid memories. I've never had that. Christmas in our house was always brilliant. It's probably why I'm so fond of all of these very silly songs. Their mid-80s purchase of *The Christmas Tape* was the start of the journey that resulted in this book.

Ghosts of Christmas present:

Huge gratitude goes to my publishers, Caroline and Andy at McNidder and Grace, for taking a chance on this quite preposterous idea, as well as to Alan Jepson for his hard work getting it on the road, and Caroline Curtis for her sharp-eyed edit. I'd also like to thank Hazel Cushion for the introduction that got the ball rolling.

Christmas cheer is also owed to Phil Jupitus, Rob Wilkins, Corrie McGuire (who doesn't know I'm about to throw this book into her workload), Greg Butler, Patrick Charlton, Vix Leyton, Juliette Burton, Andy Heintz, Jez Miller, Pete Gardner, Rich Jennings, Kimbo and the Bloom-Burrowses for their friendship and/or their help.

I'd also like to acknowledge those that gave their time and stories to help make this book what it is … whether they know it or not.

Ghosts of Christmas yet to come:

To Melanie, Oscar and Felix — here's to many more Christmas mornings.

ABOUT THE AUTHOR

Photo credit: Alexis Dubus

Marc Burrows is an award-winning author, comedian and musician, currently residing in Bristol. His 2020 biography of Sir Terry Pratchett won the Locus Award for best non-fiction and became the basis for a stand-up show that received rave reviews at the Edinburgh Fringe and has toured extensively across the UK, mainland Europe and Australia.

His second book, *The London Boys*, explored 1960s London through the lives of the teenage David Bowie and Marc Bolan and received 8/10 from *Classic Rock* and four stars from *Shindig!* He plays bass in the cult punk band The Men That Will Not Be Blamed For Nothing, writes regularly for *The Independent*, *Big Issue*, *The New Statesmen* and many more and is working on a novel and a new stand up show. He is generally quite tired. His previous book, *NIRVANA: A detailed guide to the band that changed everything* was published in November 2024.